Total War
New Perspectives on World War II

Series Editors
MICHAEL A. BARNHART, SUNY at Stony Brook
H. P. WILLMOTT

The Second World War, a conflict that literally spanned the globe, has spawned the publication of thousands of books. In fact, it seems that new ones appear almost daily. Why, then, another series on this subject? Because there is a need for brief, accessible, and affordable books that synthesize the best of recent scholarship on World War II. This series aims to differ from the vast majority of volumes published on the war. Marked by tightly focused studies on vital aspects of the conflict, from the war against Japan to the Anglo-American alliance to the rise of the Red Army, the books in this provocative new series will compel World War II scholars, students, and buffs to consider old questions in new terms. Covering significant topics—battles and campaigns, world leaders, and political and social dimensions—*Total War* intends to be lively, engaging, and instructive.

Volumes Published

H. P. Willmott, *The War with Japan: The Period of Balance, May 1942–October 1943* (2002). Cloth ISBN 0-8420-5032-9   Paper ISBN 0-8420-5033-7

Thomas W. Zeiler, *Unconditional Defeat: Japan, America, and the End of World War II* (2004). Cloth ISBN 0-8420-2990-7   Paper ISBN 0-8420-2991-5

UNCONDITIONAL DEFEAT

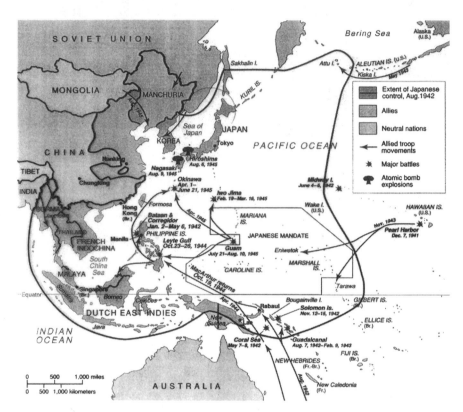

THE PACIFIC THEATER OF WORLD WAR II, 1941–1945

James L. Roark et al., *The American Promise*, vol. 2 (New York: Bedford/St. Martin's, 2002). © 2002 by Bedford/St. Martin's. Reprinted by permission of the publisher.

UNCONDITIONAL DEFEAT

JAPAN, AMERICA, AND
THE END OF WORLD WAR II

THOMAS W. ZEILER

Total War
New Perspectives on World War II
NO. 2

A Scholarly Resources Inc. Imprint
Wilmington, Delaware

© 2004 by Scholarly Resources Inc.
All rights reserved
First published 2004
Printed and bound in the United States of America

Scholarly Resources Inc.
104 Greenhill Avenue
Wilmington, DE 19805-1897
www.scholarly.com

Library of Congress Cataloging-in-Publication Data

Zeiler, Thomas W.
    Unconditional defeat : Japan, America, and the end of World War II /
by Thomas W. Zeiler
        p. cm. — (Total war ; no. 2)
    ISBN 0-8420-2991-5 (pbk. : alk. paper) — ISBN 0-8420-2990-7 (alk.
paper)
        1. World War, 1939–1945—Campaigns—Pacific Area. 2. World War,
1939–1945—United States. 3. World War, 1939–1945—Japan. I. Title.
II. Series.
D767.Z45 2003
940.54'25—dc21

                                                            2003006154

To Doug, Jeanie, and Diana

About the Author

Thomas W. Zeiler is chair and professor in the Department of History at the University of Colorado at Boulder, where he has taught since 1990. The recipient of the Bernath Lecture Prize granted by the Society for Historians of American Relations in 2001, he is the author of five books relating to U.S. diplomacy, most recently *Globalization and the American Century* (2003), and is a recent Fulbright Senior Scholar.

Contents

List of Maps

Introduction

T his book explores why and how America destroyed the Japanese military and, ultimately, Japan itself, from November 1943 onward, the time when the United States took the offensive and drove its enemy back to its own shores. Military planning and action in battle revealed that U.S. troops faced an implacable enemy who would give no quarter. Thus, although atrocities were committed on both sides, it was Japanese actions that brutally intensified the war until its grisly end in August 1945. The senselessness of Japan's fanatic defense, itself a product of blind loyalty to leaders and near-spiritual belief in the nation's quest for expansion, had a life of its own. The Japanese fought on, seemingly robotic in their willingness even to kill themselves for a futile cause. This behavior, in turn, heightened American fear, horror, and determination to crush the enemy. America's response of rage, coupled with the massive weight of U.S. industry and technology, made the Pacific war's course hard on both sides but its consequences devastating for Japan. American soldiers, as one scholar has written, "abandoned themselves to destroying their environment before it would succeed in destroying them."[1] That environment had been created by the Japanese over several years, and thus Japan would pay the ultimate price of total and unconditional defeat for its prior aggression. What follows is the story behind that tragedy.

The last half of the American war with Japan is a story of contrasts. In those final twenty-two months, from November 1943 to September 1945, the United States and its allies pushed the empire of Japan ever backward into devastating defeat. The means of victory were clarified during this period. Overwhelming material superiority and human resources, and the ability to mobilize these forces, defeated the Japanese. In turn, Japan's lack of supplies, and its inability to get these goods to the field even if it had them, meant its end. In a war of stark differences, one nation fought a fierce yet hopeless defense with diminishing resources, while the other launched a methodical, smothering attack with all the means at its disposal. The result was unconditional defeat for Japan and total victory for the United States.

The diary of a Japanese soldier captured on New Guinea in November 1943 revealed the bare essence of the conflict. "As we have no food, we fight whilst only eating grass," wrote the soldier. He fully understood the nature of his country's predicament, for "the present war is a war of supply," and his country was losing. Japan lacked the necessities not just for victory, as in the earlier phases of the war, but for adequate defense, yet the soldier also epitomized the sad plight of his nation, as he held illusions of ultimate triumph. He urged "a drastic change in our strategy" to stave off defeat.[2] By November 1943, however, the Japanese had no options except to await America's next move. Holding all the assets of war, the United States determined the methods and means of Japan's defeat. Strategy, tactics, and timing rested with the Americans, as their exertion of power proved more complete than anything imaginable by Japan.

Victory's path revealed incongruities among the protagonists. The Americans planned multiple advances in the Pacific Ocean and on the Asian mainland, using a massive number of troops, devising and adopting novel amphibious techniques, and deploying the new nuclear category of weapons. The Japanese stubbornly but desperately clung to their territory, often with the barest of defenses, including suicide attacks undertaken by a spiritual willingness to die. Differing capabilities and outlooks led to drastically varied tactics, thus making the last phase of the war a study in contrasting capabilities but shared experiences of violence.

The protagonists held one aspect of the war in common—a basic savagery. Japan's version was a cruelty begun in the 1930s and intensified during the Pacific war; U.S. fierceness came in reaction to conditions set by Japanese actions and easily matched the enemy in a fury of destruction from the skies, on the seas, and on the ground. As a result, casualties mounted on both sides, particularly among the Japanese defenders, and brutality, as well as suffering, was commonplace. Those who experienced combat witnessed the sheer hell of war. The human disaster is a tragic yet essential element to present in a war of such contrasts, for it makes meaningful both U.S. victory and Japanese defeat and points to the horror of war, no matter its cause or justification. This book examines the people who fought and lived through the conflict, as well as the top-level strategic angle.

In the period of balance from May 1942 to November 1943, defeat for Japan was certain, but the dimensions of that loss were not. America answered the question of how Japan would be brought to its knees, and by August 1945, the parameters had been rendered abundantly clear in all aspects of warfare, and in diplomacy as well. Isolated in every theater by American efforts, Japan crumbled. Japanese politics was in turmoil, the government faced rebellion, and the emperor stood on the brink of extinction. Wracked by the destruction of the homeland from the air and blockade by sea, Japanese society veered near chaos, and the people peered into the abyss of an uncertain future. America's military had experienced such horrors at the hands of Japan that the United States mercilessly unleashed a weapon of mass destruction. By August 1945 the United States had brought the war home to its enemy, but in reality, beginning in November 1943, America's offensives had pointed to only one conclusion: the unconditional defeat of Japan.

THIS BOOK HAS BENEFITED from a variety of sources. Those quoted directly are cited in the notes at the end of each chapter; the bibliography includes all studies that informed this book.

It would be remiss not to single out the authors I particularly relied on for information and analysis. The works of Williamson Murray and Allan R. Millett, Ronald Spector, and H. P. Willmott guided me in the narrative and analytical foundations, and I am indebted to them. The publications of the following authors were also especially important in the conceptualization of this study and in providing information: Joseph H. Alexander, Peter Calvocoressi and Guy Wint, Haruko Taya Cook and Theodore F. Cook, James F. Dunnigan and Albert A. Nofi, John Ellis, Edwin P. Hoyt, Douglas J. MacEachin, Peter Schrijvers, E. B. Sledge, and Harold G. Vatter. The series of U.S. Army and Marine accounts of campaigns and the publications of the Naval Institute Press were also indispensable.

Several people helped me learn about this era. Steve Pelz, David Spires, Ron Story, Ned Willmott, and Marcia Yonemoto have taught me about the Pacific war. My two children, Ella and Jackson, are just the greatest. And as usual, my wife and best friend, Rocio, remained ever tolerant with me—no mean feat. This book is dedicated to my siblings, who survived youthful combat for which I was (largely) the instigator. Like Japan, which arose from war to attain great heights, they survived me to produce wonderful lives, careers, and families.

 Notes

1. Peter Schrijvers, *The GI War against Japan: American Soldiers in Asia and the Pacific during World War II* (Washington Square, NY: New York University Press, 2002), 207.

2. Lyn Crost, *Honor by Fire: Japanese Americans at War in Europe and the Pacific* (Novato, CA: Presidio Press, 1994), 38, 39.

1

A NOVEMBER FOR OFFENSIVES

"It is not our intention to wreck the island," announced Rear Admiral Howard F. Kingman, American commander of a naval support group poised to attack the principal island of Betio on Tarawa Atoll, in November 1943. "Gentlemen, we will obliterate it."[1] Betio was a dot in the central Pacific but the allusion to ruination was appropriate. With a rage provoked by nearly two years of war against an unyielding and fanatical foe, the Americans focused their manpower and mechanical might on Japanese positions throughout the Pacific. The landings on Tarawa epitomized the brutality of the war against Japan, and signaled the demise of the empire of Japan. The United States and its allies also pursued their southwest Pacific campaign by assailing Bougainville in the Solomons and, in addition, they shored up their military and diplomatic positions in China, all to the detriment of Japan. Thus, November 1943 was a month of offensives that launched Japan toward unconditional defeat.

The various theaters of war exposed Japanese weaknesses and, even more significant, revealed ever growing American strengths. Only a government willing to sacrifice hundreds of thousands of lives to a lost cause, or at minimum to slow down its ultimate national defeat, would stand up to the U.S. juggernaut. But Japan did so from that November onward, though steadily retreating and often routed in pitched, savage battles on land, at sea, and in the air. The fact that the Japanese fought on in the face of certain tragedy also convinced Americans that only by the most merciless and expansive use of weaponry, industry, and manpower would their enemy finally end this brutal war. That is, Japan's fanaticism prompted American ferocity on a scale never before imagined in history. If the empire would not stop fighting on its own and surrender—the logical, rational choice, owing to the vast disparity in power between the two nations—then the United States would force it to do so, step by step across the Pacific.

Sources of Power and Defeat

On December 27, 1943, Prime Minister Tojo Hideki tried to rally the Japanese Diet by announcing that "the real war is just beginning."[2] He was correct, but not in the way he hoped, for his nation was headed toward catastrophe. Prior to November 1943, Japan held its ground in the Pacific and Asian theaters; after that, Japan's sorrows began, at home as well as abroad. Decisive developments in the war arose as much on the factory floors and farms of America and Japan, and in the shipping lanes in which this production flowed, as they did in battle. That is, by 1944 the United States economy, and Japan's relatively minuscule output, undergirded American victory. The Allies simply overpowered the empire by output of goods, services, and personnel. This time, David did not defeat Goliath, but rather an army of Goliaths eventually crushed its poor foe.

Japan suffered a manpower shortage. The nation mobilized 9.1 million military personnel, including university students, who had previously been exempt from combat up to the draft age of twenty years old but by December 1, 1943, were being called to take up arms against the enemy. The draft age dropped to nineteen and, by early 1944, fell to eighteen. By March 1945, youths from upper elementary school to college were being sent to work; at war's end, 3.4 million students had been drafted into war employment. To bolster the armed forces, males were restricted from employment in various transportation and other service-sector jobs, replaced by women. Military defeats, shipping losses, and U.S. bombing compelled still more stringent requirements. The government encouraged higher birthrates in an effort to maintain and raise production. Formerly the unemployed, women, and hundreds of thousands of Chinese, Taiwanese, and Koreans comprised much of the work force. Nevertheless, productivity declined because of the lack of skilled male workers and the plethora of unskilled young labor, and hardship increased as shortages wracked the Japanese military and consumer economies.

Conditions were bleak. Cereals and other substitutes such as sweet potatoes, dry biscuits, and soybeans replaced the staple of rice, which was in short supply. Caloric and protein intakes sagged below 2,400, the Ministry of Health and Welfare's nutritional standard for an adult male doing medium labor, and by 1945 the level had dropped to 1,793. Malnutrition led to health problems; cases of tuberculosis rose by 30,000 by 1944. In spring of that year, people were instructed to evacuate the cities to live with relatives elsewhere, and by August, schoolchildren were being sent away. As American bombing increased, the government created fire-prevention zones by razing buildings, which only heightened housing shortages. Japan was a nation losing a war of attrition, and its situation would only worsen as the American behemoth drew closer.

Japan had gone to war with few economic reserves in hand, and by 1944 its logistical shoestring haunted the military. Overstretched in Asia and the Pacific, the Japanese could neither hold nor ship home their valuable possessions of goods procured overseas, owing to American domination of the seas. In 1942 the military had shipped back to Japan 40 percent of oil-field production, but two years later a mere 5 percent reached the home islands. The homefront, along with pilots and the navy, faced hard times, and by mid-1943 all economic indicators began to tumble. Consumer industrial output tailed off that year, hurt by restricted production in China. Munitions-related production dropped precipitously, starting in 1944, and the stagnating output of iron, steel, coal, and other basic goods undermined the economy. Regardless of Korean slave labor, which accounted for one-quarter of all miners, normal coal supplies could not keep pace with consumption.

Shipping losses exposed the fragility of the economy. The large cities of Tokyo, Yokohama, Osaka, and Kobe lacked coal because increasing U.S. attacks on merchant vessels cut shipping capacity with each American advance across the Pacific. The surprise attack in the Truk Islands in February 1944 reduced Japan's available shipping another

10 percent—it plummeted under the 4-million-ton mark—and U.S. seizure of Saipan in July broke a major shipping route. Imperial government requisition of vessels led to decreasing imports of materials carried from overseas territories and to consequent price rises at home.

Even state intervention did not work for long. Airplane production, which rose until mid-1944, was victimized when shipping losses cut into imports of bauxite and other material needed for aluminum. Its trade cut off from abroad, Japan experienced a virtual shutdown of consumer and light industry and then great pressure on munitions factories. The economy's collapse meant the empire's doom.

Thus, the results in the field were not surprising. American troops simply overwhelmed the Japanese with quantities of industrial and technological goods. Heavyweight weapons also countered Japan's lighter guns and equipment, but it was the sheer amount of matériel that staggered the Japanese. The Americans actually wasted tons upon tons of food and industrial products. Marines abandoned truckloads of metal objects; their enemy left primitive wooden boxes attached to poles by rope. Most revealing of the supply and power gap were the words of a Japanese medical officer captured on Luzon in June 1945. After dressing the officer's flesh wound, an American doctor threw aside a half packet of sulfa powder. The prisoner grabbed the remainder, murmuring that "the Americans have so much, we have so little."[3]

As the war progressed, the United States provided a lesson in size, geography, and resources. While America became richer, Japan grew poorer. U.S. gross domestic production doubled between 1938 and 1944, only one statistic that tells the story of victory and defeat (see Table 1). Germany and Japan made high-quality armaments, but they could not produce ships, aircraft, and guns at the level that a rich, large nation could; America simply dwarfed its adversary in the war in Asia and the Pacific. In 1944, U.S. industries produced 26 tons of explosives for every ton made in Japan, and the next year the ratio jumped to 61 to 1. Indeed, "the most decisive battle of the Second World War was undoubtedly that of production," writes a statistician of the conflict.[4]

The output was staggering. The United States produced or had access to the lion's share of strategic raw materials, foodstuffs, and basic goods in 1944–1945 (see Table 2). Unlike Japan's, the U.S. economy enjoyed a miracle of massive food and fiber production and also got the goods to industry and consumers without worry of interruption by enemy forces. In 1945, Japan produced just under 600,000 gross tons of merchant shipping, compared with America's 5.83 million tons, a key component being tankers. Japan's 873,000 extant tanker tonnage at the end of 1943 plummeted to just under 267,000 tons by war's end. In addition, the American armed forces had nearly three times more personnel than Japan in 1944 and mobilized almost 16.4 million people in total (as compared with Japan's 9.1 million). These figures, added to the pooling of resources among the Allies, the vastness of the Soviet Union, and the capital-intensive high-technology nature of the U.S. and British team show that "in general terms the outcome of the war was decided by size," as one economic historian has put it.[5]

TABLE 1

Comparative Military Production, 1939–1945 (in units)

	United States	Japan
Tanks/self-propelled guns	88,410	2,515
Artillery	257,390	13,350
Mortars	105,054	unknown
Machine guns	2,679,840	380,000
Trucks	2,382,311	165,945
Aircraft	324,750	76,320
Fighters	99,950	30,447
Bombers	97,810	15,117
Transport	23,929	2,110
Naval	1,247	257
Aircraft carriers	141	16
Battleships	8	2
Cruisers	48	9
Destroyers	349	63
Submarines	203	167

Source: John Ellis, *World War II: A Statistical Survey* (New York: Facts on File, 1993), 277–80.

In the end, it hardly mattered that Japan mobilized 70 percent of its national income for the war effort, for that revenue was so much smaller than America's. Quantity largely prevailed over quality in this war. Even during the recession year of 1938, when compared on a global basis the

U.S. national income of $67.4 billion had been nearly twice that of Germany, Italy, and Japan *combined*. Turned toward the military, the U.S. economy poured in resources and achieved a limitless abundance of war matériel. Government military spending, which peaked in 1944, accounted for over 45 percent of the gross national product that year. The government also added 12 million employees to its payroll—10 million of these in the military—and financed a secret $2-billion project to build an atomic bomb as well. Rationing conserved additional goods for the war effort, while spending spurred a manufacturing, mining, and construction boom. Against such a productive behemoth, Japanese willpower, sacrifice, and even suicidal tactics were pointless. That Japan fought on despite the no-win odds, then, was perhaps due to their viciousness in desperate straits.

TABLE 2
Comparative Production, 1944–45 (metric tons)

	United States	Japan
Coal	1,085.9	62.7
Iron ore	186.2	6.9
Crude oil	449.7	1.1
Crude steel	177.7	7.3
Aluminum	2,119.6	117.0

Source: Ellis, *World War II*, 275–76.

News from the U.S. homefront dug Japan deeper into a hole. For the average American, circumstances were no worse than those of the Depression years and, in many cases, much better. As in Japan, clothing, housing, and access to petroleum were restricted, but personal consumption of food, energy, medical care, and clothing rose, albeit slowly. Hardship existed but not at the dire level seen in Japan. Food consumption showed the contrast: protein levels remained stable, while the government ensured ample supplies of vitamin C. Americans sacrificed in the war but in more moderate doses than the Japanese, and thus, in general, the civilian standard of living did not suffer greatly. Flagrant cheating, profiteering, strikes, voluntary mass migration to urban areas, the flood of women into the workforce, internment of Japanese Americans, partisan politics, minority civil rights movements, lobbying for veterans' benefits, and postwar planning for the international economic and peace structure revealed Americans to be concerned with much more than mere survival, as was the case for the Japanese. When combined with America's productivity, the November offensives gave Japan further proof of the empire's losing cause. Tokyo's response, however, was ever more fanatical resolve, which only compelled the United States to escalate the brutality.

Empress Augusta Bay and Bougainville

Until November 1943 the Pacific war was fought in two areas. In the north the Japanese occupied the Aleutians until chased from Kiska in July 1943. In the southwest, General Douglas MacArthur and Fleet Admiral William Halsey advanced up the Solomon Islands and New Guinea toward the ultimate prize of the Philippines. Victories at Midway and Guadalcanal had crippled the Japanese carrier fleet, leaving the empire with much of its aircraft force in the southwest land-based at the port city of Rabaul.

By November a third zone of operations had opened. Admiral Chester Nimitz, the commander in charge of all operations of the U.S. Pacific Fleet, approved a new strategy. Some of his new, fast carriers would seize island chains in the central Pacific to set up air bases from which the Americans could bomb Japan. As well, Nimitz would launch submarine attacks against Japanese shipping. The goal was to reach the Mariana chain of Saipan, Tinian, and Guam, from which heavy long-range bombers could pound the Japanese home islands. The first step toward the Marianas required seizing the Gilbert and Marshall Islands, which would also permit the U.S. Navy to share the action with the vain MacArthur, a man equally admired and loathed by troops as well as leaders in Washington. The general wanted all resources focused on his drive to the Philippines, Formosa, and Japan.

MacArthur and Nimitz, his superior, were at odds, not an unusual situation during the war. MacArthur had good reason to lobby for the southwest Pacific. Reconquering the Philippines had a political and emotional appeal back home, while assaulting the central Pacific, he correctly warned, would be bloodier than many imagined. Yet Nimitz also wanted to tie up the remaining Japanese Combined Fleet, based at Truk in the Caroline Islands, and thus neutralize Imperial naval power.

A central Pacific campaign would do so, although the Japanese Combined Fleet did not figure in the Gilbert or Marshall Islands defense because it was stretched too thin to fill the huge expanses of the Pacific. Thus, the Japanese concentrated most of their fleet and carrier aircraft on Rabaul. That proved to be a strategic error, for the Americans soon bypassed Rabaul in preparation for landings in the northern Solomons, as well as the Gilberts. Nimitz and MacArthur worked things out by dividing massive U.S. power between their separate though strategically linked theaters.

Before Nimitz's offensive began, the Allies targeted the large island of Bougainville in an effort to encircle and neutralize the 100,000 Japanese troops garrisoned at Rabaul. MacArthur planned an invasion of New Britain, to the west of Rabaul, to begin in January 1944 as part of Operation Cartwheel (the campaign in the southwest Pacific). Having advanced up the Solomons after the victory on Guadalcanal in early 1943, the Americans sought a toehold on Bougainville. Off the island's southern coast, troops from New Zealand landed on adjacent Treasury Island in late October, and then U.S. marine parachutists raided Choiseul Island in a feint to lure Japanese troops from southern Bougainville. All the while, Allied aircraft pounded enemy positions on the island.

The Japanese faced a predicament that froze their army units in New Guinea and the Solomons. Their loss of New Georgia and Kolombangara in the central Solomons and then Vella Lavella in early October 1943 left them with troops on Choiseul and Bougainville, and defending them would be difficult because naval and air forces also had to guard against an imminent Allied attack on northern New Guinea and New Britain. This ability to fight on multiple fronts in several theaters was a hallmark of Allied power, with the United States providing the resources to drive out the Japanese from multiple directions.

The Japanese could not hope to defend all their assets. On New Guinea, the world's second biggest island, where disease thrived in the often rain-drenched, gluey mud of impassable jungles, pockets of Japanese fought the Americans and Australians into 1945. Along the north coast the Allies finally broke an enemy counterattack around Finschhafen in late November 1943, causing at least 5,500 Japanese casualties. But slowed by the Japanese action, MacArthur now waited for the tremendous expansion of troops in the southwest Pacific area. He had 5 divisions by early 1944, with more on the way. Added in were 3 regimental combat teams, 3 engineer brigades, and 5 Australian infantry divisions, along with 1,000 combat aircraft and a growing number of landing craft, transports, and cargo vessels, plus a replenished warship fleet. Meanwhile, Japan's Eighteenth Army had endured about 35,000 casualties, leaving only 1 of its 3 divisions in eastern New Guinea near full strength. Although bogged down at times, the American-Australian advance along the north coast by December 1943 forced the Japanese to divert to the southwest area manpower and matériel that might otherwise have been used in the central Pacific.

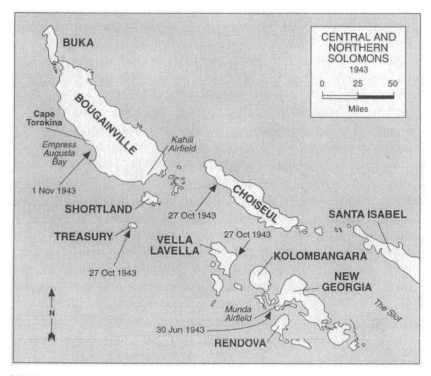

CENTRAL AND NORTHERN SOLOMONS

Joseph H. Alexander, *Storm Landings: Epic Amphibious Battles in the Central Pacific* (Annapolis: Naval Institute Press, 1997), 37.

Furthermore, to neutralize Japanese airpower the Americans bombed Rabaul's airfields, damaging shipping, ammunition dumps, and aircraft on the ground and intercepting dozens of Japanese fighter planes. By the end of October it was clear that the raids had inflicted major losses. In tandem with Marine Air Wings, heavy bombers of the Thirteenth Air Force and units of the Royal New Zealand Force left the Japanese with an estimated 154 planes in the northern Solomons, about one-third the Allied number.

Adding to his airpower shortages, Admiral Mineichi Koga, commander of the Combined Fleet, had been dealt a losing hand as American naval strength emerged in the western Pacific. Now his miscalculation undermined him further: believing no attack would come on Bougainville until December 8, the second anniversary of Pearl Harbor, he planned an offensive on New Guinea, but in so doing he positioned the Combined Fleet too far to the north and west to block the U.S. landings on Bougainville. Koga's problems magnified from there. He sought a naval showdown with the Americans somewhere in the central Pacific, guarding his fleet for this decisive event, but he could not compete with the U.S. fleet that Admiral Nimitz had rebuilt after Pearl Harbor. In addition, the Japanese had lost a large number of carriers and destroyers in the battles of the Coral Sea, Midway, and Guadalcanal as U.S. submarines wreaked havoc on precious Japanese shipping.

Koga's aircraft and naval circumstances set him at a disadvantage. He hurriedly replaced the planes lost to American attacks over Rabaul and New Britain, sending 250 aircraft from 5 carriers to the area. Then, realizing that intelligence reports had failed to pick up the landings at Empress Augusta Bay, he sent Admiral Sentaro Omori from Rabaul to search for the American task force coming up from Guadalcanal to support the Bougainville invasion. When Omori did not find them, he returned to Rabaul, only to be informed that the Americans had landed on Cape Torokino. The admiral went out again, this time with a larger force than before and one more powerful than U.S. Task Force 39, under the command of Rear Admiral Aaron Merrill. But Omori was too late.

Fourteen thousand men of the U.S. Third Marines and Thirty-seventh Infantry landed on Cape Torokina, on Empress Augusta Bay in the middle western part of Bougainville, on November 1. Bougainville's coastal plains were divided by two long mountain ranges; the broad flat beaches of the east coast around Cape Torokina were deemed best for landing. The plan was to hold this area of unoccupied jungle until 2 airfields could be hastily built for U.S. aircraft, which would attack Rabaul, less than 200 hundred miles away. Japan's Sixth Infantry Division, occupying the southern part of the island to protect 5 airfields, was far from the action. Dive-bombers from Rabaul strafed the invaders with few results, and the defenders offered minimal resistance at Cape Torokina—a godsend for the accident-prone Americans, some of whom were inexperienced in the high surf. Shortages of vessels also hindered the U.S. invasion, but within two hours the Americans secured a beachhead. The next day, raiders overwhelmed the Japanese, who either died or escaped into the interior of Bougainville.

The Japanese held on, however, adjacent to the cape. They had constructed a few dozen camouflaged pillboxes, fortified with a 75-mm. fieldpiece, by hitting some landing craft, a trench system, and rifle pits, effectively blunting U.S. naval bombardment. Chaos ensued in the shallows from machine-gun and mortar fire. As a sergeant reported after a shell hit his boat, lodging a fragment in his left thigh, "It was an awful mess. Bloody men pulled themselves off the deck and forced themselves over the side. One man had part of his back blown off." Looking back as he went into the water, the sergeant "saw that Smith wasn't going to make it; he had a wound in his head." Yet not only did the marine battalion lose just 26 men, it took the beaches, moved into the scrub bush, and attacked the pillbox entrenchments. Here, the viciousness of the Pacific war was in full display. Hand-to-hand fighting was the rule as the combatants clubbed, knifed, and punched each other in the narrow trenches. It was one of the first times that amphibious assault troops had met organized defenders who had survived naval bombardment. For that reason, reporters noted that the fighting outside the bunkers made this area on Bougainville "the bloodiest beach in the entire Solomons campaign."[6]

Other marine units and then service personnel arrived throughout the day, inching their way up the beaches. By nightfall, 8 transports had unloaded and headed back to Guadalcanal, fearful that Koga's naval force would swoop in. Rain came during the night, but the beachhead held, untroubled by Japanese army units on Bougainville but immediately threatened by Koga's fleet. Omari's task force of 4 cruisers and 8 destroyers attacked the following day, as the Allied amphibious vessels were scurrying about supplying the invading force. At stake for the Japanese was whether they could mount significant resistance in the northern Solomons. The ensuing naval engagements dashed these hopes.

A battle in Empress Augusta Bay erupted on the night of November 1. Elements of Merrill's Task Force 39, having located Omari by radar at nearly 40,000 yards away, were damaged, but the Japanese commander, incorrectly thinking that he had crippled the Americans, retreated to Rabaul. From there, 98 of the recently delivered planes took off to attack Merrill's withdrawing fleet. They scored two hits, losing 17 aircraft in the process. Merrill then struck back, sinking a light cruiser and a destroyer and damaging 2 other vessels, while suffering torpedo hits on only one ship. Task Force 39 had weathered a major air attack and guarded the American landing on Bougainville. The Battle of Empress Augusta Bay, the last major surface engagement in the Solomons, was also the final time that the Japanese fleet would challenge American dominance in the region.

From Truk, Admiral Koga determined to dislodge the Bougainville invaders, ordering the best units of the Second Fleet to join the planes at Rabaul. Under the command of Admiral Takeo Kurita, this fleet of heavy and light cruisers, destroyers, and service ships was detected steaming toward Bougainville on November 4. The normally aggressive Admiral William Halsey reacted in alarm, for his destroyers would not be able to defend the large contingent of American transports on their way from Guadalcanal. Also because Nimitz had rerouted all available ships to the Gilbert Islands, Halsey could not even procure an additional heavy cruiser. He would have to make do with Merrill's Task Force 39 and Rear Admiral Forrest Sherman's Task Force 38, which consisted of 9 destroyers, 2 light cruisers, a light carrier, and the old carrier *Saratoga*. The task forces risked defeat from both Kurita's fleet and the Japanese aircraft roaring in for the kill from Rabaul.

The dilemma made Halsey pause, but this risk-taker did not retreat. He had prevailed at Guadalcanal by boldness, and he planned to do the same off Bougainville, even though Task Force 38, with his son on board a carrier, might be destroyed. Sherman readied his Task Force off Cape Torokina, turning into favorable weather at nine o'clock in the morning of November 5 and launching all 97 of his planes—dive-bombers, torpedo planes, and fighters. Stunningly, they flew over Rabaul, dodging antiaircraft defenses and Japanese Zeros, bombing ships, and snapping photos. No ships on either side went to the bottom, but 24 Zeros and 10 American planes went down. A wave of U.S. bombers then hit Rabaul in the early afternoon, to the joy of Halsey; he proclaimed that the attack doomed the port, and the strike at Rabaul did halt Japan's defense of Bougainville. Impressed (and worried about Halsey's situation in the Solomons), Nimitz finally released a carrier group, and on November 11, Halsey drew on the additional 234 planes of this new Task Group 50.3, along with 3 carriers and Task Force 38, to attack Rabaul again. By this time, however, most of Koga's fleet had retreated to Truk.

Halsey's results were less spectacular than Sherman's run over Rabaul, but the strategic gains were sizable. The Japanese now abandoned naval action in the northern Solomons, thereby undermining resistance on Bougainville. On November 25 the last engagement occurred when American destroyers met Japanese counterparts off Cape St. George, New Ireland. The United States exhibited its outright dominance: Japan lost 3 new destroyers, while 2 others fled westward. Thereafter, the empire went on the defensive, hoping for a final battle that never came. Also, despite the delusions of some Imperial admirals, Koga's fleet and aircraft had been gravely depleted. A total of sixteen confrontations with the Americans had cost the Japanese a devastating number of planes and crew, forces that could no longer be replaced at a rate to keep pace with American production. Finally, the Americans' isolation of Rabaul made a landing on New Britain unnecessary, for Japan was unable to threaten the perimeter around Bougainville.

Infantrymen, bayonets fixed, advance through jungle behind an M4 medium tank on Bougainville. U.S. Army, *United States Army in World War II: Pictorial Record: The War Against Japan* (Washington, DC: Department of the Army, 1952), 143.

As for the island itself, the marines and army benefited from the reduction of air strikes from Rabaul by expanding their own perimeter. By November 5, in the midst of the first raid on Rabaul, their lines extended almost 3 miles inland. Three days later the Japanese countered with a bombing attack that killed 5 and wounded 20 on a transport, but the Americans had nearly 20,000 men on Bougainville by this time and repeatedly attacked against disorganized resistance, inflicting heavy casualties. Pushed up the trails in the swampy areas as the marines struggled to secure a safe zone within which airstrips would be built, the Japanese regrouped. They engaged the Americans at point-blank range on November 9, only to lose over 150 men in retreat. Yet the defenders retained forward defenses, ambushing the Americans on November 13 with machine guns, mortars, and sniper fire. Although American tank commanders grew disoriented at times, they pushed on into the loose but deadly resistance, the kind that drove U.S. troops to fight as ferociously as their enemy.

The Third Marine Division then fought the week-long Battle of Piva Forks. Beginning on November 19 with the most intense artillery fire yet in the Pacific war, the battle pitted U.S. forces this time against organized and fierce Japanese defenses. A battery near a coconut grove hit the marines head-on. Noted an observer, a "deafening roar" joined "the sharp terrifying sound of a shell exploding close by, . . . the agonizing moans of men shouting for corpsmen, for help, for relief from burning torture, . . . the maniacal screams and sobs of a man whose blood vessels in his head have burst from the blast concussions of high explosives." The Third Battalion suffered 14 dead and many wounded in just five minutes. An eerie silence ensued as marines walked through a "weird, stinking, plowed-up jungle of shattered trees and butchered Japs. Some hung out of trees, some lay crumpled and twisted beside their shattered weapons, some were covered by chunks of jagged logs and jungle earth, a blasted bunker, their self-made tomb."[7] Farther up the streams the marines encountered a dug-in enemy that focused on the flamethrowing engineers but spared nobody in inflicting several dozen U.S. casualties. Although the Japanese defended every yard gained by the marines at Piva Forks, the battle ended on November 25 and marked the last of the organized resistance around Empress Augusta Bay. By mid-December, 50,000 American troops had advanced 4 miles into Bougainville and begun building air bases. The first short runway reached completion at Cape Torokina on December 10, and nine days later a plane landed on the first U.S. bomber airstrip on Bougainville.

Bougainville was important for its airfields. The runways under construction in late November 1943 in the Cape Torokina area are supplied by a Douglas Transport C-47 and protected behind a defensive perimeter five miles deep. U.S. Army, *United States Army in World War II: Pictorial Record: The War Against Japan* (Washington, DC: Department of the Army, 1952), 133.

The earlier celebration of Thanksgiving, back on November 23 during the Battle of Piva Forks, hinted that Allied victory in the war was just a matter of time. Troops in the rear ate a warm dinner that day, a luxury not available to the reeling Japanese. Amazingly, even U.S. combat soldiers at the front received turkey dinners from runners ducking sniper fire. Still, life in the supply and staging areas was hardly comfortable, as personnel were victims of bombing, scorching temperatures, stultifying humidity that rotted clothes and caused skin ulcers, insect bites, and even some tropical maladies such as elephantiasis, in addition to the more common diarrhea. Marines counted 1,107 enemy dead, though more bodies disappeared in the swamps. Likely all the Japanese wounded died before reaching aid. The marines suffered 115 casualties.

Off Bougainville, the Japanese defeat loomed even larger. Because of the naval and air losses the Japanese in the Gilbert Islands could not count on adequate support; therefore, the defense of Tarawa was doomed in the face of smothering and seemingly limitless American power. Koga's fleet would not dare make a move from Truk. As a result of that quiescence the U.S. campaign in the central Pacific started uncontested at sea. This lack of naval resistance granted the Americans a great advantage on land, even though Japanese defense of their turf amounted to much more than just smoke and mirrors.

The Gilbert Islands

Seizure of the Tarawa, Makin, and Apamama atolls in the Gilbert Islands began the central Pacific offensive called Operation Galvanic, which ended eleven months later with the capture of Peleliu, a few thousand miles west of the Gilberts. At that point the campaign merged with MacArthur's southwest operations after the liberation of the Philippines in November 1944. The landings in the Gilberts, the Japanese-held islands closest (1,600 miles southeast) to Hawaii, represented the first transoceanic amphibious operation by the U.S. Navy. Troops traveled over 1,000 miles, a distance unprecedented in military history, and advanced 4,200 miles from Hawaii to Peleliu—an average of 400 miles a month. Success on such an enormous scale displayed America's unrivaled power.

Japan could not miss the meaning of the central Pacific campaign. Clearly, U.S. naval leaders harbored no doubts that they could push back the Japanese Combined Fleet. By November 1943 the United States, adopting a doctrine of using more to lose less, enjoyed numerical and qualitative superiority in ships and equipment. In the central Pacific, unlike Guadalcanal, the Americans drew on their staggering numbers and disparity in equipment to devastating effect. By the time of Galvanic, Japanese merchant shipping had suffered prohibitive losses, and the central Pacific then became a graveyard for military transports as well. U.S. submarines overcame organizational and operational defects—

specifically by corrections to the explosion device on the Mark XIV torpedo—and by summer 1943 had increased the number of their sailings from Pearl Harbor and Australia. The resulting swarm of torpedoes against Japanese shipping (nearly 900,000 tons of which went to the bottom in the central Pacific alone), further submarine penetration from U.S. bases in the central Pacific, and the first-time addition of amphibious support from carriers rendered Japan's strategic plans increasingly pointless.

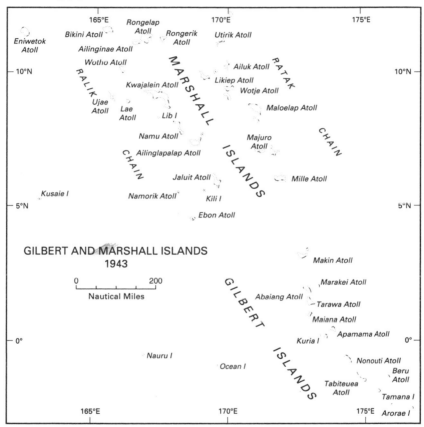

GILBERT AND MARSHALL ISLANDS

U.S. Army Center of Military History, *U.S. Army Campaigns of World War II: Eastern Mandates* (Washington, DC: Government Printing Office, 1993), 7.

Yet because the Japanese remained as aggressive as ever—perhaps more so because they now assumed a desperate defensive posture—the Gilberts had to be taken quickly and air bases swiftly built. American military planners gave the invading force just a few days to overrun the atolls before hopping to the neighboring Marshall Islands six weeks later. Otherwise, not only might Japanese subs and planes attack slow U.S. transports from bases in the Marshalls, but the Combined Fleet might impede the invasion itself. Under the command of Admiral Raymond Spruance, who rotated fleet command with Halsey, the U.S. Fifth Fleet (called the Third Fleet under Halsey) would drive across the central Pacific in a display of amphibious power. A veteran of Midway and the clever chief of staff to Nimitz, Spruance took to heart his boss's urging to get in and out of the Gilberts, and rapidly. To their relief the cautious Nimitz and Spruance soon learned from intelligence that the Japanese had only about 5,500 troops in the Gilberts while the Imperial Fourth Fleet—comprising 1 naval air flotilla, 3 light cruisers, and 28,000 troops—remained near the Marshalls to the west. Thus, the potential for naval conflict was slight. More worrisome were the actual landings on the atolls.

Wisely, Nimitz focused on the Gilberts only, making extensive preparations for America's first offensive in the Central Pacific. The participation of various services complicated planning, for Nimitz drew on the Pacific Fleet to bring the Twenty-seventh Infantry Division of the U.S. Army from Hawaii and the Second Marine Division from New Zealand to the Gilberts. The Army's Seventh Air Force sortied over the Gilberts a week before the landings, dropping 173 tons of bombs, while battleships and heavy cruisers bombarded from the sea, and then planes from carriers strafed the beaches. Bombproof shelters protected the defenders on Tarawa, as U.S. commanders soon realized, and just as worrisome was the specter of Japanese subs and planes coming out of Truk.

Makin Atoll, which garrisoned a Japanese seaplane base of 800 soldiers (only 300 were combat troops), seemed a relatively easy operation because U.S. troops at least doubled the number of Japanese, who had few heavy weapons. Yet the Twenty-seventh Infantry Division (which had no prior amphibious training) expended four days in taking the atoll, slowed by Japanese harassment of the green U.S. troops; the outmanned defenders cursed and threw firecrackers, causing panicked Americans to shoot back wildly and thus allow the Japanese to pinpoint their positions. Nearly all the defenders were killed, however, whereas the Americans lost 64 soldiers, though Japanese submarines also sank an escort carrier, the *Liscomb Bay*, killing 644 U.S. sailors. But there was no time for mourning, or rest. By the time Makin was cleared on November 23, the notorious battle for Tarawa was under way.

The target on Tarawa Atoll was Betio, the principal island, roughly the size of New York's Central Park. Its airstrip would allow photo reconnaissance planes to reach Kwajalein in the Marshalls, the next stop on the island-hopping campaign. Awaiting the Americans was a garrison of 4,836 naval infantry and engineers, untested but trained under Rear Admiral Keiji Shibasaki. In September the Japanese military had adopted a new operational policy, opting for defense and delaying tactics rather than rapid advances as Imperial Headquarters readied for a massive counteroffensive in the south and central Pacific in spring 1944. Shibasaki's sailors took part in the customary ceremony of reciting the Imperial Rescript, which reminded them of the reward of death in battle. Many in the garrison wore "semin bari" cloths around their waists—with each of a thousand stitches sewn by a different person—to give them protection, while others wore the Rising Sun emblem. They were determined to fight and die, with hopes of glory but the knowledge that they faced long odds, for the emperor.

Actually, although surprised by the American assault, Japan's military leaders believed that the defenses on Betio would hold. The island was guarded by nearly 200 cannon and hundreds of machine guns embedded in bunkers. Besides, despite the pounding from U.S. carrier aircraft, ships, and long-range bombers from the Ellice Islands, Shibasaki suspected that the invasion was really a feint to distract the Japanese from the southwest Pacific. He realized his error once he spotted the vessels, including troop transports, of a landing force on the morning of November 20. Training the coastal guns on the formations, Shibasaki's men did little damage. Worse, they were still two weeks away from encircling Betio with mines; thus the lagoon approaches remained open. Recalling his own amphibious landings on the China coast, the admiral hoped that Tarawa's coral reefs and receding tide would provide protection. His wish initially seemed fulfilled when American bombing suddenly ceased, and he peered from his bunker to see landing craft still offshore to the north of the island. Shibasaki then moved his guns from the south beaches to hit these sitting ducks, but he came in for another surprise: the Americans sped to shore not in wooden boats but in amphibious vehicles that rolled over the coral reefs. The invaders launched fusillades of machine-gun fire into the pillboxes, instigating a new sort of warfare that signaled a turning point in the Pacific war.

Nevertheless, the Americans by no means had it easy in this first amphibious assault of its kind by the marines. The three-hour bombing

—the largest preliminary naval bombardment of the Pacific war to date—turned out to be insufficient. Despite the fact that ships and aircraft dropped 6 million pounds of explosives on Betio, or 1,300 pounds of ordnance for each of the island's defenders, the shells did not pierce the pillboxes. They did, however, knock out some coastal guns, 3 tanks, and aboveground buildings as well as depleting supplies of ammunition and undermining communications. Still, American commanders worried that if Shibesaki had survived the war's biggest bombing assault, how could the marines hope to achieve amphibious landings without carnage? The lack of accurate coral reef maps, combined with misjudgments about the local tides (nobody knew the depth of submerged reefs), wreaked havoc on the landing craft. Furthermore, the amphibious tracked landing vehicles called amtracs had just recently been tested. The 50 that arrived from San Diego hours before the invasion were the only quick way to get from ship to shore, across the 1,000-yard reefs.

On the first day, stranded amtracs disgorged thousands of marines as far as 500 yards from shore, forcing them to wade to the beaches in waist-deep water. Since bombardment had not routed the defenders, disciplined Japanese soldiers held their fire and then let loose with devastating waves of firepower that killed men in the amtracs and ignited their fuel tanks. Five of the 14 new Sherman tanks, lacking the necessary fording kits that protected against flooding, stalled in the water. Men were sprawled everywhere, their commanders yelling at them to evacuate in the face of sheets of bullets. Tarawa was a destructive affair that cost the Americans 5,000 casualties the first day, including about 1,500 battle deaths. Two companies landing at Red Beach lost half their men; 4 of every 5 members of the amphibious tank crews lay dead or wounded. The second day brought better planning. Landing craft forged to the beaches with enough marines to assault the Japanese garrison, and by the fourth day all but 146 of the defenders lay dead—4,690 in all. Only 17 Japanese surrendered, along with 129 Korean laborers. The marines had 956 dead and the navy 29—nearly half of whom died in the water— along with over 3,300 wounded. In six months of fighting on Guadal-canal, the Second Marine Division had lost 263 men; in seventy-six hours of fighting on Tarawa, nearly ten times that number perished. In six months of battle, Guadalcanal had claimed 4,123 American lives; just over three days on Tarawa, an island less than 3 square miles, saw over 2,500 men killed. A reporter found dead Americans bunched together before pillboxes, with a half-dozen defenders killed inside; others were suspended on barbed wire strung on coral reefs. Some fortifications revealed the charred remains of dozens of Japanese fighters. It was a "furious blood-letting," write two historians.[8]

The carnage on Tarawa was horrific, but the United States captured the atolls, including Makin, Apamama, Ocean, and Naura. As one officer boasted to his troops, just before dying in machine-gun fire as he waded ashore, "This is the first time a landing has been made by American troops against a well-defended beach, the first time over a coral reef, the first time against any force to speak of, and the first time the Japs have had the hell kicked out of them in a hurry."[9] Tarawa witnessed the worst fighting over an intense, short period of the entire central Pacific campaign. The victory also took several more days than expected because well-concealed defenders forced the marines to pay a bloody price for Betio and the capture of the twenty-four other islands of the atoll. But Tarawa was American on December 6, 1943, two years after the attack on Pearl Harbor.

Although the many mistakes made in planning had cost hundreds of lives, most errors were remedied before the campaign for the Marshall Islands. Bombardment exercises on replicas of pillboxes were held at the naval gunnery range in Hawaii, for example, to study how to destroy these defenses. Amphibious warfare doctrine had been tested and proved, carried out by three different services (army ground and air forces, navy, and marines) despite problems with cooperation. Furthermore, the U.S. Navy showed that it could remain in an area, in control, during a land operation, an ability that served as the basis of offensives in the Pacific from then on.

The commander of the V Amphibious Corps, which oversaw Galvanic, later claimed that Tarawa had no particular strategic importance, but most American military leaders, as well as the Japanese, believed that the invasion made the next operations in the Marshalls easier. Admiral Koga, commander of the Imperial Combined Fleet, had miscalculated that the Americans were going to attack Wake Island and paid the price in the Gilberts. He had also mistakenly focused his attention on reinforcing Rabaul and thus suffered Halsey's air raids in the southwest Pacific. By December 1943 the Japanese were in trouble in both theaters.

For Admiral Shibasaki, the defender of Tarawa, the message was clear before his death during the first day of battle. Confident that he could hold the atoll, he nonetheless recognized that he faced a huge invading force employing the unremitting tactic of storm landings, as the Japanese called them. The United States successfully took a fortified island by the vast and innovative means at its disposal, including amphibious warfare, more powerful and speedy *Essex*-class fleet carriers, fast submarines, destroyers, minesweepers, landing craft, and an increasingly efficient and massive replenishment and supply system. The storm landings (from Tarawa to Okinawa sixteen months later) were offensive, fast, long-range (protected by carrier fleets), sustained, and lethal. On Betio the overwhelmed Japanese understood the message that America "had suddenly, and savagely, breached Japan's outer perimeter in the Central Pacific."[10] Yet Tokyo would not abandon the fight.

To be sure, Tokyo tried to put its plight in a good light. Focusing on American casualties on Bougainville, Japanese newspapers reported that Galvanic in the Gilberts was a ploy to divert attention from the death count in the southwest Pacific. The government continued its propaganda campaign, developed since Pearl Harbor, which vilified the enemy, called on great sacrifice from the people, and predicted glorious victory. Censorship ensured that the public did not hear about the battlefield reverses, or if they did, the government lied about the outcomes. When the Americans hit Rabaul and invaded Bougainville, Imperial Headquarters called the battle on Cape Torokina a victory and described the ruination of the U.S. fleet. The military could not trick perceptive listeners with such falsehoods, yet in general, the Japanese people believed that although the future would be difficult at the very least and that greater sacrifices were in order, the end would be triumph for Japan and its Pan-Asian Co-Prosperity Sphere. Suicidal charges and holdouts—on Tarawa and Bougainville—were reported as splendid fights to the death that honored the emperor, and Tarawa's garrison "died heroically to the last man," announced the government.[11] Still, a difference from the triumphalist messages of the now distant past of 1942 was evident, as censors disguised only the eventual fate of the nation. Like Shibasaki's forces on Tarawa, the people of Japan would fight to the last person if the government and emperor deemed it necessary.

There was no doubt that Tarawa was a horror show. One correspondent reported that in a U.S. marine assault, a flamethrower caught a Japanese defender of a pillbox in a "withering stream of intense fire. As soon as it touched him, the Jap flared up like a piece of celluloid. He was dead instantly but the bullets in his cartridge belt exploded for a full sixty seconds after he had been charred almost to nothingness."[12]

The nightmare on Tarawa also brought the war home to the American public. In order to prepare them for the expectedly brutal subsequent battles in the Pacific, the marines showed photos and films of the Tarawa landing—the first images of slaughter revealed during the Pacific war.

Nimitz, visiting Betio, was sickened by the sight, as was a stunned and repulsed American public just learning, like people in Japan, the meaning of war's cruelty. Tarawa began to condition people to this war without mercy and the recognition that Japan could be brought to its knees only by horrific annihilation, which could also cost tens of thousands of American lives. As Admiral Spruance concluded, Tarawa showed the need for "violent, overwhelming force, swiftly applied."[13] That lesson the Americans would teach Japan again and again as they took to the offensive.

China

Beyond the Pacific theaters the United States brought its diplomatic as well as sheer military power to bear against Japan in November 1943. Regarding China, America had two strategic goals. The first was to tie down Imperial Japan's forces there and prevent their deployment to the Pacific by bolstering Chinese armies against the Japanese invaders. The second was to secure air bases in southern and central China from which to bomb Japan itself. Achieving these objectives would take considerable diplomatic effort, and ultimately, neither was fulfilled. The first goal met the resistance of Chinese ally Jiang Jeshi, although enough aid flowed into China to compel the Japanese to maintain a sizable number of troops there; the second turned out to be unnecessary, given the success of the island-hopping campaign in the central Pacific.

Since the war in Asia had begun in 1937, the Chinese had shouldered the brunt of the fighting. Nationalist Goumindang leader Jiang Jeshi, based in Chungking, as well as the communists in the north, led by Mao Zedong, fought this ground war with U.S. military advice and supplies. Yet neither Generalissimo Jiang nor Chairman Mao was strong enough militarily or had enough indigenous support to drive the Japanese from Chinese soil. They had also long fought each other in a civil war that polarized China and thus further inhibited the war effort. A unified Chinese counteroffensive against Japan seemed impossible, despite U.S. efforts, mainly because Jiang in particular had much less interest in defeating Japan than in routing the communists.

In addition, in U.S. planning, China—a remote theater—occupied a military status secondary to Europe and the Pacific. American commitments elsewhere, as well as production bottlenecks early in the war, rendered the Allies incapable of overcoming the vast distances in China to equip and train Jiang's army. Internecine warfare among warlords, demands for patronage from the generalissimo's cronies, and the struggle against communism stymied further help. Some supplies came through India by sea and were then airlifted from Burma over the Himalayas, but this dangerous operation proved too meager to build an adequate army in southern China. The Americans urged Great Britain to reconquer Burma, which the Japanese had seized in 1942, but the British were too weak. Given the insufficiency of the Burma supply route, the opportunistic Jiang took what U.S. aid was available but used much of it for his internal purposes. To Washington's dismay, Jiang's corruption and focus on Mao depleted his effort against Japan.

Faced with Chinese civil war and domestic rivalries, enormous logistical problems, a befuddling web of political intrigue, and disparate cultures, President Franklin D. Roosevelt still managed to keep Jiang in the American corner and the Japanese occupied in China. He promised large deliveries of airlifted supplies for China's air force and army, but diplomacy was the key to his success. A master politician, Roosevelt orchestrated a charm offensive in November 1943, one that built on his longtime flattery of Jiang by nominating China one of four leaders in the postwar world. He thought China would help America stamp out imperialism in Asia by freeing the subject peoples of the British, French, Dutch, and Japanese empires—grand illusion on Roosevelt's part, for Jiang was incapable of assuming this role. FDR's mistaken conviction that China could contribute to the decolonization movement undermined American foreign policy after World War II. Yet during the war, his misguided policy of embracing Jiang caused no more than frustration on the part of U.S. officials working for the defeat of Japan in China.

In fact, it was a practical option. Because America could not supply China with enough matériel to drive out the Japanese, FDR figured that coddling Jiang's ego would aid the war effort with minimal U.S. involvement. The military situation in China had not improved; supplies from India were at a trickle; Allied plans to liberate Burma were canceled owing to the Pacific and Mediterranean campaigns; and U.S. General Claire Chennault's idea of air bombing operations on Japan from China seemed untenable. Thus, at his only meeting with Jiang—in Cairo, November 22–26 and again from December 4–6, 1943—Roosevelt encouraged the anticolonial crusade. Once Japan surrendered, Korea was to be given its independence after a period of trusteeship under Chinese tutoring, but in reality, Korea, Formosa (Taiwan), and Manchuria would all be returned to China. Adding to Jiang's glory, Roosevelt proclaimed that China must lead "on an equal footing in the machinery of the Big Four Group and all its decisions" after the war.[14] The subsequent Cairo Declaration presented this rosy picture as well as a demand for Japan's unconditional surrender. Jiang acclaimed President Roosevelt as China's great friend.

The Cairo Declaration, designed to appeal to Asians as well as bolster Jiang, came just weeks after the Japanese had solidified their own anti-imperial alliance. On November 5 the Diet in Tokyo had formalized the Greater East Asia Co-Prosperity Sphere: Japan, Manchukuo, Burma, India, Indonesia, and the Philippines. This Asian federation of formerly Western colonial holdings, the Japanese hoped, would join the empire in its war against America, China, and the West, in return for nominal independence. That the Imperial Army held power in all these areas, and had no plans to leave, was glossed over as Tokyo bureaucrats pledged supposed self-government for the members of this united Asian bloc based on racial solidarity.

Japan rolled out the red carpet in a display of unity. Thousands of schoolchildren greeted the delegates outside the Imperial Palace and 100,000 people at Hibiya Park heard Premier Tojo Hideki and the German ambassador proclaim certain victory in the war. The conferees announced five doctrines—or war aims—predicated on coexistence, mutual prosperity, respect for Asian traditions, and racial equality to serve as a counter to the Anglo-American Atlantic Charter of 1941. Officials and journalists fantasized that Asia would no longer bend under the yoke of Western domination. But attaining such universal principles, much less winning the war, was out of the question. Japan had already become the new imperialist, and a racist one at that, which would never give up power in its occupied territories unless pried from them by force. But the rhetoric, however illusory, promised freedom from imperialism and thus gave those under Japanese control an alternative to FDR's ideal of the Big Four policemen.

Within months, Roosevelt revealed his renowned caginess. He sidled away from Jiang as a key element in the postwar world. Even in Cairo, he had confided to the chief U.S. military adviser in China, Joseph Stilwell, that he would support the next leader if Jiang were deposed. In addition, Soviet willingness to enter the Asian war once Hitler was defeated rendered Jiang irrelevant on the mainland. Still, FDR placed greater stock in diplomatic overtures than actual power relationships when it came to China. The Cairo Declaration firmed up the Asian alliance and, when added to the promise of Soviet entry into the Asian war, represented formal approval of plans discussed in Washington and Chungking. Regarding the disposition of Japanese territory after the war, the declaration affirmed that "Japan will also be expelled from all other territories which she has taken by violence and greed." To be sure, the Japanese were correct in surmising that Roosevelt assented to such a pledge merely to court Jiang Jeshi and cover up growing divisions between the Nationalists and the Allies. Yet having China as a partner was one more element in the offensive against Japan. The blunt Cairo Declaration, along with an American air bombardment of Formosa from Chinese bases at the time of the conference, emphasized that point. From across the Pacific and across China the "Japanese-American war was steadily coming closer to the Japanese homeland."[15]

American-Chinese diplomacy went hand in hand with the military assaults in the Pacific, and all were key elements of America's November 1943 offensives. The United States had fought a two-front naval and amphibious war in the Pacific and had done so largely alone. Within six weeks of each other, Halsey had landed on Bougainville, MacArthur's First Marine Division had gone ashore at Cape Gloucester in New Britain, and Nimitz had taken Tarawa. The conflict against Japan would be won not by an Asian land war but by advances across the Pacific. At Imperial Headquarters, Japanese military leaders no longer thought in terms of offensives; their military swagger of previous years was replaced by the realization of fighting an already powerful enemy growing stronger by the day. Yet the Japanese showed a remarkable persistence in the face of the invincible United States.

 Notes

1. Joseph H. Alexander, *Across the Reef: The Marine Assault on Tarawa* (Washington, DC: Marine Corps Historical Center, 1993), 7.

2. H. P. Willmott, *The Second World War in the East* (London: Cassell, 1999), 126.

3. Schrijvers, *The GI War*, 234.

4. John Ellis, *World War II: A Statistical Survey* (New York: Facts on File, 1993), 281. See also Schrijvers, *The GI War*, 244.

5. Mark Harrison, "The Economics of World War II: An Overview," in *The Economics of World War II*, ed. Harrison (Cambridge: Cambridge University Press, 1998), 19.

6. Harry A. Gailey, *Bougainville, 1943–1945* (Lexington: University Press of Kentucky, 1991), 73.

7. Ibid., 108, 109.

8. Williamson Murray and Allan R. Millett, *A War to Be Won: Fighting the Second World War* (Cambridge, MA: Belknap Press, 2000), 345.

9. Charles T. Gregg, *Tarawa* (New York: Stein & Day, 1984), 66.

10. Joseph H. Alexander, *Storm Landings: Epic Amphibious Battles in the Central Pacific* (Annapolis, MD: Naval Institute Press, 1997), 44.

11. Haruko Taya Cook and Theodore F. Cook, *Japan at War: An Oral History* (New York: New Press, 1992), 264.

12. Ronald H. Spector, *Eagle against the Sun: The American War with Japan* (New York: Vintage Books, 1985), 265.

13. Alexander, *Storm Landings*, 49.

14. Gaddis Smith, *American Diplomacy during the Second World War, 1941–1945*, 2d ed. (New York: Alfred A. Knopf, 1985), 92.

15. Akira Iriye, *Power and Culture: The Japanese-American War, 1941–1945* (Cambridge, MA: Harvard University Press, 1981), 154, 155–56.

2

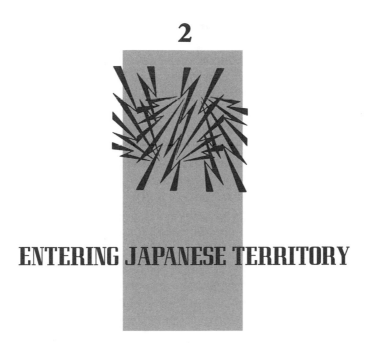

ENTERING JAPANESE TERRITORY

Offensive-minded U.S. troops, equipped with a formidable array of weapons and fortified with ample supplies, aggressively moved on to their next targets. In the central Pacific they headed into the Marshall Islands, while General MacArthur's forces aimed for the Philippines by progressing northward across New Guinea. The Japanese blocked, resisted, and counterpunched. But both American campaigns relentlessly rolled them back in furious warfare.

The Marshall Islands

The Marshalls—two island chains roughly 125 miles apart but only 70 square miles in area—rested 2,200 miles southwest of Hawaii and a few hundred miles northwest of the Gilberts. Some of the nearly two thousand reef-enclosed islets and islands were tiny, like Kili, yet Kwajalein was the largest atoll in the world. The Japanese highly prized the Marshalls, which had been mandates since 1914.

The operation to seize them, code-named Flintlock, represented a significant effort against the empire. As the American learning curve regarding amphibious warfare shot upward after the troubles at Tarawa, U.S. leaders undertook a bold strategy of bypassing some Japanese strongholds and heading for the center of Japanese strength, on Kwajalein. A clear message accompanied the campaign. The Americans had retaken lost ground in the Solomons and Gilberts, but in the Marshall Islands in 1944 they registered a major additional victory by penetrating Japanese territory for the first time. Enemy bases, built throughout the Pacific since World War I, had never been touched by U.S. forces. Now that isolation ended under Flintlock, the initial step—through Japanese lands—toward Tokyo.

The Marshalls drew the attention of strategists on both sides. The islands allowed Japan to extend menacingly into the eastern Pacific, threatening the U.S. Navy as well as transportation and communication lines, and remained defensive barriers blocking the heart of Japan's outer ring of defense in the Carolines and Marianas. Since the 1920s, American naval planners had crafted ways to take the chain as a step toward recapturing the Philippines, which they correctly predicted would be conceded to Japan in war. Japanese strategists had determined in mid-1943 to bog down the Americans in the Marshalls, thereby buying time in the more important Carolines. American successes in the northern Solomons and Gilberts forced realistic thinking about the Marshalls. Although Japan would ultimately write off the islands as indefensible, they would reinforce the Marshalls and fight to the death, making America pay a dear price for victory. Such resistance provoked a campaign of violence from the United States.

The U.S. Navy relished the challenge. From mid-December into January 1944, air attacks hit the heavily defended easternmost Marshalls, which Rear Admiral Forrest Sherman had decided to skirt in favor of zeroing in on Kwajalein Atoll. Deciphered enemy military codes showed that the bulk of Japan's forces had been shifted to the outer Marshalls in anticipation of an American attack there. Sensibly but audaciously, Sherman went after the interior of the chain, even though fellow commanders—Spruance included—opposed the plan. Air bases on four surrounding islands protected Kwajalein, they argued, and the island also lay within range of planes from the Marianas and Carolines, making communications difficult and occupation impossible. Yet Sherman countered that a new fast carrier Task Force 58 in the Fifth Fleet could handle the Japanese planes. Besides, Japanese air reprisals against the American attacks of January had been ineffective. Nimitz agreed, and with Task Force 58 ready to detour around the eastern atolls and attack Kwajalein, D-day was set for January 31.

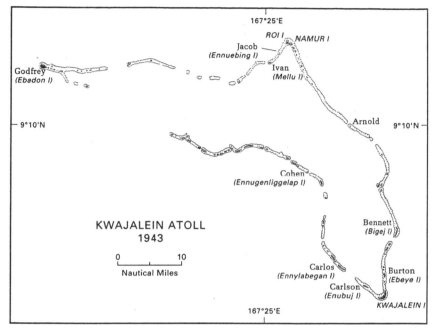

KWAJALEIN ATOLL

U.S. Army Center of Military History, *U.S. Army Campaigns of World War II: Eastern Mandates* (Washington, DC: Government Printing Office, 1993), 12.

Having learned the hard lessons of amphibious warfare in the Gilberts, the American military improved its air and fire support during Flintlock. Commanders crafted another set of assault groups, which would draw on the same warships that had served off Tarawa, although this time they would benefit from more time, support vessels, firepower, and air cover. The Gilberts provided a base for combat and photographic reconnaissance by U.S. warplanes. Thus, Task Force 58 readied for action in the last days of January 1944, with 12 carriers, 8 new fast battleships, several escort cruisers and destroyers, and 650 aircraft under the command of the veteran aviator Vice Admiral Marc Mitscher, who had begun to perfect the new carrier warfare after a bad performance as captain of the *Hornet* at Midway. Guided by British ULTRA reports taken from decrypted enemy cable traffic that pinpointed Japanese planes, the four air groups under Task Force 58 swept aside the estimated 235 Japanese planes in the eastern atolls in just two days.

Crescent-shaped Kwajalein Island, at the southeast tip of Kwajalein Atoll, and a pair of islands to the north—Roi and Namur—were the American objectives. The center of Japanese aviation operations, Roi had to be seized, along with the nearby Namur support base only 400 yards away. The two islands dominated the northern entrance to the Kwajalein lagoon, where U.S. troops would land. Forty-four miles away, Kwajalein Island housed a large Japanese garrison and a nearly completed 5,000-foot airstrip—ideal for American long-range bombers. Like Roi and Namur, Kwajalein was surrounded by flat, shallow coral reefs of the type that had made landing on Betio so harrowing. Accessible beaches without heavy surf were fortified by seawalls and log palisades.

Military intelligence warned of impending threats, for Kwajalein was 955 miles east of Truk, the command center of the Combined Fleet. It was unlikely that Admiral Koga would sail into the Marshalls, but he might send a light striking force. In addition, nearly two dozen submarines cruised the area. Although U.S. air assaults neutralized Japanese airpower, some 560 aircraft were available at Truk and Saipan as reinforcements, in addition to planes at airfields on Maloelap, Jaluit, and Wotje Islands in the Marshalls. On Eniwetok, at the western end of the chain, there were air and naval bases, a seaplane anchorage, and 1,000 troops. Furthermore, Japan stationed 35,000 ground forces in the Marshalls, putting over one-quarter on Kwajalein. U.S. intelligence predicted that its defense would be "of a more permanent nature and consequently more formidable" than Tarawa's.[1]

Japanese forces were at the disposal of Vice Admiral Masashi Kobayashi, who had the task of punishing the Americans. As the air attack commenced, he withdrew his forces to Truk; major elements of the Imperial Navy would never again enter the Marshalls. Task Force 58's further destruction of shore-based airplanes led to the evacuation of all remaining planes by February 1, which left Japan bereft of airpower in the Marshalls. Yet on the ground, several thousand troops had arrived from Truk, the Philippines, Manchuria, and the home islands. Kobayashi distributed many of them to the outer eastern islands, on the mistaken assumption that the Americans would land there first. On Kwajalein, the reinforcements were divided evenly between Kwajalein Island and Roi-Namur.

Taken by surprise, the Japanese had not sufficiently readied their defenses on Roi-Namur and Kwajalein; 2 tin-mount 5-inch naval guns, cannon, and machine guns in pillboxes guarded the three islands. Underwater and beach obstacles, mines, and barbed wire were scarce and of bad quality, and four massive blockhouses could not make up for the dearth of concrete structures. On Roi-Namur, 3,000 naval aviation, ground defense, service, and construction personnel awaited the Americans, but Kwajalein and Roi-Namur together had only the same number of defenders as Betio, though compelled to cover three times the area.

The full American force descended on Roi-Namur and Kwajalein Island on January 29. Task Force 58, having whipped through the outlying Marshalls, pounded all three and eradicated Japanese air power. Under the command of Rear Admiral Richard L. Conolly, the Americans shot down 11 of the last 20 fighter planes on Roi in a few minutes and destroyed the island's air base. Kwajalein and Namur came under a similar withering attack. Carrier planes and then battleship and destroyer bombardment also took care of Wojte and Taroa Islands as the amphibious groups threaded through the Marshalls in preparation for landing.

On D-day, January 31, the American troops—given forty-two days' rations—huddled on the landing craft. Transporting the Fourth Marines, who were raw recruits in the Pacific war, were 240 amtracs and 75 armored amphibians. For the first time on a large scale, 2.5-ton amphibian trucks carried to shore the division's howitzers. Their novelty and number, added to communications snafus, led to repeats of the transport jam that had occurred off Tarawa. Amtracs and boats were separated or followed the wrong route to shore, some artillery ended up on the beaches hours before the soldiers; radios failed. Fortunately, Japanese fire was minimal. Amtracs churned over the reefs toward Ennuebing Island, an outcropping 2,500 yards from Roi. Company B of the Twenty-fifth Marines were the first Americans to land on Japanese territory in World War II. By nightfall, the V Amphibious Corps had met all its objectives, taking nine islands plus Majuro Atoll, which fell into American hands without bloodshed. Roi and Namur would be attacked the next day.

Before dawn on February 1, Admiral Conolly brought his battleships in close to the islands. Chaos ensued. Air strikes and heavy bombardment did not eliminate the Japanese battery on Roi; confusingly dispersed landing vehicles, crossed orders and commands, mechanical failures, and rain squalls that knocked out radios caused Conolly to delay the assault for several hours. The marines who finally went ashore suffered high casualties because of the surf, reefs, and sunken amtracs. Some landings met no resistance, but others confronted disorganized yet determined defenders. Two Japanese rushed the Twenty-third Marines' Company E with bayonets. A few yards inland, dazed defenders fought from open trenches. Small-arms fire bothered the invaders; more substantial opposition came from one of the huge blockhouses until marines lobbed grenades through the entrance. Company C's marine tank and amtrac commanders, impatient to seize the air base, rumbled too far ahead of support to the northeast corner of the island. Meeting Japanese resistance from gun emplacements and pits, Company C retreated and then grouped in a coordinated attack in the late afternoon.

The marines saw few living Japanese. Death was quick and brutal. Mopping up, Company C came across a trench holding 40 defenders, most of whom had committed suicide. Several hundred Japanese were victims of bombardment, their bodies strewn in debris. Isolated soldiers popped out of ditches. The adrenaline-pumped Americans often shot wildly, mistaking coral reefs for swimming Japanese. Individual tragedies occurred, such as when Private Richard Anderson fell on a hand grenade to save his comrades. Second Lieutenant John Chapin recalled the chaos of the landings. As he turned to talk to his platoon sergeant, who was manning a machine gun next to him, Chapin realized the man was dead—"the whole right side of his head disintegrated into a mass of gore."[2] Yet the lessons of Betio bore fruit on Roi: the landing went more smoothly and discipline was largely the rule on land.

Just a few hundreds yards away, however, Namur proved more harrowing for the Twenty-fourth Marines. As on Roi, bombardment softened up the island, but disorderly scheduling of amtrac movements hindered the marines. The bombing had destroyed the central communications and intelligence building on the island, however, killing ranking officers (including Vice Admiral Michiyuki Yamada, air commander in the Marshalls), which impeded organized resistance. After the 7 remaining officers perished together while scurrying toward a bomb shelter, individual Japanese soldiers fought for themselves. In one instance, when 3 tanks became stuck in soft sand, the Americans killed 30 onrushing enemy, while the Japanese killed only 1 U.S. soldier. There was incredible heroism and sacrifice on both sides. When First Lieutenant John Power's Company K assault team set a demolition charge outside a pillbox, Power was severely wounded by return fire. Holding his left hand over the injury, he rushed the opening made by the explosion and emptied his weapon with his right hand. As he paused to reload, he was shot twice and killed.

Namur caused more problems than Roi before falling into U.S. hands. Marines blew up a large blockhouse, not knowing it contained torpedo warheads, and the subsequent explosion shook the island, temporarily halting bombardment. A column of smoke shot more than 1,000 feet in the air, and soldiers offshore saw the island disappear in a cloud of brown smoke as palm tree trunks and concrete shot through the air. A hole the size of a swimming pool was all that remained. The blast launched one American 50 yards out to sea, where he was rescued. But 20 of his comrades died, and 100 more were wounded in the destruction of the blockhouse and two subsequent explosions, accounting for nearly half the American casualties on Namur.

Pockets of defenders hidden in dense undergrowth on Namur were tougher to root out than on Roi. Shell holes, fallen trees, and jungle slowed the advance. Japanese climbed up the sides of tanks, only to be swept aside by raking machine-gun fire. Captain James Denig, a tank commander in Company B, got separated from his unit. While he was getting his bearings, Japanese defenders climbed on his tank and dropped a grenade into an open port, killing him and his driver and wounding 2 other crew members before rescuers burst upon the scene. Heavy machine-gun fire hampered the invaders in other parts of Namur. The two sides also engaged in vicious hand-to-hand combat. More often, the defenders fell to the combination of infantry backed by tanks. Near the end of the battle a group of Japanese jumped into an antitank ditch, firing upon advancing marines until tanks entered one end of the ditch. Americans, reported an observer, dumped deadly canister and machine-gun fire "down its length, piling dead Japanese three deep."[3] It was this kind of fanaticism that hardened American troops toward the violence they committed. Namur's seizure on February 2, after a day and a half of fighting, cost the marines 313 dead and 502 wounded. Over 3,500 Japanese died.

Meanwhile, the crescent of Kwajalein Island to the south was being contested by the well-trained U.S. Army's Seventh Infantry. On January 31, islets in the lagoon and fortifications on Kwajalein had been boldly shelled from vessels just 1,500 yards offshore, while Task Force 58 launched 96 sorties against the island. Amtracs came ashore, infantry crouching behind them, to secure the beachhead with minimal resistance from a handful of the 5,000 diehard defenders garrisoned on the island.

As on Roi-Namur, the defense was fanatical but disorganized, limited to mortar fire and attempts to infiltrate American lines. The Japanese faced long odds but never thought of giving up.

Machine guns and automatic rifles cover infantrymen on Kwajalein, as a tank and tank destroyer advance. U.S. Army, *United States Army in World War II: Pictorial Record: The War Against Japan* (Washington, DC: Department of the Army, 1952), 230.

By the first night, with 6 battalions ashore, the Americans reached one end of the airfield. Troops advanced across the island, occasionally eliminating survivors of the bombardment who had holed up in wrecked shelters and pillboxes, necessitating close combat. Private First Class Julian Guterrez fired his M1 rifle into a spider hole, causing a Japanese soldier inside it to commit suicide by turning a grenade on himself. Guterrez threw a grenade into a patch of palm fronds, which erupted in flesh and gore, prompting the private to flee to the lagoon to clean himself off. Vomiting, he was unable to gather himself together for several minutes.

After repulsing Japanese small-arms fire behind their own lines, the Americans began mopping up on February 4, the fourth and final day of the Kwajalein battle. In a rare instance of surrender, 49 Japanese (along with 125 Korean laborers) were taken prisoner. Enemy desperation and dementia were recurrent. In one instance, Japanese riflemen walked into American lines carrying palm branches to shield their naked bodies. In another, a Japanese officer rushed out of his pillbox and doused a U.S. infantryman with a fire extinguisher before being incinerated himself by a flamethrower. The gruesome task of burying some 1,200 Japanese bodies strewn over the island in the baking hot sun went on for days afterward.

Far fewer Americans perished on Kwajalein than on the equally large and well-defended Tarawa because the earlier costly assault had loomed large in the minds of American military planners. They responded with improved coordination of navy, air, and ground units. As a result, of the 41,000 U.S. troops involved in Flintlock, 372 were killed (at Tarawa, over 3,300 had died). The Japanese dead numbered 7,870 of the 8,675 soldiers on the island. Adding Majuro Atoll, which was taken without a loss, Kwajalein represented a resounding victory on Japanese soil. Still, resistance did not end: a dozen or so Japanese seaplanes retaliated for the invasion of the Marshalls on February 12 by bombing ammunition dumps on Roi, killing 30 Americans and wounding 400 more, destroying most of the U.S. supplies and buildings on Roi, burning 2 landing vehicles, and damaging a large amount of construction equipment. Yet even before this deadly raid, eight days after D-day, U.S. combat teams and transports were being removed from the atoll in preparation for the seizure of Eniwetok.

Truk and Eniwetok

The capture of Kwajalein, marking the initial invasion into Japanese territory, cleared the way for taking the Marshalls, neutralizing the huge naval base at Truk, and moving into the Mariana Islands to the west. Nimitz's daring strike into the Marshalls also paid off in other ways. The Fourth Marines received valuable experience in amphibious combat, which it would bring to bear later on Saipan, Tinian, and Iwo Jima.

Furthermore, Spruance had guarded his reserves of troops, which had sailed in transports to the Marshalls; casualties had been kept low. Momentum in the island-hopping campaign continued, and the tempo of the war against Japan quickened. So encouraged were military planners that they advanced their timetable from May to mid-February 1944 to attack the westernmost island of the Marshalls: Eniwetok. Nimitz sought to build a major fleet base on that island, and at the same time, Spruance's carriers advanced far to the west toward Truk to dismantle this principal Japanese naval base in the central Pacific and thus open the way to the successful conclusion of the Marshall Islands operation.

The Japanese knew that Truk was no longer viable as a base once the Gilbert Islands fell. With American carriers and submarines roaming the central Pacific, it was increasingly perilous for the Japanese to resupply vessels at the huge complex. As a consequence, in early February 1944 the Imperial Navy began moving the Combined Fleet back to Japan itself, and just in time, too. Task Force 58's 6 battleships, 9 carriers, and dozens of other vessels launched the first of 2 major attacks on Truk on February 17. In 30 raids each involving in excess of 150 planes—a more potent force than in Japan's two assaults on Pearl Harbor—Marc Mitscher's forays destroyed 270 of the nearly 400 planes on the airfields over a three-day period. Two dozen transports and a dozen warships escaped, but Mitscher hunted down another 24 transports, 2 cruisers, 4 destroyers, 2 submarines, 5 auxiliaries, and 24 merchant ships. A Japanese torpedo bomber hit the carrier *Intrepid*, putting it out of action for several months, and shot down four American planes, but on the second day of attacks not one Japanese plane rose off the ground.

The raids shut down Truk, the first time in history that carrier air-craft had forced a big base to cease operations. The Japanese never again stationed large naval and air forces on Truk, although they did place enough aircraft and ships there to prompt a second U.S. carrier and battleship assault on April 29–30, which took out another 100 airplanes and destroyed or chased off the remaining ships. Once Truk's use as a mid-Pacific air base was eliminated, the United States never had to launch an amphibious attack there (as the Japanese had long expected), and the facility served mostly as a Japanese prison camp for the remainder of the war. With over two-thirds of Truk's aircraft destroyed and its ships on the bottom or on the run, U.S. forces had a free shot to Eniwetok.

On the same day that Truk was first attacked, the final stage of Flint-lock also began, 670 miles to the east. Coconut palm- and mangrove-covered Eniwetok Atoll was 326 miles northwest of Roi-Namur, only 1,000 from the Mariana Islands, and 2,500 from Japan. It held about 3,500 Japanese on four principal islands that formed a rough circle around a lagoon. The Japanese First Amphibious Brigade, numbering 3,940 men, had arrived there in early January 1944 to reinforce the atoll's only air base, on Engebi, and to garrison the other three islands of Eniwetok, Japtan, and Parry. With Kwajalein's fall, 110 airmen evacuated to Eniwetok en route to Truk were now left stranded on the atoll.

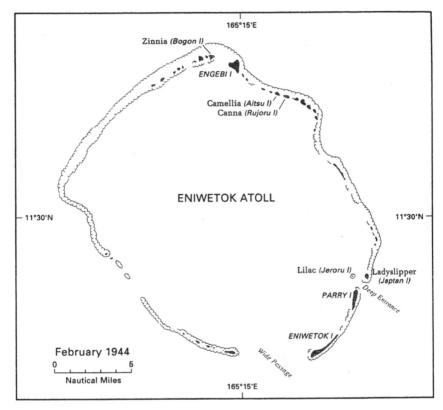

ENIWETOK ATOLL

U.S. Army Center of Military History, *U.S. Army Campaigns of World War II: Eastern Mandates* (Washington, DC: Government Printing Office, 1993), 21.

The defenders dug trenches and dugouts protected by logs, built networks of "spider traps" composed of oil drums set in the ground and lightly covered, and constructed weakly reinforced but well-camouflaged pillboxes, having learned from the Tarawa invasion to erect more effective defenses. They were armed with flamethrowers, naval guns, mortars, grenade dischargers, machine guns, and rifles. Engebi's commander predicted that the Americans would bombard the atoll from all sides in advance of an amphibious landing in order to secure the inner lagoon. Surf and rugged reefs would hinder them, however; thus, the commander determined to "make complete use of every available man and all fortified positions, carrying out each duty to the utmost. Plans must be followed to lure the enemy to the water's edge and then annihilate him with withering fire power and continuous attack." If necessary, the atoll would be defended by "creative night attacks." Defense works and tactics on Eniwetok and Parry were similar, though the latter also benefited from the largest force of men as well as minefields. In all cases the Japanese were prepared to fight to the end, "die gloriously," and in so doing convince the Americans that only the most furious, vengeful assault would lead to victory.[4]

U.S. forces, now reinforced from the Kwajalein operations to over 10,000 men, readied to land in Eniwetok. Mistaken intelligence reports indicated that only 800 (as opposed to 3,500) Japanese were on the atoll, and that most were on Engebi (not Parry). D-day for Eniwetok was February 17, with Rear Admiral Harry Hill commanding the amphibious units. Before landing, the Americans began a tremendous bombardment of the islands, meeting no return fire. In the entrance passage of the lagoon, minesweepers also destroyed a minefield—the first encountered by the U.S. Navy in the war against Japan. Taking some small islets the first day and softening up the Japanese with shelling from inside and outside the lagoon, the Americans prepared to land on Engebi the next day.

On February 18 the amtracs roared ashore, amid some minor confusion but generally in an orderly fashion, as they worked toward Engebi's airstrip. Bypassed in the assault, defenders collected weapons and fired on the Americans from the rear. U.S. commanders realized that more enemy troops than previously thought were on the island, yet the defense was feeble, and Engebi fell that day. Eniwetok was the next target. In the belief that it, too, was lightly defended, Eniwetok received light bombardment relative to Engebi and, later, Parry. That belief was mistaken and proved fatal for some Americans. Eniwetok proved tougher than expected to capture. A high bluff, spider traps, and Japanese fire caused congestion in the landing. One group met a fierce counterattack of 400 defending troops who were eventually thrown back but managed to bog down the U.S. advance. Tank and infantry companies fought stiff opposition, while small groups of Japanese, numbering 6 to 10 men, attacked through the night. The hidden network of Japanese trenches, foxholes, and pillboxes, out of which the defenders could snipe at the Americans' flanks and rear, dragged the campaign for Eniwetok Island into a three-day affair. In so doing, it delayed the invasion of Parry, the last island. In addition, horror, fear, and sadness were ever present. Crawling forward to ask a fellow soldier to locate the Japanese in a coconut grove, a marine found a dying comrade with wounds in his head. "So it came over me what this war was, and after that it wasn't fun or exciting, but something that had to be done."[5]

With Eniwetok Island in mind, Admiral Hill bombarded Parry with great intensity, as did artillery from Eniwetok and Japtan Islands, to complete the capture of the atoll. On Parry, some men in the landing teams succumbed to a land mine, while others died rooting Japanese from spider traps. Japanese mortar and machine-gun fire grew severe, prompting two U.S. Navy vessels to shift their position out of harm's way. After continued naval bombardment, marines moved forward behind tanks, encountering enemy strong points of tunnels and barracks that required vicious fighting to subdue. By nightfall of February 22, Parry was taken. For the first time in the war, American ships illuminated a battlefield all night: star shells lit up the island and allowed the marines to cut down bands of surviving Japanese. Parry cost the Americans over 300 casualties; the Japanese had more than 1,000 killed. But the capture of Eniwetok Atoll was complete. Some 3,400 Japanese had died, whereas the marines buried 262 and had 757 wounded. Exhausted and dirty but thankful to be alive, the marines finally rested. One recalled his amazement at being intact and that there "was not much jubilation. We just sat there and stared at the sand, and most of us thought of those who were gone—those whom I shall remember as always young, smiling, and graceful."[6] The result was even greater resolve to revenge those fallen comrades.

The campaign in the eastern mandates formally ended in June 1944, although mopping up and reinforcing the Marshall Islands continued into April 1945, and the dull business of bombing the islands that had been initially bypassed continued under the marines until Japan's surrender. Enemy garrisons withered away, many of their occupants starved to death, dying of disease, or barely subsisting until surrendering at war's end. They occasionally shot down a marine pilot, but their own physical and emotional deterioration was their biggest threat.

Operation Flintlock succeeded beyond earlier predictions because of the lessons learned at Tarawa about amphibious warfare. The Marshalls campaign taught the Americans that close air support and heavy naval gunfire were imperative; they were not any longer an exception to be used haphazardly. Scheduling of landing vehicles would be further perfected. The Japanese, likewise trying to adapt after Tarawa, had discovered that they could not withstand the fierce naval bombardment, and so they, too, made adjustments in readying for the assault on the Mariana Islands: they would simply heighten their brutally senseless resistance.

That the stronghold of Eniwetok fell in February—not May, as first planned—allowed Admiral Nimitz to speed up his invasion of the Mariana Islands by thirteen weeks. He had proved that the central Pacific, in contrast to MacArthur's route from the southwest, would be the most efficacious approach to Japan. With the further conquests of Saipan and Tinian, he could place long-range bombers in reach of the home islands. The quick seizure of the Marshalls, moreover, had saved lives, and the troops were ready for action in the Marianas. With Truk out of the picture, Japan's eastern perimeter continued to contract. Once deemed "unsinkable aircraft carriers" by the Imperial Navy, the Gilberts, the Marshalls, and Truk had been put out of service. The setbacks revealed the devastating power of the United States to advance at will toward Japan.

Isolating Rabaul: The Admiralty Islands

General Douglas MacArthur worried about military planning. The central Pacific campaign had gone forward, and to MacArthur's chagrin, his theater of operations seemed to play second to island-hopping in the thinking of Washington, D.C. Army and navy competition for resource allocation might swing against him, for air force planners, eying the Mariana Islands to the northwest as bases from which to operate the new B-29 bomber, also pushed for Chester Nimitz's advance. The Joint Chiefs leaned toward the central Pacific operations as well but still supported MacArthur, believing that U.S. forces could be transferred from one area to the other in a two-pronged attack. (The China theater had been rele-gated to the back burner.) But MacArthur insisted on elevating the southwest Pacific theater by a focus on isolating Rabaul on the way to the ultimate recapture of the Philippines.

In late January 1944, U.S. brass met at Pearl Harbor. Interservice rivalry yielded a temporary victory for MacArthur when Nimitz acquiesced to moving toward the Philippines rather than north to the Marianas. Admiral Ernest King, intervened, however. This chief of naval operations was the foremost proponent of the central Pacific drive, and that campaign would continue in order to guard against Japanese flanking attacks. The Joint Chiefs agreed, to the consternation of MacArthur, who still would continue his advance in the southwest.

By the time of D-day in the Marshalls, forces in the southwest Pacific had greatly expanded. Five infantry divisions were present, along with 3 regimental combat teams, 3 engineer special brigades, and 5 Australian infantry divisions. On the way were 3 more U.S. divisions. With these, added to the 1,000 combat aircraft under the command of General George Kenney and the Seventh Fleet under MacArthur's new naval commander, Vice Admiral Thomas Kinkaid, plus Admiral Halsey's South Pacific force and a growing amphibious fleet, MacArthur had tremendous assets at his disposal. For the Japanese, the future looked grim. Unable to replace their air, sea, and ground losses, they frenetically bolstered their forces in western New Guinea while awaiting an American-Australian onslaught on the eastern part of the island.

In mid-December 1943, MacArthur began operations to quarantine Rabaul and to move toward the Philippines by the New Guinea route. He hit Madang, across the straits separating New Guinea from New Britain, and then crossed the straits to assault Arawe at the opposite tip of New Britain from Rabaul. Japanese defenses, air raids, and counterattacks at the end of the month inflicted casualties, and during the initial assault, Japanese machine gunners sank most of the rubber landing boats. Although U.S. soldiers swam for their lives, 16 did not make it, and 17 others were wounded. Successive landing waves got separated, but superior firepower trounced the Arawe defenders. A Japanese air counterattack on the two infantry battalions yielded little—just 1 transport sunk and 8 auxiliary vessels damaged. Meanwhile, the Japanese Sixth Air Division from Wewak on New Guinea lost all its bombers, and an additional 19 bombers and 22 fighter planes of the 11th Air Fleet from Rabaul went down. Nonetheless, it took another month and an additional marine corps tank company and infantry reinforcements to drive off the defenders in the swamps, mud, and jungles of New Britain. On January 16, 1944, the Arawe Peninsula was America's, but at the cost of 118 dead, 353 wounded, and 4 missing.

At the western end of New Britain, at Cape Gloucester, the Guadalcanal veterans of the First Marine Division took the Japanese airfield and garrison on December 29. On New Year's Day, while clearing out the

Japanese from the jungles, they met fierce resistance. Having constructed a camouflaged bunker complex along a stream later aptly nicknamed Suicide Creek, the Japanese held off the marines for two days until U.S. tanks rumbled down a makeshift log road to annihilate them. The operation cost 310 marine dead and 1,083 hurt, further evidence that the Japanese would pointlessly fight to the bitter end. But now MacArthur had control of the entire western end of New Britain, as well as the west side of the straits between New Britain and New Guinea. The Americans used the airfield at Cape Gloucester, rather than establishing a PT-boat squadron at Arawe, for the rest of the war. Responding to this pressure on Rabaul and American victories in the central Pacific, Japan withdrew from both New Britain and New Guinea most of its air power, which was then no longer a threat to Allied operations in the Bismarck Archipelago. To be sure, MacArthur could not seize Rabaul by overland travel because of the terrain, but his next moves on New Guinea and in the Admiralty Islands, 360 miles west of Rabaul, made holding the port irrelevant.

The Australians had taken Finschhafen, on New Guinea, in early December 1943, and they progressed up the coast in pursuit of the Japanese. On January 2, 1944 a U.S. amphibious combat team landed at Saidor, unloading men and cargo so efficiently that 6,700 troops and their equipment were ashore by nightfall, with only 6 casualties. Capturing Saidor's airstrip and splitting General Hadazo Adachi's Forty-first Division at Madang from his beleaguered Twentieth Division at Sio were their two objectives, both of which were fulfilled. After the bombardment that preceded the U.S. landing teams, 50 defenders garrisoned at Saidor retreated inland over rugged mountain trails toward Adachi's main forces up the coast at Madang. During this death march, conducted at night to avoid Allied air attacks, starving and dysentery-ridden troops confronted intense rain that caused small streams to overflow and block their path. Many drowned, and many died from malnutrition. In the rain they "marked their line of retreat with corpses."[7] Uneasy American troops took notice of this ultimate sacrifice on the part of their enemy.

MacArthur's gains mounted. He had a staging area on either side of the straits between New Britain and New Guinea and had forced the Japanese to retreat. Even more significant, the Japanese left behind a virtual gold mine: as they fled, soldiers of the Twentieth Division dismantled their radio equipment to carry over the mountains, but a heavy steel trunk full of codebooks was too heavy to take and too wet to burn, so they buried it. The Allies found the trunk near a stream and hustled the material to Australia, where it was dried out, copied, entered on IBM computing machines, and decrypted. The find allowed the deciphering of the Japanese Army's communications, not the first or the last time that intelligence would give the Allies a big edge. Aided by thousands of Japanese American and Native American linguists, code-breakers, and code-talkers throughout the Pacific and Asia and at the Pentagon in Washington, U.S. officials uncovered decisive information. In this case the Japanese never caught on and so did not take sufficient measures to change their codebooks, and thus they paid a price. The intelligence coup tipped off MacArthur to impending Japanese air raids on New Guinea, exposed enemy convoys, and revealed that 4,000 Japanese were on the Admiralty Islands, 250 miles to the north—though U.S. planes flying over the islands had reported no signs of activity at the main airfield of Los Negros Island. MacArthur decided to "put the cork in the bottle" of the Solomons-New Britain campaign by attacking the Admiralties.[8]

As MacArthur prepared, Halsey added to his carrier-based attacks on New Ireland, just to the east of Rabaul, by securing a land base for PT-boat raids on the Green Islands, 60 miles east of New Ireland. On February 15 the Third New Zealand Division, backed by the U.S. Navy, landed on the largest island, Nissan. Japanese resistance evaporated, and Halsey began building his PT-boat bases and airfields which, in combination with the seizure of the Admiralty Islands, meant the encirclement of Rabaul. Moving ahead of a scheduled April attack on the Admiralties by drawing on ULTRA information, General Kenney's planes destroyed a squadron of Japanese planes on the island of Los Negros in the Admiralties and silenced the main airfield on January 24. A month later, reconnaissance by three medium bombers above Los Negros and Manus, the other big island of the Admiralties, found no enemy activity. MacArthur ordered a probe of Los Negros by 1,000 assault troops, who were rounded up from shore leave in Brisbane, Australia, crammed into destroyers, and pointed toward the island.

A 6-man reconnaissance force landed on Los Negros on February 27, finding it "lousy" with Japanese. Indeed, ULTRA reported 3,250 enemy garrisoned on the island.[9] Los Negros was nearly flat, separated from the larger, mountainous Manus Island by a narrow strait that fed into the natural Seeadler Harbor, itself an ideal spot for an anchorage. The patrol had encountered elements of the Japanese garrison, which had been so well camouflaged that the low-flying bombers passing over earlier had missed them.

Regardless of the misinformation, the commander on the island, Yoshio Ezaki, helped the invaders by deploying his troops along Seeadler

Harbor. MacArthur and Admiral Kinkaid watched the initial assault on February 29 at the beach of Hyane Harbor, on the opposite side of Los Negros. Believing Hyane too narrow and its beach too small for the Americans, Colonel Ezaki had placed only a handful of artillery, anti-aircraft batteries, and machine guns at the harbor entrance. Taking advantage, waves of U.S. boats came ashore as Japanese fire on the first morning was nullified by naval bombardment and a rainstorm. By that afternoon the Americans had encircled the Los Negros airfield. Mac-Arthur landed to inspect the perimeter; he conferred a Distinguished Service Cross on Second Lieutenant Marvin Henshaw, the first soldier on the beach, and left orders for General William Chase to hold the airstrip at all costs.

MacArthur called for reinforcements to the Admiralties while General Chase, lacking barbed wire, contracted his perimeter around the airfield. Ezaki instructed his battalions to "annihilate the enemy who have landed. This is not a delaying action. Be resolute to sacrifice your life for the Emperor and commit suicide in case capture is imminent."[10] Still focused on Seeadler Harbor, however, he held back many of his troops. A few Japanese managed to infiltrate the lines, compelling wounded Americans to remain in their foxholes throughout the night, receiving treatment from medical personnel who used instruments sterilized in buckets of campfire-heated water. At one point a group of Japanese donned life preservers and swam around to the rear of the U.S. lines, isolating a platoon of E Troop, which hung on for life. Chase's perimeter was still holding by the dawn of March 1, at the loss of 7 Americans killed and 15 wounded, while 66 of the infiltrators were killed. Taking Ezaki's words to heart, 15 defenders rushed Chase's command post in the afternoon, to be mowed down by machine guns or later to commit suicide. Further probes and piecemeal attacks were repulsed until by the next morning, March 2, the perimeter was secure. Coming ashore, 1,500 more troops and 400 Navy Seabees towed along artillery, ammunition, heavy equipment, and other supplies.

The worst fighting was still to come. With the Seabees forming an inner perimeter, artillery and mortars in support, and destroyers using ULTRA to bombard the Japanese, Chase's regiment fanned out across the airfield. It took Ezaki a day to realize that Hyane Harbor was, indeed, the center of action. That night, March 3, he launched an attack, engaging tired U.S. soldiers linked by solid defensive positions of artillery, mortar, and minefields. A destroyer came up close to shore to barrage the Japanese attackers, but Ezaki's troops did not quit. They yelled false commands in English, tricking one mortar group into abandoning its post, though other American units ignored pleas to cease firing. Meanwhile, the Japanese advanced with abandon—talking, shouting, and even singing as they approached machine guns. They overran or infiltrated points on the perimeter, inflicting heavy casualties. Sergeant Troy McGill of G Troop found his group reduced to 2 just 35 yards in front of the main perimeter. He sent his compatriot back to safety while he defended the position alone until his rifle jammed, when he wielded it as a club until he eventually perished. Yet by the morning of March 4 the Japanese were on the run, suffering over 750 dead to the Americans' 61 soldiers lost. No prisoners were taken; all Japanese survivors obeyed orders and committed suicide.

Now veteran observers of such fatalistic behavior, the Americans took another two weeks to secure the Admiralties. After seizing some islets, with casualties, the Americans moved on to Manus on March 15, moving across the island and encountering heavy fire from pillboxes. Tanks and Australian fighter planes based on Los Negros eliminated the defenders with 500-pound bombs, and the next day, Manus's airfield fell into U.S. hands. Retreating to the island's interior, 200 defenders made a stand from their quickly fortified pillboxes at the village of Old Rossum, from March 19 to 25, but air and artillery power eventually overwhelmed them; survivors staggered into the jungle to die or to subsist on dog meat until hunted down. On April 1, U.S. troops attacked two small islands in native dugout canoes, the only time in the Pacific war that such vessels were used for an amphibious assault. All told, only 75 Japanese surrendered in the Admiralties, while nearly 3,300 of their comrades died. The Americans lost 330, with 1,189 wounded.

By taking the Admiralties, MacArthur hoped to close out the campaign against Rabaul and press on to the Philippines. It would not be so easy. On Bougainville the Japanese prepared a counterattack against the expanded American perimeter at Empress Augusta Bay. Lieutenant General Hyakutaka Harukichi spent early 1944 mobilizing some 19,000 troops. When he realized that the Empress Augusta Bay invaders represented the main U.S. force, he moved across the mountains. He had mistakenly estimated the enemy troops at around 30,000 but found himself facing more than double that number. To make matters worse for him, Japanese Army plans had been decoded, which prevented a surprise attack and allowed optimal placement of American defenses. In addition, the Japanese lacked air cover, and Halsey's occupation of the Green Islands cut off their reinforcements and supplies from Rabaul.

Major General Oscar Griswold let the Japanese come to him. He waited behind a 23,000-yard perimeter, which was a series of hills flanked by swampy ground and rivers. The Japanese faced long odds, but they were able to observe the Americans from higher terrain than the U.S. perimeter. Griswold readied mines and booby traps, a large number of rifles and extra machine guns, searchlights and other illumination devices, and oil drums each containing a torpedo surrounded by scrap metal. Eight howitzer battalions, 6 cannon companies, and numerous gun batteries, supported offshore by all available destroyers of the "Bougainville Navy," were in place by early March 1944.

Hyakutaka inspired his men: "Attack! Assault! Destroy everything! Cut, slash and mow them down" and seek revenge "with the blood of the American rascals."[11] On March 8 the Japanese commenced an artillery barrage that compelled the Americans to evacuate their planes from the airfield, Hyakutaka's only clear victory in the Empress Augusta Bay counterattack. From there, he planned two simultaneous ground assaults, followed by the main thrust. His first target was the steep Hill 700 on the northeast side of the U.S. perimeter, upon which the Japanese advanced near midnight on March 8 until two companies were blocked by the Americans. U.S. forces then destroyed an infantry battalion before the attackers took a saddle between the Hill 700's two highest points. Yet Griswold cleared the hill the next day, finding over 300 Japanese dead on top, joined by 78 Americans. The next night, at Hill 260, the Japanese seized the 150-yard saddle between its two highest points and stormed up the steep slopes, maniacally screaming threats in English and singing songs to unnerve the waiting soldiers. The Japanese took South Knob, despite wave after wave of U.S. attacks that left 98 dead and 581 injured. Four days of vicious fighting with flamethrowers and an artillery barrage of over 10,000 rounds finally dislodged Hyakutaka's troops. They suffered 560 deaths, and survivors fled into the jungle.

The main Japanese thrust came on March 11 near the center of the perimeter in an assault on the U.S. 129th Infantry of the Thirty-seventh Division. Ferociously, Japanese officers brandished their prized sabers and blindly rushed forward screaming, "San nen Kire!" or "Cut a thousand men!"[12] Although they merely overran a few pillboxes before U.S. infantry and tanks restored the defensive lines, the fighting was gruesome. In one encounter an American search party entered the charred remains of a pillbox to hear the click of a grenade in the corner. As they dove for safety, a Japanese soldier—bleeding, face seared, clothing burned—threw a grenade and died. Japanese "dead were strewn in piles of mutilated bodies, so badly dismembered in most cases that a physical count was impossible. Here and there was a leg or an arm or a blown-off hand, all to show for the vanished and vanquished enemy. At one point, Japanese bodies formed a human stairway over the barbed wire," noted one American. Bulldozers, their drivers nearly overwhelmed by the stench of decaying bodies, scraped up the remains and covered them in mass graves.[13]

The combat was gut-wrenching, and more such savagery was on the way, but Hyakutaka would not give up. On March 15 his forces penetrated 100 yards into the perimeter before being driven back with 190 Japanese dead. The remainder regrouped in the jungle for their last try on March 23. Again, superior U.S. firepower pounded the attackers, 7 artillery battalions erupting for twenty-five minutes in the heaviest concentration of firepower yet seen in the Pacific war. The Japanese retreated, leaving behind wounded and heavy equipment. Sporadic fighting ensued as the Americans, including the first black infantry unit (the new Twenty-fifth Regiment) to engage in combat during the war, gave pursuit. Mopping up on Bougainville took until November 1944. Although 263 Americans had died in defense of the perimeter, more than 5,500 Japanese expired; rot and dismemberment prevented a full count. Even the reported numbers, however, represented enough carnage to end the northern Solomons campaign on a grisly note.

With Rabaul's isolation complete and Bougainville secure, MacArthur moved on. Although the Australians would continue the Solomons campaign in 1945, the failed Japanese counterattack at Empress Augusta Bay in March 1944 ended any real threat to the Allies. Cartwheel had wrested the southwest Pacific area from Japan's hold, and successive clashes interrupted supply routes, leading to the attrition of the empire's air, sea, and ground forces. The Japanese could not stand up to the multi-faceted American attack on the theater's several fronts. The nineteen-month northern Solomons campaign over, MacArthur could turn toward New Guinea, and the Philippines beyond.

In the Admiralties, MacArthur had been lucky; had Ezaki concentrated his troops on Hyane Harbor, Chase might have been routed. MacArthur could thank ULTRA and bad enemy decisions for his good fortune. Allied forces seized Emirau Island to the east of the Admiralties, thereby completing the Bismarck Archipelago campaign, and began building bases. From Los Negros, planes hit New Guinea and the Carolines to the west, while Seeadler Harbor's superb anchorage became a major facility for Allied ships. The U.S. Army erected hospitals and depots as a staging area for invading the Philippines. Kavieng and Rabaul remained in Japanese hands, but they were surrounded and impotent. Imperial forces had been dedicated, but they were not enough in a war dependent on resources. Stretched thin, Japan could neither protect nor reinforce its holdings. "In the final analysis, the American home front, the source of a seemingly unending flow of supplies and equipment, combined with the fighting skills of the American soldier to make victory possible," noted a U.S. Army account.[14]

The occupation of the Admiralties, Bougainville, and the Marshalls led MacArthur and Nimitz to accelerate their plans for victory. Triumphant in the southwest Pacific, the general boldly looked to an April landing at Hollandia, 580 miles behind enemy lines up the New Guinea coast. It was a leap well beyond previous plans, but vision could become reality now that the huge Japanese bases at Rabaul and Truk were paralyzed. For his part, Admiral Nimitz eyed the Marianas. The American military machine had moved more proficiently than ever thought possible, for in the five months since November 1943, U.S. forces had reduced Japanese land-based air power, and the Imperial Navy had withdrawn to the west, its forward bases obsolete. Amphibious landings were being perfected, Japanese territory captured. Perhaps wondering why Japan would fight on, Nimitz nonetheless prepared for further deadly assaults. In the next four months the Americans would advance from the south and east toward the two big prizes: the Philippines and Japan itself. Both were within reach, but not without brutal combat.

 Notes

1. Robert D. Heinl Jr. and John A. Crown, *The Marshalls: Increasing the Tempo* (Washington, DC: Government Printing Office, 1954), 28.

2. John C. Chapin, *Breaking the Outer Ring: Marine Landings in the Marshall Islands* (Washington, DC: Marine Corps Historical Center, 1994), 6.

3. Heinl and Crown, *The Marshalls*, 97.

4. Ibid., 120.

5. Chapin, *Breaking the Outer Ring*, 24.

6. Ibid., 27.

7. Edward J. Drea, *MacArthur's ULTRA: Codebreaking and the War against Japan, 1942–1945* (Lawrence: University Press of Kansas, 1992), 92.

8. Spector, *Eagle against the Sun*, 281.

9. Leo Hirrel, *U.S. Army Campaigns of World War II: Bismarck Archipelago* (Washington, DC: Army Center of Military History, 1993), 14.

10. Ibid., 16.

11. Stephen J. Lofgren, *U.S. Army Campaigns of World War II: Northern Solomons* (Washington, DC: Army Center of Military History, 1993), 27; Gailey, *Bougainville*, 147.

12. Ibid., 154.

13. Ibid., 155–56.

14. Hirrel, *Bismarck Archipelago*, 26.

3

THE CHINA-FORMOSA-LUZON LINE

Regardless of American advances and Japanese losses, both sides suffered from delusions. Three were in evidence. First, Douglas MacArthur continued to believe that the route to victory lay in the Philippines and then China, refusing to concede that his southwest Pacific campaign and pursuit of the strategic front that ran from China to Formosa to Luzon in the Philippines came second to Nimitz's island-hopping campaign. The second delusion was Jiang Jeshi's belief that China remained a pivotal theater in the war. The Allies fought to reopen the Burma Road but otherwise increasingly ignored China. Yet, neither MacArthur nor Jiang, men with inflated senses of their own grandeur, ended up as wartime failures. That was not the case for the Japanese high command, men who perpetuated the war under a third and most striking delusion: they erroneously held to the hope of victory, or at least negotiated peace. By midsummer 1944 this pipe dream would have been laughable if it had not brought such tragic suffering to the Japanese people and their soldiers. In the oldest war theaters—Asia and the southwest Pacific—Japan simply could not hold. By trying to do so anyway, this stubbornly irrational nation heightened American wrath.

Japan in Crisis

Imperial General Headquarters actually had been encouraged by the defense at Tarawa, which gave the military time to regroup its naval and its air forces in the Marianas and the Philippines. Yet after the Marshalls, Truk, and Rabaul disasters, admirals and generals began blaming one another for their nation's declining fortunes. Prime Minister Tojo lashed out at all the services, demanding that each provide a plan to halt the United States, bolster the nation's defenses, and maintain access to raw materials. In February 1944 he fired his navy chief of staff, rejected the army's advice to focus on the Philippines as the main line of defense, and assumed the position of minister of war. Such were the desperate acts taken by Japanese leaders, acts destined not to bring peace but to extend a punishing war.

The Japanese homefront was also collapsing, in the main because of U.S. submarine warfare. By January 1944 the number of submarines had doubled from that at the beginning of the war and then rose another 50 percent by the end of the year. Improved hulls, engines, guns, torpedoes, and communications made these predators ever more effective. They hindered Japanese redeployment to the Philippines and Marianas, forcing to the bottom the equivalent of two divisions between March and mid-June, when the Marianas campaign began. Seven of nine transports carrying two divisions to New Guinea were lost to torpedoes, for Japanese antisubmarine forces became consigned to protecting incoming oil tankers but were helpless to guard personnel headed for battle. Soon, even the safety of the oil tankers was in doubt: as the tanker fleet was reduced by 60 percent in 1944, a scant one-tenth of the oil produced in 1944 and 1945 arrived in the home islands. So destructive were the U.S. submarines that American sailors soon complained about the lack of enemy shipping targets.

Japan also faced the prospect of U.S. strategic bombardment. When the Americans found a base close enough to the home islands to send the new B-29 Superfortress bombers, the Japanese, who lacked sufficient antiaircraft defenses, would suffer. Into the summer of 1944, however, the B-29s focused on the Marianas campaign. Furthermore, engine problems and technological challenges plagued production. The Superfortress was expensive (although innovative design had brought the cost for each down to $700,000 by 1943, in comparison with the B-17's price tag of $240,000), and engineering glitches delayed its mass production by Boeing Aircraft. Yet though receiving fewer than 100 planes by June 1944, army air force leaders salivated, eager to test this highly publicized weapon.

Impressed, outraged, but undaunted, Tojo resolved to change strategy. He harbored doubts about the entire war effort but dared not publicize them, for superpatriots assassinated anybody who sought peace. Thus, Tojo protected himself by responding intrepidly. He ordered the military, incredibly, to return to the offensive in 1944, hoping to defeat the Allies once more and persuade them to negotiate a peace settlement. The offensive would be three-pronged: attack the Commonwealth army in India, go after the Chinese Army and U.S. air bases in western China, and inflict a defeat on the American Fifth Fleet in the Marianas. He would almost ignore (although harry) MacArthur's advance along the north coast of New Guinea, awaiting the general in the Philippines. The strategy spelled impending disaster. As historians have written, these "many sequential and parallel decisions of early 1944 took Japan's armed forces to catastrophe."[1]

Burma and India

Until early 1943, Anglo-Indian forces had been routed in Burma. Britain had infiltrated the Myitkyina-Mandalay area, prompting Japan to conquer Burma by late 1942 and cut the last overland supply route to China. This victory frustrated Lieutenant General Joseph Stilwell, chief of U.S. forces in the China-Burma-India theater, who was charged with building Jiang Jeshi's army into a viable force. Jiang's main base at Kunming in southwestern China could only be supplied by the dangerous airlift over the "Hump"—the high Himalayas—so Stilwell focused on reopening the land supply route by taking northern Burma with Chinese troops. His failure was due to logistical difficulties in India throughout most of 1943, plus competition for resources from Major General Claire Chennault and his "Flying Tigers," who demanded that the Hump supplies support his air force rather than Stilwell's Chinese ground forces. In the end, Allied leaders approved both efforts. Chennault's planes inflicted some losses, but because they never achieved air superiority, Japanese forces drove his planes from advance bases in east China. Stilwell's limited offensive in central and northern Burma, however, got another chance.

Or so it seemed. In October 1943, Vice Admiral Lord Louis Mountbatten, the supreme commander of the Southeast Asia theater, also sought to reconquer Burma and open the Burma Road. He ordered Stilwell to send two Chinese divisions toward the communications center of Myitkyina, 175 miles southeast of Ledo in India, a town that lay at the end of a planned road through Burma to China. But at the Cairo Conference in November, Anglo-American strategists decided to minimize the role of Chinese forces and send resources to other theaters, with China playing an air base support role. From February to October 1944, nearly 18,000 tons of supplies flew over the Hump to support the B-29 bombing campaign on Japan, while Jiang's armies got morsels.

Nonetheless, despite Mountbatten's orders to desist, Stilwell persevered with his Burma plan. To get at Myitkyina, he moved three Chinese divisions through rough terrain of underbrush, jungle, and mountain ranges to engage crack Japanese troops. The Chinese outnumbered the occupiers, but Imperial commanders were more experienced and committed. Stilwell resorted to threats and blackmail to mobilize the Chinese officers—to no avail: his forces had bogged down in Burma by February 1944, moving so ponderously that defeat was snatched from victory. Stilwell also had the first U.S. combat unit in the theater, the Galahad commando force of hardened veterans—mixed with psychiatric misfits —who had shipped voluntarily from the Pacific theaters. Assigned to Brigadier General Frank Merrill, who had escaped from Burma with Stilwell in 1942, it was nicknamed by a reporter "Merrill's Marauders." This unorthodox band joined Orde Windgate's superb Chindit fighters and the Kachin Rangers—northern Burmese tribesmen serving as scouts —to overcome Chinese reluctance to fight.

The Japanese, therefore, confronted a myriad of forces. Stilwell's Chindit, Kachin, Marauder, and Chinese groups plus the British Fourteenth Army challenged them in north Burma, while the Chinese Army in Yunnan and African and Indian divisions under General William Slim were deployed in northeast Burma near the Indian border. Unfazed, Japanese forces went on the offensive against Slim at the same time that Stilwell launched his campaign on Myitkyina and the Chinese made a thrust on the upper Salween River south of the Burma Road. Imperial

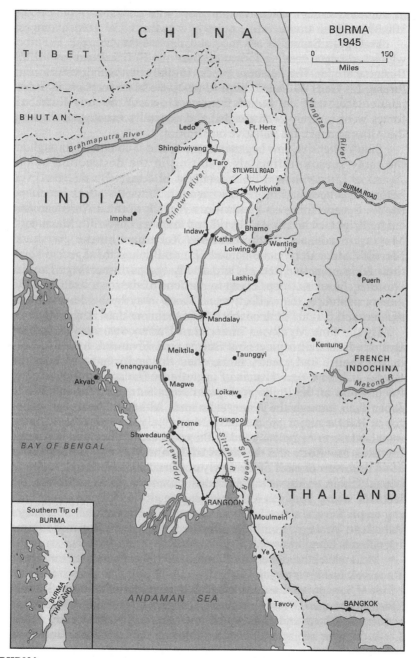

BURMA

U.S. Army Center of Military History, *U.S. Army Campaigns of World War II: Central Burma* (Washington, DC: Government Printing Office, 1996), 5.

troops faced numerically superior armies and air forces in three areas, but they nearly emerged victorious.

In February 1944, Stilwell's forces tried to block the withdrawal of Japan's Eighteenth Infantry Division from Burma. Aware that they were trapped between Merrill's Marauders and the slow-moving Chinese, the Eighteenth decided to attack the Americans. The Marauders held them off at Walawbun, however, and then a Chinese tank force cut the division in half. Retreating to the south, the Japanese incurred heavy losses— roughly 800 died—but ultimately escaped, for Stilwell failed again to trap the enemy. Encouraged by the chase, he sent the Marauders in a wide loop around the Japanese to cut off their retreat. Chinese troops attacked from the front, and two of Merrill's battalions set up their block in the Inkangahtawng jungle, about 20 miles north of Kamaing. But this time the Japanese forced Merrill back into the surrounding hills with a counterattack that nearly destroyed the U.S. force.

Encouraged, in March the Japanese Eighteenth Division outflanked the approaching Chinese and attacked. Stilwell sent Merrill to Nhpum Ga, an exhausting jungle march away. Merrill put a battalion on top of a hill near the hamlet and another 3 miles away at Hsamshingyang, where an airstrip supplied his forces, but the Eighteenth bombarded them, cut the trail to the airfield, and took the Americans' water hole. Water was airdropped to help the Marauders survive until the Japanese tired, and then Merrill's battalions moved toward each other on the road between the two villages in a vicious pincer attack. After a Nisei interpreter in Merrill's band learned of a Japanese plan to attack part of the U.S. perimeter, the Marauders booby-trapped their foxholes. When elements of the Eighteenth Division attacked, the Americans opened fire, causing the invaders to jump into the mined foxholes. In early April the Eighteenth gave up on Nhpum Ga but not until the cruel campaign had convinced the Americans that their enemy could be beaten only by reciprocal ferocity and cunning. Among Merrill's men there were mental breakdowns as they witnessed, said one, "the waste of battle and the fate that might befall the entire force."[2]

Stilwell was not done with the Marauders, despite their weakened state. Casualties and disease cost them 700 men, and the insufficient calories of short-term K rations caused their average weight to plummet over 20 pounds. A heart attack had taken Merrill himself out of action. New Chinese units, 5 brigades of Windgate's Chindits, and 400 Kachin Rangers reinforced the Marauders, but the 4,000 Chinese could not be expected to fight any better than had those before them, and Windgate had been killed in a plane crash. His leaderless Chindits were as exhausted and depleted as the Marauders, having been in the jungle deep in central Burma for four months.

Recognizing the precarious situation, Stilwell nevertheless wanted Myitkyina airstrip and ordered the Marauders over the 6,000-foot Kuman Mountains. Three weeks later the tired, diseased commandos—their will sapped by a muddy, drenching, insect-infested trek over steep mountain trails—miraculously emerged at Myitkyina and captured the airstrip on May 17, surprising a small detachment of Japanese. Stilwell had achieved his mission, despite British bureaucratic holdups and Japanese violence, by sheer endurance as well as an unexpectedly good showing by the Chinese.

The Chinese continued to perform well around Myitkyina, yet trouble at once arose when it was discovered that the Japanese had more soldiers in the vicinity than the Allies had thought. Japan's commanders rushed reinforcements to bolster the town, from which the Chinese troops could not dislodge them. As the monsoon rains arrived, a 2-1/2 month siege of Mytikyina began. The Marauders were spent, with dysentery so bad that members of one platoon cut away the seats of their pants for relief. Yet Stilwell was unrelenting, ordering hospitalized men back into battle. Committing his troops gave him leverage with Jiang and the British to send more of their soldiers, but he was just too hard, rarely rewarding the Marauders with medals, promotions, or supplies. Although the pressure from Japan on the Asian mainland required such Allied sacrifices, the accumulation of physical and psychological blows undermined the capabilities of the Americans in Myitkyina.

Fortunately, the Japanese overestimated the forces arrayed against them, for a counterattack that would have likely routed the Allies never developed. The Imperial occupiers held on, undersupplied and isolated in their defense of Myitkyina. The Chinese fought well, even capturing the key town of Kamaing in June and chasing the Japanese from the vicinity. Finally, on August 3, 1944, the town of Myitkyina fell to the Allies. Though victory came at a high cost of lives, the Ledo Road now could be completed into northern Burma, connecting India and China. Logistics teams were already in the area clearing the highway and building support facilities, including gas pipelines, and transport planes flying over the Hump could use the Myitkyina airfield, which gave them a shorter and safer route to China. Deliveries to Jiang's forces had nearly doubled between May and July 1944. For their part, Merrill's Marauders had been evacuated; reduced to nonoperational status in late May 1944, the unit had ceased to exist altogether by August.

Crises occurred elsewhere. Hundreds of miles west of Myitkyina, on the Indo-Burmese border, the Indian towns of Imphal and Kohima became the focus of the Japanese Burma Area Army, which checked the advance of the British Fourteenth Army from the east. Led by 100,000 soldiers of the Fifteenth Army under the command of Lieutenant General Masakuazu Kawabe, the Japanese offensive reached Imphal in late March 1944 and Kohima in early April. Outnumbered, British commander William Slim was forced into a desperate defense on the Indian frontier. Airlifted supplies and men allowed the British and Indian troops to move quickly where needed, and Allied troops held on to Kohima until relief came on April 18. The Japanese formations were soon outflanked and eventually destroyed.

The first convoy truck moves up the Ledo Road, a key supply route in northern Burma near the Chinese border, on January 28, 1945. U.S. Army, *United States Army in World War II: Pictorial Record: The War Against Japan* (Washington, DC: Department of the Army, 1952), 437.

With similar results, the fighting for Imphal to the south was nevertheless a far cry from Kohima. Imphal involved a bloody, drawn-out battle of attrition that has been likened to the horror of Verdun during World War I. Having run beyond its supply lines, the Japanese offensive bogged down in the face of the well-supplied British, who controlled the air. On June 22 the siege collapsed, and elements of the Fifteenth Army straggled back across the Burmese border, reduced by two-thirds of its force of 85,000 soldiers. "Nowhere in World War II—even on the Eastern [European] Front—did the combatants fight with more mindless savagery," conclude two historians.[3] What had started as a rousing Japanese victory in India ended in humbling retreat as Slim readied to drive the enemy east toward Thailand, reconquer Burma, and destroy the Fifteenth Army.

Beginning in the second half of 1944, the Japanese withdrew from Burma under the pressure of the Allied counteroffensive. Although this remote theater was of little strategic importance to winning the war, the push persisted and exemplified the ongoing brutality caused by Japanese tactics and Allied responses. Slim commanded a coordinated multinational force, including Indian, African, Chinese, American (the Mars Task Force—survivors of Merrill's Marauders combined with a national guard unit from Texas), Burmese, and European elements. All had a hand in drubbing the 100,000 (at best) men of the Burma Area Army when the counteroffensive began in January 1945. Slim's Fourteenth Army had 260,000 men, plus 2 infantry brigades and 2 armored brigades, and support from 183,000 U.S. and 72,000 Chinese troops. Against 250 Japanese aircraft the Allies had 800 combat planes and 250 transports with which to press General Slim's advantage. The Japanese were so desperate that they executed wounded colleagues in the field rather than carry them out.

Slim's Fourteenth Army divided into three corps. Two marched on Mandalay to the east, and a third headed south by land and water toward Rangoon. Slim's forces crossed the Irrawaddy River at Meiktila, south of Mandalay, and routed the Fifteenth Army from its fortifications (including a maze of pagodas), taking the city on March 20, 1945. The Japanese incurred four times as many deaths as the Allies—6,500 to 1,600. Ahead of the coming monsoons and aided by a British airborne landing, the Allies took Rangoon in May, causing Japanese casualties to nearly triple the number (7,000 to 2,500) of their own. Remnants of the Fifteenth slipped away, but then, shockingly, these desperate troops counterattacked, mistakenly believing that the heavy rains would slow Slim down. They would simply not give up, even in circumstances that meant certain death. Their miscalculation proved fatal: an Indian division killed nearly 11,000 Japanese, and an additional 10,000 perished along the Sittang River. Japan had seized Burma and Malaya in 1942 with the loss of 5,000 lives in the theater. By the time they surrendered in Asia on September 12, 1945, Imperial forces had suffered 97,000 deaths since the start of the Imphal offensive just fifteen months before.

The Allied campaign in Burma had opened the Stilwell Road but with less impact than originally desired, for the rugged terrain still favored the Hump airlift. It was not the first time a theater faded in importance. The Aleutians campaign, deemed a shortcut to Tokyo, had been abandoned for the central Pacific, and the India-Burma-China route to victory likewise fell by the wayside. Slim had effectively coordinated multicultural units and dearly punished the fanatical Japanese. The resources that the empire diverted to the Indian subcontinent justified the sending of a relatively small contingent of U.S. troops to the region, but unlike the Americans, Japan could not afford to overstretch.

China

In China, the Japanese had more lasting success. One reason lay in Jiang's inaction. The Cairo Declaration pledged his military support, but he was unwilling to begin a major offensive. Indeed, the Japanese withdrew five infantry divisions to the Pacific, an indication that they feared little from China. Stilwell repeatedly complained to Roosevelt and the army's chief of staff, George C. Marshall, that Jiang was more devoted to blockading the communists in Yenan than to fighting the invaders. Meanwhile, Mao Zedong had so effectively fought guerrilla actions against the Japanese in northern China that in February 1944, FDR asked Jiang to let American observers visit Yenan to gather intelligence. Incensed, the generalissimo refused. Moreover, he continued to hold back. The 15-division Y-Force was supposed to support Stilwell's offensive in northern Burma, but Jiang delayed, claiming that U.S. lend-lease supplies were insufficient to equip his troops. Roosevelt intervened on April 3, demanding that Jiang attack the weakened Japanese Fifty-sixth Division, stationed near the Burma Road in western Yunnan province. The president then threatened to divert Y-Force supplies to the U.S. Fourteenth Air Force, the first time he seemed to have tired of Jiang's procrastination.

The threatened cutoff, and incessant prodding from Stilwell, forced Jiang to send General Wei Li-huang across the Salween River on the night of May 11–12, 1944, hoping to trap the Japanese and continue into Burma to support the Myitkyina operation. With surprising strength, they halted his advance, although the Y-Force laid siege to several Imperial strong points. To the south, Wei only reached the Burma Road before a Japanese counterattack pushed him back on June 16 and the Y-Force ran out of steam. Worse, Japan launched its own offensive in east China. Jiang pulled back the Y-Force, sending Stilwell into a paroxysm of rage that eventually led to his recall. He knew Wei was on the verge of chasing the Japanese from the Ledo Road, but not until September did the Chinese secure the key town of Tengchung in the Salween campaign.

In east China, Japan's success was stunning. On April 19, 1944, the Japanese launched a series of offensives, called Ichigo, to boost Imperial power at American expense. Troops seized Allied airfields, thereby denying Chennault his bases and jeopardizing B-29 raids from east China.

In July 1944, Chinese troops cross the Salween River into Burma from the east as part of the operation to take Myitkyina. These soldiers would meet Allied forces in Burma in September 1944. U.S. Army, *United States Army in World War II: Pictorial Record: The War Against Japan* (Washington, DC: Department of the Army, 1952), 427.

Then the offensives opened an overland communication and supply route from Korea to Indochina to replace the dangerous maritime route scouted by U.S. submarines. Finally, Ichigo secured the key railroad lines running north to south in China, as well as seizing the central Chinese

Wuchang-Liuchow line. Jiang's Nationalist Army fled into western China
as the Japanese marshalled 15 divisions, totaling 820,000 men, to partici-
pate in the grand scheme.

The initial April offensive routed the Chinese Z-Force, eliminating
resistance to Japan in the central Honan province, and Japanese momentum seemed unstoppable. Chinese troops and the U.S. Fourteenth Air
Force harassed the invaders, but the Z-Force, despite outnumbering the
Japanese, could not stop the advance. A string of Imperial victories followed from May into August 1944. Japan swept through Hunan province,
capturing communications centers without encountering much of a
fight. At Heng Yang, Chinese troops backed by Chennault from the air
held them off for six weeks, but that was an exception; the old rule of
Chinese Army inefficiency, corruption, and insubordination generally
prevailed. For instance, in Hunan, Chinese generals were Jiang's political
enemies; they did not want to help him by sending reinforcements. China
was in crisis. In May, the Japanese took the Chengchow-Hankow railroad,
opening supply lines and providing a staging area from which to attack
Hengyang and thereby expose American air bases.

This next phase of Ichigo began on May 27. Although the Japanese
pushed the Chinese armies around, the latter put up enough of a fight to
slow the advance. In mid-June, Changsha fell, and Hengyang came under
siege a few weeks later. A few Chinese commanders held the town—
without help from Jiang—until it fell on August 8. Imperial forces moved
on, but now at a slower pace, taking until November 1944 to capture
Kweilin and Liuchow to the south. Occupying central and southern
China, Japan enjoyed a complete line of communications from Singapore, through Indochina, to Manchuria. Fleeing Nationalist troops, some
of whom were killed by angry locals who had long despised Jiang's
corruption, abandoned resistance. Because they did not hold a secure
railroad network, however, the Japanese earned few tangible gains from
the offensive.

Still, Ichigo caused a crisis in the China-Burma-India theater because
it was the first major Japanese offensive in China since December 1941.
Jiang panicked, casting blame on the Allies for delaying supplies and
warning that he would withdraw Wei's Y-Force from northern Burma to
defend southeastern China. Jiang undermined the effort to break the
Japanese blockade in the theater, but pressured by Marshall, Roosevelt
urged the generalissimo to place Stilwell in charge of all ground forces in
China. For several weeks, Jiang refused. Then, in October 1944, Stilwell
was fired from his post, FDR being aware that criticizing the popular

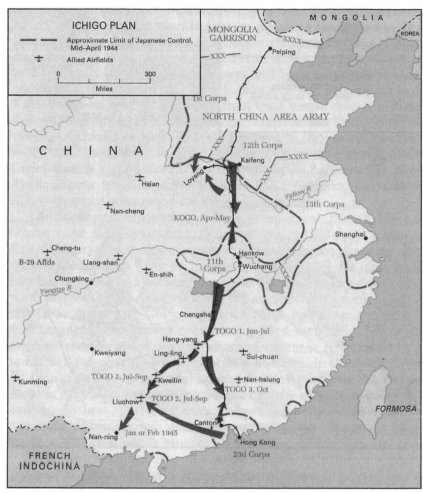

ICHIGO PLAN

U.S. Army Center of Military History, *U.S. Army Campaigns of World War II: China Defensive* (Washington, DC: Government Printing Office, 1993), 18.

Chinese leader might cost him reelection votes a month later. The Americans slowly turned their back on Jiang, yet they remained beholden to him. He was ever effective at marshaling public and congressional opinion, for the rest of the war and well beyond it.

In autumn 1944 the Allies divided Asian commands between the British in Burma and India and the Americans in China. Lieutenant General Albert C. Wedemeyer, an experienced military planner, took over from Stilwell, and Patrick Hurley, a Republican sympathetic to Jiang, became the ambassador to China. Both hoped that increased lend-lease supplies would prompt a Nationalist-American offensive by the end of the year that would recapture lost territory. Both were disappointed. The Allied march to Germany had stalled, preventing the transfer of more troops to Asia; U.S. forces in the Pacific were concentrated on the liberation of the Philippines; and the vehemently anticommunist Hurley scuttled talk of cooperating with Mao in northern China. Jiang's secret service chief plotted with American intelligence to run their own partisan offensive and thus topple Jiang from power. Adding to the tangle of political, military, and diplomatic intrigue were the Soviets. At Yalta in February 1945 they promised to enter the Asian war ninety days after the defeat of Germany; Roosevelt had pledged them more lend-lease aid and the restoration of Manchuria and other territories. Jiang viewed the Yalta Accord with some ambivalence. On the one hand, he initially backed the plan, for he could cynically use Red Army soldiers to fight the Japanese while he unleashed his own forces on Mao. Yet on the other, he chafed at potential Russian gains of Chinese lands.

Stalemate on the China front was the upshot of this mess. Indeed, Japan's Ichigo offensive ground to a halt in early May 1945 when Chinese forces held off an assault on a U.S. air base in Chihchiang. Also, the Salween campaign ended, aided by the Allied counteroffensive in Burma which freed up Chinese and American troops. But it was the deteriorating position of Japan in the Pacific war, rather than such moderate Allied military success, that dictated events in China. By spring 1945, defense of the home islands grabbed the attention of Imperial Headquarters, which ordered troops redeployed to Japan from the Asian mainland. Despite the pullout, Wedemeyer's pursuit was still slow, as the Japanese backed into northern and central China, held on to Shanghai, and by the end of July were preparing to defend the coastal areas and other strongholds. Chinese forces moved into vacuums left by the withdrawing troops; more than likely they would otherwise have failed to push out the Japanese. In the end, China was liberated by the atomic bombs of early August 1945, not by Chinese and American troops.

China turned out to be a military sideshow, its fate determined elsewhere in the war. Chinese internal politics remained center stage for the United States because of Roosevelt's commitment to Jiang as a postwar leader in Asia. Yet support for Jiang Jeshi throughout the war resulted in neither a stable government nor an effective military force but perilously mired America in the intrigues of Chinese infighting. The consequences of the Chinese quagmire were a Red scare at home, political recrimination once Mao overthrew Jiang in 1949, and the Cold War's arrival in the region during China's civil war and the Korean and Vietnam conflicts.

New Guinea

Difficulties in China and Burma contrasted with sweeping successes on New Guinea as General MacArthur headed for the Luzon line. Victory in the Admiralties impressed Washington, and thus planning in the southwest Pacific sprang forward. With Rabaul quarantined, MacArthur raced toward the Philippines, figuring on jumping 580 miles up the north coast of New Guinea, past Hansa Bay where the Japanese had 3 divisions, to attack Hollandia. The move was bold but logical.

Because the Admiralties had fallen two months ahead of schedule, MacArthur wanted to cut time off the southwest Pacific campaign (and compete with Chester Nimitz for resources) by swift movement. Air bases in the Admiralties extended the range of U.S. fighter planes past Wewak, the center of Japanese air power, to Hollandia, while the assault on Truk had forced the withdrawal of the Japanese fleet westward to the Palaus and Singapore. Without protection from the Imperial Fleet, Japanese forces at Aitape and Hollandia were now exposed. And although planning was going ahead for the invasion of the Marianas, the U.S. carrier fleet was free at the moment and could thus support MacArthur on New Guinea.

To be sure, Nimitz was alarmed, believing his central Pacific drive would stall because of MacArthur's campaign and the advent of the typhoon season. The Joint Chiefs settled matters, ordering MacArthur to take western New Guinea, including the extreme tip of the Vogelkop Peninsula, and then prepare to invade Mindanao in the southern Philippines by mid-November 1944. Nimitz was to isolate Truk, take the Marianas by mid-June, and advance on the Palau Islands east of Mindanao by mid-September. Halsey's south Pacific force would be split between MacArthur and Nimitz, with the former receiving most of the army units and the latter the naval forces. The Joint Chiefs, buying MacArthur's unprecedented plan to leap up the New Guinea coast, provided him with the necessary support.

Once ULTRA decrypts revealed that the Japanese expected an attack at Hansha Bay or Wewak, MacArthur was all the more certain that he

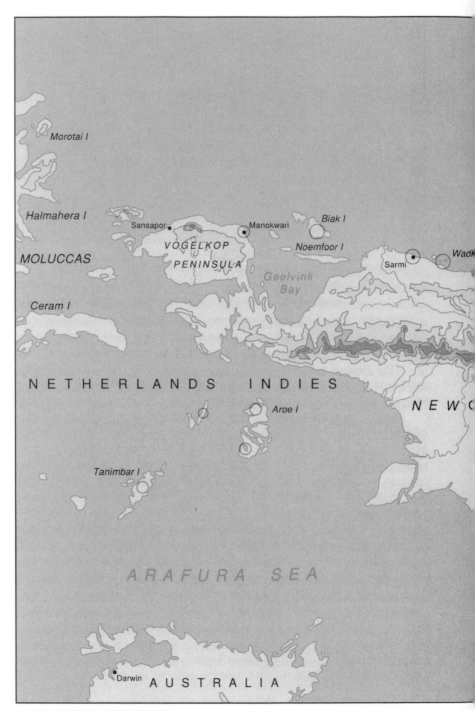

NEW GUINEA OPERATIONS
U.S. Army Center of Military History, *U.S. Army Campaigns of World War II: New Guinea* (Washington, DC: Government Printing Office, 1994), 20–21.

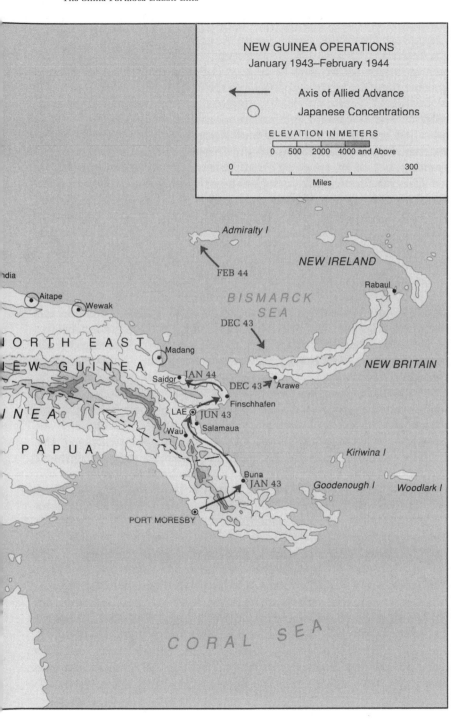

NEW GUINEA OPERATIONS
January 1943–February 1944

should strike at Hollandia, farther west. Hollandia was a major air base that the Japanese were reinforcing, but it lacked land defenses. At the end of March 1944, meeting Nimitz for the first time during the war, MacArthur and his commanders soothed the admiral's worries about the dangers to his carriers from Japanese aircraft. Thus, Nimitz permitted his largest vessels to dally only a day off the New Guinea coast, but allowed his smaller escort carriers to stay a week to support MacArthur's attack force—which, appropriately for Nimitz, was code-named Reckless.

The Hollandia landing was MacArthur's most decisive operation of the war and also the death knell for the Japanese on New Guinea. Valuable for two good harbors, the Hollandia area contained large Lake Sentani, surrounded by level plains on which the 11,000 defenders—of whom only 500 were combat troops—had built three airfields and had two more under construction. If they were seized, General George Kenney's army air force could dominate western New Guinea and support Nimitz in the central Pacific by bombing Palau Island in the Carolines. Hollandia could serve as a base for Allied troops, and the Japanese garrisons at Wewak and Hansa Bay could be isolated. For Japan, Hollandia represented the fringe of a retracting empire, the last outpost of the Second Army's New Guinea operations. Tokyo was ready to defend the area, but, fully expecting MacArthur to go after Wewak and Hansa Bay, General Hatazo Adachi delayed sending reinforcements to Hollandia. MacArthur cultivated Adachi's fear: in mid-March the Seventh Fleet shelled Wewak, as if to soften it up, and Kenney's pilots bombed airfields with an intensity that destroyed 168 planes on the ground and stripped trees of their foliage. Dummy parachutists and empty life rafts from submarines completed the ruse of an imminent U.S. landing.

Kenney had another surprise. The Japanese had placed their remaining 350 planes around Hollandia, believing they were out of reach of his planes, but the value of Nimitz's help soon became apparent. MacArthur planned to hit Aitape, 140 miles east of Hollandia, to provide for an airfield. Nimitz offered 8 escort carriers to protect the Aitape landing, which he then moved off Hollandia once his big carriers had departed for the Marianas. The technologically resourceful Kenney, capitalizing on Nimitz's support at Aitape, was now free to target Hollandia. He equipped his P-38 fighter planes with 300-gallon wing tanks, thereby extending their range from 350 to 650 miles. On March 31, Kenney launched over 100 of the new models, accompanied by bombers, and found 139 Japanese bombers and 125 fighters lined up wingtip to wingtip. "Bombing gorgeous, entire target uncovered," reported an observer.[4] Initial raids destroyed 199 Japanese planes at Hollandia, and all told, Kenney destroyed 400 aircraft (losing just 4 of his own), leaving U.S. warships nothing to shoot at, he later boasted. Japanese airpower in the area had evaporated.

The shallow draft of U.S. landing ship tanks (LSTs) allowed them to run up to shore and disperse up to 2,000 tons of cargo. These LSTs are anchored near Saidor on New Guinea and were used along the coast during MacArthur's operation. U.S. Army, *United States Army in World War II: Pictorial Record: The War Against Japan* (Washington, DC: Department of the Army, 1952), 273.

The barrage off Hollandia was just as impressive. A small transport, cruisers, and destroyers let loose with everything they had, at point-blank range. Wrote a witness, "The rocket guns fired. Then came the planes. Like a grasshopper scourge they filled the sky. Dive bombers screamed as they sped earthward. Soon, fires and black smoke rose to great heights. Here and there appeared a feeble answer. The enemy's guns, whatever they had, had been silenced."[5]

A huge armada of 217 ships sailed more than 1,000 miles to transport a total of 84,000 U.S. Army troops to Aitape and Humboldt Bay in the Hollandia area. Three amphibious landings deep behind enemy lines brought 53,000 soldiers ashore in three days, including 23,000 engineers, who overcame the typically difficult terrain on New Guinea. In addition to Kenney's air raids, the feint at Hansa tricked Adachi. On April 22, Lieutenant General Robert Eichelberger led unopposed units ashore at Hollandia, 25 miles apart. To ease congestion, engineers labored to clear the shallow waters, the beaches, and the swamps beyond of obstacles. Then combat teams landed at Aitape without encountering the enemy. MacArthur was ecstatic. That night, he invited his commanders for ice cream on his cruiser before departing for Australia. In one swoop, Japanese defenses had been cut in half, and the Eighteenth Army in eastern New Guinea was completely cut off from home.

The U.S. Twenty-fourth Infantry Division moved east, and the Forty-first Infantry advanced west in a pincer movement around Hollandia's aerodromes. A lone Japanese plane dropped bombs on one of the Forty-first's beaches, however, exploding an abandoned ammunition dump and igniting a fire that swept the beach for two days. It killed 24 Americans, injured over 100, and forced U.S. troops to half rations. Nevertheless, the Americans inched their way over swampy trails and unbridged streams, eventually attacking the 7,600 underarmed and untrained defenders.

Within four days of the Hollandia landings, Allied troops had dispersed the Japanese into the jungle. MacArthur had 5 air bases, which could support 200,000 men once Eichelberger had cleared the roads, but the Americans soon realized that construction on Hollandia was not worth the effort. The aerodromes had been badly built, and loaded bombers would be unable to land because the ground was too soggy and the mountains too close to the airstrips. Life there, as elsewhere on New Guinea, was made miserable by sticky weather, malaria, and boredom.

Although the Hollandia operation succeeded in general, this phase of the New Guinea conflict reflected the pitiless nature of combat in the war.

Whereas a relatively low total of 152 Americans were killed and 1,057 wounded, the Japanese garrison of 10,000 suffered 3,300 dead and 611 captured, and Adachi's three divisions of 55,000 soldiers were stranded, surviving on roots and berries until making a desperate counterattack in July 1944 at the Driniumor River. During July and August the 10,000 soldiers of the Eighteenth Army died, while nearly 3,000 Americans (including 440 killed) fell, making that two-month period MacArthur's costliest campaign in terms of casualties since Buna. Moving east toward Wewak, the Australians closed in on Adachi in December 1944, and in May 1945, Wewak fell, as did 7,200 Japanese and 451 Australians. Adachi fled to the hills with 13,000 troops, most of whom perished from disease, starvation, and exhaustion. He surrendered in September 1945 and later committed suicide rather than face hanging after his trial in Rabaul. Yet amazingly, he had chosen to fight on rather than surrender months before.

MacArthur's lightning strike had sawed off about two months of the New Guinea campaign, permitting him to arrive at the Philippines sooner than he had first thought possible. Maintaining momentum, MacArthur rushed up the north coast to capture more airfields to replace Hollandia's swamps as long-range bomber bases. The Forty-first leap-frogged west to Wakde Island and the airstrips at Sarmi on the coast. After Kenney destroyed 52 planes, leveled the town of Sarmi, and set the island on fire with heavy bombing, 4 rifle companies raided tiny Wakde on May 18, 1944. The assault was not easy, as nearly 800 defenders fought from spider holes, coconut log bunkers, and coral caves. Japanese machine gunners hit the U.S. assault waves, which were easy marks as they ran parallel to the Wakde shore before reaching positions on the beach. The first night was long for the Americans, harassed by Japanese fire, grenades, and attacks from groups of infiltrators. It took two days of brutal fighting, 40 dead, and 107 wounded to take the island on May 20. But MacArthur gained an airstrip close enough to support the Biak Island assault farther west and send the first B-24 reconnaissance planes over the southern Philippines a week later. Four Japanese prisoners and 759 corpses remained behind.

The Sarmi area provided tougher going. General Walter Krueger wished to protect the foothold at Maffin Bay by clearing out the Japanese from the overlooking hills, and although intelligence told him of enemy preparations, he underestimated the number of defenders. At Lone Tree Hill the 158th Regimental Combat Team confronted 3 infantry regiments led by veteran troops from the Chinese theater, who had constructed a complex of caves, pillboxes, and dugouts covered by camouflaged mountain guns. A giant tree stood over the area. Four days of fighting caused 400 casualties in the 158th, which retreated to the beachhead and then deployed farther west. Krueger sent the entire Sixth Infantry Division to Sarmi on June 14. Lone Tree Hill finally fell after ten days of intense fighting. The division suffered 1,200 casualties (including 114 dead), while counting almost 1,000 enemy killed and dozens more sealed in the fortified caves. The Wakde-Sarmi operation cost 630 American dead, 41 missing, and 1,742 wounded; five times as many Japanese perished. Krueger believed that the experience would toughen the Sixth for the next round, on the Vogelkop Peninsula.

It took until the end of August 1944 to secure the area, but by that time, MacArthur had pushed westward to Biak Island, which dominated strategic Geelvink Bay. Steamy, equatorial Biak was just east of the Vogelkop Peninsula, at the tip of New Guinea. Its airstrips were located at the end of a 7-mile road that went inland from the coast, the road itself flanked by caves and topped by large shrubs growing on 200-foot cliffs. The 11,000 Biak defenders, led by Colonel Naoyuki Kozume, had fortified the caves with supplies, communications facilities, artillery, mortars, and antiaircraft guns, and they were ringed by pillboxes and bunkers.

On May 27, as Kozume completed his defenses, the Forty-first Division attacked. Overheated, thirsty Americans met little resistance as they came ashore near Bosnek, the main town on the island, but as they advanced up the road to within 200 yards of the airfields, the troops walked into a Japanese trap. Imperial troops ambushed the Americans with a barrage of well-aimed automatic fire and mortars from the caves and then drove a wedge between two companies of the Third Battalion of the 162d Infantry. The Americans managed to withdraw by nightfall, covered by the 162d's Second Battalion, but the next morning, Kozume pulled a surprise attack with light tanks that isolated the Second itself. Unusually, this time around the Japanese enjoyed the superior power of armored vehicles.

That advantage did not last long, but it did prove terrifying until heavy U.S. Sherman tanks rushed in to rip apart the light tanks and evacuate the Second Battalion to safety. A few days later, on June 1, reinforced American troops came down the road again, supported by artillery and air power, while two battalions edged along the ridge overlooking the Biak airfield. Combat was vicious. Lacking water, some men died while crawling to replenish their canteens from water holes.

The Americans could not budge the Japanese from the ridges after a week of hard fighting. Angered, the impatient MacArthur relieved General Horace Fuller and appointed Eichelberger in his place. The infantry, descending from its high ground under continual pounding, ran into another ambush as it tried to take the airfield. Writes one historian of the New Guinea campaign, "The Americans were like fish in a barrel."[6] Yet a tidal wave of firepower, unleashed with a devastating fury, eventually engulfed the Japanese and drove them from their positions.

Japanese strategists then pulled the plug on Biak. The Imperial Navy, preparing to defend the Marianas and Carolines in the central Pacific, wanted Biak to protect its flank; thus the High Command called for the annihilation of U.S. forces on Biak, but the plan never materialized. Japanese forces scuttled back to the Philippines in late May, expecting a naval engagement there. Two weeks later, when the Marianas campaign began, most of the Japanese abandoned Biak, not realizing that they might have inflicted sufficient damage to delay America's timetable in the Pacific war. Yet the Japanese Navy preferred to wait in the Philippine Sea, leaving the remnants of the garrison to fight off the Americans. The defenders of Biak were tough but, in the end, overwhelmed.

Still, the victory was by no means total for the United States. The ridges above the airfield were not emptied of Japanese artillery until June 20—too late to support Nimitz in the Marianas—and the bloodletting was relentless until mid-July 1944. There was no usual mopping up, for the Japanese offered concentrated resistance in the interior equal to their defense from the caves. Biak was a largely wasted effort; it cost MacArthur's forces over 400 killed and 2,000 wounded, an abnormally high number. Although Japan lost a staggering 4,800 dead, the defenders had stalled MacArthur's offensive, and in doing so they had gained valuable time for building a new line of defenses in the extreme west of New Guinea. There would be a few more battles before MacArthur bagged New Guinea, his last step to the Philippines.

As the carnage on Biak continued, the Americans leaped another 60 miles westward to Noemfoor Island, MacArthur hoping to use this tiny, 15-by-12-mile island for an air base in place of Biak. General Kenney mercilessly dropped 8,000 tons of bombs on Noemfoor, dazing the small garrison into submission. Parachutists suffered a 10 percent casualty rate because they jumped from less than 400 feet to a hard airfield covered in coral, Japanese aircraft, and supply dumps. The defenders launched sporadic charges, causing 411 American casualties. The Japanese defenders had 1,759 killed, while 889 surrendered, mostly laborers.

As the Japanese reeled westward, U.S. forces landed on the Vogelkop Peninsula on July 30, meeting little opposition. Airplanes had dropped tons of DDT up to a mile inland to rid the area of malaria-carrying mosquitoes. A week later the infantry had still not engaged in combat, so the troops began building air bases, which were ready for fighter planes by mid-August. With the September 1944 seizure of Halmahera and Morotai Islands, MacArthur had clear sailing to Mindanao in the Philippines, and the New Guinea campaign was over.

The Allies had incurred substantial losses on New Guinea, but things could have been worse. The key to the campaign was speed. MacArthur's leapfrogging tactics prevented the "meatgrinder" encounters that the Japanese sought and thus saved lives. Until Saidor in January 1944 there had been 24,000 Allied casualties, 70 percent of these Australian, as the Allies advanced 300 miles in twenty months. After the landings at Hollandia in April the casualties had numbered 9,500, mainly American, but in just over three months, some 1,300 miles had been covered. The Japanese incurred 11,000 deaths; 30,000 more suffered in isolation, and another 96,000 soldiers and sailors were stuck on New Britain. Mac-Arthur, writes one analyst, "left [the jungle] to devour the Japanese soldiers isolated in its interior."[7] Such losses, however, further impressed upon Allied troops the rabidly committed nature of their enemy to fight on. Regardless of its lack of great conquests and epic battles, the capture of New Guinea allowed MacArthur to move on to the Philippines.

Helped by ULTRA, shrewd planning, bold tactics, sheer power, and enemy mistakes, MacArthur arrived on Morotai on September 15, 1944, less than two hours after troops had gone ashore. This island was a mere 300 miles from the Philippines. Recounted one of his aides, MacArthur "gazed out to the northwest almost as though he could already see through the mist the rugged lines of Bataan and Corregidor. 'They are waiting for me there,'" he said.[8]

 Notes

1. Murray and Millett, *A War to Be Won*, 349.

2. Gary J. Bjorge, *Merrill's Marauders: Combined Operations in Northern Burma in 1944* (Washington, DC: Army Center of Military History, 1996), 32.

3. Murray and Millett, *A War to Be Won*, 350.

4. Stephen R. Taaffe, *MacArthur's Jungle War: The 1944 New Guinea Campaign* (Lawrence: University Press of Kansas, 1998), 86.

5. Morris Coppersmith Diary, http://topshot.com/dh/Victory.html.

6. Taafe, *MacArthur's Jungle War*, 160.

7. Edward J. Drea, *The U.S. Army Campaigns of World War II: New Guinea* (Washington, DC: Army Center of Military History, 1994), 31.

8. Spector, *Eagle against the Sun*, 294.

4

IN RANGE OF THE HOME ISLANDS

Before Douglas MacArthur's ultimate triumph of liberating the Philippines, the campaign in the central Pacific had already assumed the leading role in the unfolding drama of Japan's defeat. The main show moved westward as veterans of the Gilbert and Marshall Islands shipped out 1,100 miles from Eniwetok, readying for landings in the Marianas. Playing second fiddle to the stars at Normandy in June 1944, the actors on Saipan, Guam, and Tinian achieved a tremendous result as they pierced Japan's inner defensive perimeter. About 27,000 U.S. casualties were the price, not unexpected considering that the Americans had entered the "Absolute National Defense Line" and come within sustained bombing range of Japan itself.[1] While D-day in France stole the headlines, the central Pacific campaign took the bulk of naval forces and logistical support. The immense, and intensely fought, effort resulted in victories in the Mariana Islands, as well as at sea, and sent the Japanese reeling.

Planning the Marianas Campaign

With reservations, Admiral Chester Nimitz zeroed in on the Marianas'
large islands (running north to south) of Saipan, Tinian, and Guam,
which all offered new conditions and terrain. Except for Guam, the
Marianas held no promise of friendly natives, for the islands—Japanese
mandates since World War I—had been home to thousands of Imperial
citizens. Moreover, not only had the Japanese military begun construction of installations ten years before—in violation of disarmament treaty
provisions—but the geography was deadly: not the flat atolls of the
Gilberts and Marshalls but jungles, mountains, swamps, and caves full of
bunkers and gun emplacements, all fringed by coral reefs.

Approaching this forbidding landscape, Admiral Raymond Spruance
commanded the U.S. Fifth Fleet and transported its 127,000 troops and
integrated amphibious units, with over 400 ships and assault vessels
under Vice Admiral Richmond Kelly Turner in support. They faced
59,000 Japanese troops on the Marianas' three main islands, and the
Combined Fleet also lurked about. Nimitz worried. He had gambled and
won at Japan's outer ring of defenses in the central Pacific, but the inner
sanctum of the Marianas, heavily defended and populated, were likely to
prove entirely different. Besides, they were 3,300 miles from the fleet base
at Pearl Harbor and over 1,000 from the Marshalls. But his boss in
Washington, Ernest King, had been impressed by the rapid headway
across the Pacific in 1944 and would not halt the momentum, regardless
of MacArthur's lobbying for the southwest or warnings from his own
staff (and Nimitz) that the distant and large Marianas would be too
difficult to seize. In March 1944, King had made the final decision. Taking
the Marianas would shorten the war by moving U.S. forces west,
interrupting Japanese supply routes, creating bases from which the B-29
bombers could hit the home islands, and drawing the Combined Fleet
into battle. Vice Admiral Marc Mitscher's Task Force 58—15 carriers, 7
new battleships, 69 destroyers, 21 cruisers, and 891 aircraft—was ready
to storm into the Marianas. In fact, after months of raids, Mitscher's and
other planes based in newly won territory had nearly eliminated Japanese
airpower in the islands.

Halsey's Third Fleet and Spruance's Fifth Fleet would lead the
campaign. Because naval production was clicking along, the European
theater required few carriers, and Eisenhower did not use amtracs at
Normandy, King was able to gather a huge force. Operation Forager
numbered 166,000 troops and 535 ships. Improvements in amphibious

landing tactics, such as sustained preliminary bombardment and amphibious feints, were in the works, and training in all conditions, demolition, and landing took place for months. Forager required substantial logistical planning because the Marianas were so large and well defended.

King also expected a showdown with the Combined Fleet, and the Japanese admirals obliged by massing ships for a confrontation in the Philippine Sea. They hoped to replay the defeat of the Russians at Tsushima in 1905. Admiral Toyoda Soemu oversaw the reorganization of the First Mobile Fleet, comprising surface and carrier battle groups, under the aggressive Admiral Ozawa Jisaburo. As U.S. intelligence homed in, the fleet expanded to 6 battleships, 9 carriers holding 500 aircraft, 13 cruisers, and 28 destroyers. The First Air Fleet sent nearly 1,000 torpedo and bomber planes, accompanied by Zeroes, to airfields around the Philippine Sea. Playing war games and engaging in operational analysis, Toyoda and Ozawa readied for a showdown they had been waiting for since Midway.

The massiveness of their power was deceiving, yet the Japanese would stand and fight using any means to slow the Americans rather than sue for peace. Out of desperation, even the emperor observed the naval exercises, hoping for a miracle. Inexperienced pilots with less than six months of flying time planned to attack and then flee; land-based bombers would refuel and rearm in the Marianas, using as little of the precious reserve of aviation petroleum as possible. If Imperial forces could defend the airfields on Saipan, Tinian, and Guam, then Ozawa's high-tech fleet could steam into battle for a night surface engagement, which remained the last tactical weakness of the U.S. Navy. Yet Japanese sailors and commanders were untrained in exploiting their ships' technological superiority, and the Americans knew Ozawa's every move through decoding. They were ready for battle, well prepared to meet the First Mobile Fleet's impressive array of firepower.

As part of the preparation, Spruance divided his forces into a Northern Attack Force to move on Saipan and then Tinian, and a Southern Attack Force that would assail Guam last. He first wanted to soften up Saipan, so Mitscher's planes issued more pre-landing strikes in the Mariana and Bonin Islands to the northwest in order to neutralize the First Air Fleet before marines landed. The attacks reduced the air fleet's numbers by half. Admiral Toyoda delayed until Spruance began the invasion of Saipan before ordering the Combined Fleet to set sail from the Philippines. Linking up with oil tankers and other elements of the

First Mobile Fleet on June 16, the Combined Fleet—totaling 222 fighter planes and 200 dive and torpedo bombers on 9 carriers—headed for the Marianas.

Meanwhile, on Saipan, Tinian, and Guam, 59,000 combat troops awaited the U.S. attack, determined to hold the airfields so that Ozawa's decisive naval battle could succeed. Saipan held 32,000 of the ground force, joined by 48 tanks and a civilian population of 20,000 that had emigrated two decades before from Okinawa. The American air attacks since late February, and relentless submarine operations, had interrupted transports of supplies and soldiers and prevented completion of fortification networks in caves and on mountainsides. Insufficient amounts of weapons, matériel, men, and time would curse the defenders. The western Pacific was no longer Japan's to control, but Imperial troops could still create chaos and casualties.

The Americans had other obstacles to overcome besides. The problem of providing support for such a distant landing on a scale far greater than ever before caused logistical headaches. Shortages of cargo ships and trucks would hamper the taking of the islands, for extended fighting required more ammunition than previous operations. Ammunition and gasoline were loaded on transports at Pearl Harbor, but the vast quantities needed for the Forager mission led to disorganized and dangerous stockpiles. On May 21, overloaded ships berthed tightly together in the West Loch of Pearl Harbor ignited, the blast killing 163 and injuring 396 people. Six landing craft were destroyed, and the cargo vanished. The haste of mobilizing for the campaign explained the disaster, yet Spruance refused to lose momentum. His Fifth Fleet sailed for the Marianas to join Task Force 58, which was clearing the skies above Saipan.

Saipan and the Battle of the Philippine Sea

The V Amphibious Corps, commanded by General Holland Smith, headed ashore on Saipan on June 15. "Howlin' Mad" Smith was just as aggressive as the amphibious doctrines he had helped pioneer before the war. In the early morning darkness the landing ships waited 5,500 yards offshore, bow doors open and ready to launch their amtracs in an effort to avoid the traffic jam of Tarawa and Kwajalein. But the Japanese had been tipped off. They sent out range markers along the reefs for their artillery to hit, and Lieutenant General Yoshitsuga Saito positioned his seasoned artillery officers to cover all beaches.

After a landing feint at 6:00 A.M., transports in a first wave roared speedily toward the coral reefs and beaches, and the defenders opened fire. Japanese aircraft were almost nonexistent, but to avoid mines, the U.S. Navy had bombarded Saipan from far out at sea, which lessened the effect of the bombing. Thus, the amtracs and new armored amphibians with 75-mm. guns in their turrets were exposed to heavy firepower. The American commanders had learned their lessons, however; there was no repeat of Tarawa, for the marines did not have to wade in. A company of the Sixth Marines did receive a direct hit; several died, and their vessel was set adrift in the surf. Still, the marines lost only 20 of the preloaded vehicles that carried 8 assault battalions in 719 tractors to the beaches. Within less than thirty minutes, 8,000 marines and the amtracs were on Saipan, though not all where they had intended. Some units landed in the wrong place because of strong currents that swept them off course, and others were pinned down by a vicious barrage from Japanese guns. Naval and air strikes saved the First Battalion of the Twenty-fifth Marines from being driven back into the sea from their 12-yard deep beachhead, but other units lost commanders, stalled under enemy fire, or spent the entire day getting to their original target positions.

Noting that the Japanese were dug into mountains and caves, General Smith had warned his commanders just before D-day that "a week from now, there will be a lot of dead Marines."[2] His premonition was correct. A lieutenant recalled that "around us was the chaotic debris of bitter combat: Jap and Marine bodies lying in mangled and grotesque positions; blasted and burnt-out pillboxes; the burning wrecks of [landing vehicles] that had been knocked out by Jap high velocity fire."[3] From mountain observation posts, the defenders unleashed unrelenting barrages that stunned the battered Americans, who countered with their own artillery fire with mixed results. Japanese snipers picked off their victims, and landing craft piled up supplies on the beaches or spilled their contents on the reefs as U.S. casualties mounted. Yet 20,000 marines, with 7 battalions of artillery and 2 tank batallions, had established a beachhead by nightfall of D-day, preparing for the expected brutal action ahead.

That night the Japanese counterattacked three times, beginning an intense free-for-all that heightened the rage of the Americans. Naval star shells illuminated U.S. troops, and Japanese artillery and intense machine-gun fire pierced American tanks. The defenders' first charge of 2,000 men faded, with 700 killed, including a bugler who was shot through his instrument. Two other charges failed to dislodge the Americans, who in the next few days pushed into the swamps and linked up with previously dispersed divisions. The marines stumbled across groups of defenders, fighting them ferociously at close quarters; a counterattack the second night withered under intense fire from rocket and grenade launchers, artillery, and tanks. The third day, June 18, brought more U.S. advances but also heavy casualties as the marines occupied an empty airstrip, cleaned out a coconut grove, and fended off counterattacks. That night the Second and Fourth Marine Divisions counted over 5,000 casualties.

The marines were not privy to the most critical event of the Saipan campaign. When on June 18 they gazed out to sea, to their amazement they saw no supply ships or transports. The troops now feared a repeat of Guadalcanal, when marines had been stranded, although this time, 33,000 tons of cargo had been unloaded to sustain them. Still, Raymond Spruance had withdrawn his ships, having learned from tracking submarines that Japan's First Mobile Fleet, the Combined Fleet's principal task force, was approaching. Spruance had called back 2 carrier groups of Task Force 58 from their strikes on the Bonin Islands, and leaving battleships and a handful of other vessels to guard Saipan, he decided to link Task Force 58's carriers with Admiral Turner's cruisers and destroyers west of Tinian. Long-range seaplanes would scout to the east and strike at Guam and Rota. The Americans readied to engage Admiral Toyoda in a decisive sea conflict.

That encounter was disastrous for Japan. The Americans had nearly double the First Mobile Fleet's planes and carriers. To be sure, Ozawa's aircraft, lacking armor and heavier fuel tanks, could range farther than U.S. planes, and Ozawa also banked on land-based planes at Guam, Rota, and Yap to inflict damage. But since Mitscher's prior attacks had reduced the number of Japanese planes, the admiral had been misinformed; as well, his pilots were far less experienced and skilled than the Americans. Nonetheless, Ozawa closed in on Saipan, bent on sinking the U.S. carriers and then destroying the amphibious forces.

Spruance tucked away his amphibious ships and let loose Task Force 58. He had not yet located Ozawa's fleet, but his four carrier groups were spread out west of the Marianas as the first wave of Japanese fighters appeared on June 19. Well-schooled officers on the carriers used radar to track the planes and estimate their flight patterns, making complex

A Japanese dive bomber plunges toward the sea, hit by American Navy antiaircraft fire during the Battle of the Philippine Sea, which decimated much of Japanese airpower. Grumman Avenger torpedo bombers sit on a U.S. aircraft carrier in the foreground. U.S. Army, *United States Army in World War II: Pictorial Record: The War Against Japan* (Washington, DC: Department of the Army, 1952), 242.

calculations to intercept them. These communications technicians listened in as Ozawa's squadron commander directed his pilots, who therefore unwittingly tipped off the Americans to their whereabouts. Veteran U.S. Hellcat pilots decimated the first wave while losing only one of their own, and battleships took care of the remnants of the attack, incurring only minor damage.

The Battle of the Philippine Sea had begun. So had the so-called "Great Marianas Turkey Shoot," as a U.S. pilot dubbed the aerial destruction of the Japanese planes at the hands of experienced American flyers. Over 125 aircraft roared down in a second attack wave, but almost all were destroyed by U.S. fighters and antiaircraft fire from Task Force 58. A third wave made its way around the battle line defenses and swarmed at one of the carrier task groups, but Hellcats and naval fire nullified this raid. The fourth and final assault wave self-destructed, inept aviators becoming separated and attacking sporadically on their own. Many never found the U.S. fleet; others died trying to ditch on Guam. In total, 373 Japanese planes had attacked, but fewer than 100 returned to their carriers. A mere 29 U.S. planes were shot down in the Turkey Shoot.

As the aerial destruction was occurring, U.S. submarines found the First Mobile Fleet, sinking the carriers *Shokaku* and Ozawa's flagship, *Taiho*, which forced the admiral to transfer to a destroyer. Mitscher could not locate the rest of the fleet by day's end on June 19, and scout planes had no better luck the next day until late afternoon, when Ozawa's forces were sighted 275 miles away. Despite the distance and the mere three hours of daylight that remained, Mitscher boldly launched his planes, risking tricky night landings on carriers, for which his pilots had never trained; some would have to ditch in the ocean. Nonetheless, the chance to wreak destruction on the Japanese Navy won the day. More than 200 aircraft took to the skies in less than twenty minutes as Mitscher got word that the Japanese were actually 60 miles farther west than previously believed. The American pilots, exhausted and worried about their return, pressed onward. They torpedoed and sank the carrier *Hiyo* and two oilers and devastated three other carriers. As Ozawa scurried west under the cover of darkness, the U.S. pilots frantically turned back, guided by carrier signal lights, searchlight beams, and star shells. Even so, 80 planes went down in accidents or for lack of fuel; although most were rescued during the night and the next day by patrols, 49 crewmen on the planes were lost. For the Japanese, however, the event was catastrophic; they lost 330 of 430 planes.

Debate endures about the Battle of the Philippine Sea. Despite the rout, Admiral Spruance actually failed to destroy the Combined Fleet. His commanders were disappointed that the enemy had escaped, and they blamed Spruance, arguing that he had cautiously turned back east toward Saipan on the eve of battle rather than let Task Force 58 search out Ozawa to the west. Later critics added that his caution had risked the loss of the carriers in a bigger battle, if one had occurred, for in racing to protect the marines on Saipan, Spruance had mistakenly sought to protect the amphibians rather than the carriers, which were more valuable to the Marianas operation. Had he been more aggressive, writes one expert, the engagement "could have been decisive and the Battle of Leyte Gulf might never have taken place."[4] Yet what was wrong about worrying over the marines? His mission, as he later explained, was to take Saipan, not to chase the Japanese fleet. Besides, Task Force 58 did achieve triumphs on several fronts. Fighting defensively, Spruance had so destroyed the First Mobile Fleet that Ozawa never again fully reconstituted his carrier groups, even though Ozawa had held an advantage of location, able to surprise the Americans. In Admiral Spruance's defense, one historian rightly concludes that "the success recorded on 19/20 June was probably as much as could be reasonably expected."[5]

Back on Saipan the victory in the Battle of the Philippine Sea left the Japanese garrison and its commander, Saito, without a savior. On land, the marines were well stocked and could count on ample assistance, thanks to U.S. domination of the seas. For General Saito there was now no hope for reinforcements to arrive. The garrison was doomed as American supply ships returned to Saipan to unload thousands more tons of cargo.

From June 19 to 22, U.S. infantry closed off the southern part of Saipan, captured the airfield at Nafutan Point, and then spent days trying to eliminate the defenders. Marine and army troops headed north to engage Saito's main forces on Mount Topatchau and in the dreadful terrain of ravines, caves, and cliffs. The defenders fought fanatically over their territory, only adding to the ferocity of the American offensive. Marine divisions attacked along Saito's lines, the Twenty-fourth sealing off caves along Magicienne Bay on the east side of the island, while the Second Marines labored west through ridges and gullies and up Topatchau. Holland Smith committed the reserve Twenty-seventh Division to the center of the line, but it bogged down on June 23, hit by fire from concealed Japanese artillery and machine guns in hillside caves along "Death Valley." Within a few days the marine general caused a famous controversy when he convinced Spruance and Vice Admiral Richmond Turner to relieve Army General Ralph Smith of his command over the Twenty-seventh, a division composed of National Guardsmen. The move did not sit well with the exhausted troops, who felt insulted, and commentators back home got wind of the request and took sides on Smith versus Smith.

Meanwhile, American forces slowly advanced, seizing central Saipan by June 30. They blasted away at caves, trying not to kill the many Korean and Chinese laborers and Chamorros residents hiding in them. The

Fourth Division progressed through canefields before meeting well-camouflaged Japanese snipers. Running out of water in the parching sun, the troops encountered caves in the cliffs overlooking the ocean on Kagman Peninsula. With a great effort they cleared them but came upon a pitiful sight of shell-shocked and starving civilians, many ill with leprosy, dengue fever, and elephantiasis. Nafutan Point, falling after a banzai charge, revealed 500 enemy bodies; the Japanese seemingly preferred to die rather than live. By June 30, fifteen days past D-day, U.S. troops took Death Valley, Hell's Pocket, and Purple Heart Ridge, the names symbolic of the brutal fighting. Typical was Flame Tree Hill. A smoke screen following an artillery barrage tricked the defenders into running from their caves in attack mode. Exposed in the open, they were wiped out by U.S. mortar and machine-gun fire. Why did—or, for that matter, how could—the Japanese continue to fight, wondered battle-weary American troops?

Taking the north island was Smith's final objective. Some Japanese regrouped in a final defense line above Garapan, while others hid in rock crevices, unsuccessfully trying to stave off hunger by eating grass and bark. The defenders lacked completed fortifications and so resorted to cave warfare or using civilians as decoys. Company A fell for the trick, losing 12 men. Other U.S. companies had been severely reduced: 6 officers and 315 enlisted men remained from a group of rifle companies that had begun with 28 officers and 690 soldiers; 22 of 29 officers in another battalion, and 490 of their troops were killed or wounded. Fearful of the decoy and other ruses, such as the defenders smearing themselves in blood and lying still to await unsuspecting Americans, the marines bayoneted all bodies they encountered. "If it didn't stink, stick it" was their gruesome motto.[6]

General Saito was cornered. Smith feared that the desperate Japanese would race forward in a final suicide attack, and indeed, Saito ordered the banzai charge, then committed hara-kiri on July 6. The next day, waiting in their foxholes with ammunition clips close at hand and fixed bayonets on their rifles, the tense marines heard preliminary yells and screams, then silence—an ominous signal. Screaming "banzai," 3,000 Japanese rushed the Americans with drawn swords, though some were armed only with a rock or a knife on a pole. The marines fired off round after round, their machine guns growing hot. "Haunting memories can still visualize the enemy only a few feet away, bayonet aimed at our body as we empty a clip into him," recalled a marine. "The momentum carries him into our foxhole, right on top of us. Then pushing him off, we reload and repeat the procedure." The Japanese seemed "like a savage animal, a beast, a devil, not human at all, and the only thought is to kill, kill, kill."[7] Until it all ended, American rage matched Japanese fury.

The carnage did not end there. The attackers shot through a gap between two battalions of the 105th Infantry, Twenty-seventh Army Division, inflicting enormous casualties, and they then overran the marine artillery. To Smith's disgust, a regiment of the Twenty-seventh failed to move forward to relieve their comrades, but the battalions were eventually rescued by amtracs and destroyers. By evening, the suicide assault halted, bringing an end to a day of terror. The two battalions had lost 918 men, and the artillery company suffered 127 casualties. Three marines received the Medal of Honor: one dived onto a grenade; another smothered a Japanese grenade to his chest in order to block the turret opening of his tank; and the third ran into enemy fire to rescue two wounded comrades. Several hundred Japanese lay dead, killed during their suicide mission or victims of shelling.

The remaining defenders either killed themselves with grenades or had officers decapitate them, but the most sickening spectacle occurred when thousands of civilians jumped off the high cliffs around Marpi Point. They were deaf to the pleas of American interpreters yelling through loudspeakers as the water turned red, hundreds of corpses blocking U.S. patrol boats. Nearly two-thirds of the 12,000 civilians committed suicide. The scene of a woman's nude corpse with a baby's head protruding, the mother having drowned while in labor, was one example of the ghastliness. The Japanese would not permit the civilians to surrender; they killed many of them by gunshot, lobbed grenades into their midst, or forced them into the sea. American soldiers looked on, pondering the beastly nature of the human race.

Saipan was officially secured in the afternoon of July 9, 1944. Just 736 prisoners were taken, 438 of these Korean laborers. The known Japanese dead numbered 23,811, but thousands more were sealed away in caves or charred in the wreckage left by flamethrowers. American troops suffered a startling 16,612 casualties, including 3,225 dead and 326 missing in action.

The Americans and Japanese had both learned hard lessons. The former would improve air support for ground troops, and U.S. planners also remedied the confusion of offloading supplies on the beaches by creating a permanent shore party charged with the movement of cargo from the beach to dumps. The Americans also realized that they would face formidable obstacles in their next moves, for hilly terrain honey-combed with complex cave networks susceptible only to flame-throwing tanks awaited them. For the Japanese, the lessons were clear. Just as Holland Smith concluded that Saipan opened the door to the home islands, General Saito had proclaimed before his suicide that Saipan would decide the empire's fate. Indeed, Japanese leaders realized after the battle that with the Combined Fleet routed and Saipan's capture the war had been lost. Yet they would still not abandon the field. Rather, they urged the troops to continue to die in defense of the empire.

In the halls of government in Tokyo, the two defeats shook Imperial Headquarters. After Saipan a consensus emerged among the General Staff that Tojo Hideki should sue for peace with the United States. The Japanese people got wind of the disaster first through a translated issue of *Time* magazine, and the defeat had a depressing psychological effect. Saipan, like Formosa, had been an old part of the empire, a place where many Japanese had settled. It was a foreign but not remote outpost. Now the recognition of defeat dawned on millions. Because "Japan has come to face an unprecedentedly great national crisis," Tojo was soon relieved of his position as head of the army. On July 18 his cabinet resigned, and General Kuniaki Koiso took over as premier, "charged with giving 'fundamental reconsideration' to the problem of continuing the war." The admirals understood that the chances of turning the tide of war had slipped away. Guadalcanal had shifted them from offense to defense, and now Saipan and the Battle of the Philippine Sea meant that effective defense had ended. As Fleet Admiral Osami Nagano warned, "Hell is on us," creeping ever closer to Japan's front door.[8] Four months after Saipan, 111 U.S. bombers took off for Tokyo from the Marianas, led by B-29s. Over the next year, the Superfortress would return to the capital and dozens of other cities as well, unleashing a destructive fury. Yet honor, fear, and bureaucratic gridlock defied logic, and Japan fought on, helplessly but with heightened cruelty.

Guam

Spruance planned to invade Guam and Tinian next, but he postponed the landings for a month until he was certain that Ozawa's fleet would not return to the Marianas. The delay frustrated the Seventy-seventh Marine Division, well-trained newcomers to amphibious warfare, as well as Major General Roy Geiger's southern landing force. The marines whiled away the days on ships out at sea and than enjoyed a few hours of rest back on Eniwetok's desolate beaches, drinking warm beer. Finally, on July 21, two weeks after Saipan had been secured, the near simultaneous invasions of Guam and Tinian began. The daring Admiral Richard "Close In" Conolly provided naval support by bringing his ships dangerously near to Guam on July 8 to launch a thirteen-day barrage, one of the longest preliminary bombardments of the war. After it was over, the landing force—comprising Bougainville veterans of the Third Marines, the First Provisional Marine Brigade (the equivalent of a full division), and the Seventy-seventh—prepared to go ashore.

Guam took on an emotional aspect, having been a U.S. possession since 1899; the marines had a long relationship with its natives and had studied it well. The small U.S. Marine garrison had fought a losing cause against the Japanese there on December 10, 1941, and about 20,000 Guamians, all U.S. nationals, had been spared only by the quick surrender that day. The Americans had vowed to return. But Guam would be difficult to capture: 35 miles long and 9 miles at its widest, it was three times larger than Saipan, had more mountains and jungles, and possessed fewer good beaches. The Japanese under General Hideyoshi Obata numbered 13,000 army soldiers and 5,500 naval troops who, now unable to return to Saipan, had ended up on Guam. Tactical command fell to Lieutenant General Takeshi Takashina, seasoned in Manchurian campaigns. These officers surmised, wrongly, that the Americans would land at Tumon Bay, where the Japanese had come ashore in 1941. The Third Marines attacked a smaller beach, however; the First Provisional Brigade hit another five miles to the south, and the two units would try to link up over rough, exposed ground. That the Japanese had erred again did not doom them, for they could cover the 15 miles of potential beach sites. A commander announced that the American soldier, "overconfident because of his successful landing on Saipan, is planning a reckless and insufficiently prepared landing on Guam. We have an excellent opportunity to annihilate him on the beaches." Tojo added that the troops should "to the very end continue to destroy the enemy gallantly and persistently; and thus alleviate the anxiety of the Emperor."[9] In the face of such determination, the Americans could not help but meet Japanese barbarity with their own.

On D-day, naval and aerial bombardment intensified as attack aircraft—85 fighters, 65 bombers, and 53 torpedo planes—blasted away at Japanese defenses, drowning out the noise from the landing ships and amtracs. Conolly came close in, firing with deadly accuracy. His supporting force of 274 ships, holding the 54,000-man landing units and their equipment, readied to storm ashore. The bombing rattled the defenders, and even worse for them, underwater demolition squads came right up to the beaches, cleared away mines and debris, and opened a 200-foot-wide hole in the coral reef for unloading. They left a sign welcoming the marines!

Such assurance belied the risks of the operation. Dazed but resolute, the Japanese resisted the Americans even after the tremendous pounding. They manned guns on the beaches to the south, using one 75-mm. gun to disable almost two dozen landing vehicles before marines at the rear overwhelmed them. Meanwhile, the Seventy-seventh Division was initiated into amphibious warfare by having to wade ashore from the reefs under enemy fire. Reverting to Saipan form, the defense was ferocious; both sides suffered numerous casualties.

The Third Marines led the northern landing to the far left of the Asan-Adelup beachhead, while other units drove into the interior. The Third absorbed intense enemy fire from the steep cliffs in the battle for Chonito Ridge, a vicious affair in which marines perished by machine-gun barrages and by grenades rolled down the incline. They retreated to ravines for a full day before others took the ridge from the rear, and the Japanese finally pulled back. On the southern beaches, at Agat, the First Brigade discovered even more resistance. Impervious to Conolly's bombardment were machine guns, 2 75-mm. guns, and a 37-mm. gun placed in a blockhouse. It took hours of sustained effort to overrun the Gaan Point blockhouse, as well as heavy losses by the Twenty-second Marines. Japanese junior officers urged suicide charges, many of which were barely repulsed. In one case, 750 men rushed a U.S. battalion poised on a hill at night. The attackers all died but not before taking several Americans with them. Another battalion of the Ninth Marine Regiment encountered 7 such frontal attacks and lost half its men.

The Third Marines to the south pursued the retreating Japanese over the ridges, but as they approached, the defenders raked them with machine-gun fire. The division had suffered over 2,000 casualties by the third day of battle. Meanwhile, the Japanese were readying a large counterattack to prevent the linking of southern and northern marine units. Takashina brought reserves into the hills along the Mount Tenjo Road, and on July 25 he began the most intense fighting yet on Guam, on Fonte Ridge. The Third Marines held despite the relentless firefights. One company commander, the thrice-wounded Louis Wilson, led marines in hand-to-hand combat for ten hours, repelling counterthrusts and mortar barrages that killed most of his patrol. By the next morning, 600 Japanese lay dead. Two more days were needed to secure Fonte Ridge and allow the marines to advance north, but before they did, a banzai charge swept over them. The Japanese overran a marine roadblock below the Mount Tenjo Road; infiltrators ran through the lines; and 50 of them reached the division hospital. Terrified American doctors and the wounded, as well as cooks, bakers, and corpsmen, killed 33 of the attackers but lost 3 men of their own.

Pushed out of the south part of Guam, 5,000 Japanese sailors determined to hold the base at Orote and drive the Americans off the island. In the early morning of July 26, Takashina ordered a go-for-broke counterattack from the mangrove swamps. Revealing their desperation, some of the assailants were drunk and used only their samurai swords, while others entered the marines' foxholes with fixed bayonets. A massive U.S. artillery barrage of 26,000 shells stopped the attack. Daylight exposed 400 Japanese bodies lying in the mud. The marines moved forward into the swamp, rooting out the defenders from dug-in defenses and minefields. Not unusually, an intrepid Imperial officer would charge a tank with only his sword. By July 28 the airfield and old marine barracks that had been abandoned in 1941 were in U.S. hands, thus undermining Japanese morale. As a result, many defenders committed suicide by jumping off cliffs, exploding grenades, or cutting their throats. The next day, the American flag rose over Orote, and the day following, the airstrip on the peninsula was back in use. A week later, 12 U.S. aircraft squadrons landed at Orote Field.

More counterattacks and masses of Japanese deaths followed on Guam in the face of the steady U.S. advance. Americans liberated some Guamians from detention camps, while other natives provided key medical assistance and food and shelter. Pockets of defenders fought to the end; hundreds died, and thousands fled into the jungles as U.S. troops neared Ritidian Point, the northernmost spot on Guam. A last-resort mortar attack on August 8 preceded a U.S. barrage against 2,000 Japanese hiding in the jungles. Most died. Two days later the last Imperial tank was destroyed, and on August 11, General Obata succumbed after sending the emperor news of the defeat.

On the day Guam was secured following the three-week battle, Admiral Nimitz arrived in Apra Harbor. Five days later he declared Guam his new headquarters and remained there until the war ended. While 10,971 Japanese had perished, some 10,000 more remained. Their will to survive was remarkable; although most died in the jungle from starvation, suicide, or dysentery, some were found in hiding as late as 1972, unaware that the war had ended. American patrols rounded up about 80 prisoners per day for a while, and over the next year they killed or captured 8,500 men. The Marines' III Amphibious Corps lost 1,190 men in action and 377 from wounds; 5,308 more were wounded. The Seventy-seventh Division suffered 177 deaths and 662 injured. On the positive side, Geiger and Conolly had worked well together, unlike the marines and navy on Saipan. Yet the negative—so many casualties lost in such horrible circumstances—left an indelible imprint on the Americans.

Tinian

Unlike the smooth interservice relations during the conquest of Guam, argument erupted about where to land on Tinian. A relatively flat island, compared with Saipan's mountains and Guam's ridges, Tinian—less than 4 miles southwest of Saipan—had few beaches suitable for a landing. The Japanese strongly defended the best ones near Tinian Town, at the south end of the island. Rear Admiral Harry Hill, in command of the invasion, and Holland Smith, fresh from Saipan, wanted to land at the tiny northern beaches, which were well in range of Saipan's artillery and were lightly defended besides. Yet these so-called White beaches could receive only 4 to 8 amtracs together, not anywhere near the 96 that had come ashore in each wave on Saipan. Admiral Turner demanded that the attack be made at Tinian Town, but Spruance intervened and chose the White beaches. He also authorized a clever feint at the southern beaches.

Tinian was smaller than Saipan, but it possessed excellent airfields that could serve as the biggest base for B-29 bombing runs over Tokyo. (The *Enola Gay*, for example, took off from Tinian to drop its atomic bomb.) The island was softened up by bombardment in the days preceding the landing, and then, on D-day minus one, the navy let loose massive air strikes using over 350 planes. Aircraft dropped 500 bombs, 200 rockets, 43 incendiary clusters, and 91 of the napalm bombs invented earlier in the year at Eglin Air Force base in Florida. Composed of diesel oil, gasoline, and metallic salt from the naphtha used in soap, these "fire" bombs were used for the first time ever in the combat on Tinian. Each napalm explosive cleared out an area between 75 and 200 feet, charring Japanese soldiers in their tracks. The U.S. military adopted napalm for flamethrower tanks, for ground troops in the Philippines, on Iwo Jima, and in the bombing of Japanese cities.

On July 24, three days after the initial landing on Guam and after days of bombardment, the Second and Fourth Marine Divisions went ashore on Tinian. Four army amphibian tractor battalions, 13 artillery battalions, and 1 engineer battalion backed them. As the Fourth Marines headed for the White beaches, the larger and experienced (from Guadalcanal, the Gilberts, and Saipan) Second Division moved toward Tinian Town. The Japanese expected them, watching as U.S. vessels opened fire with 3,000 rounds from 3 battleships, 7 destroyers, and 1 cruiser. Transports sent landing craft crashing toward the beaches as Japanese gunners, part of the nearly 9,000 Imperial troops stationed on Tinian, let loose from their camouflaged coastal defense batteries. The defenders cheered as the Americans halted 400 yards offshore and then retreated back to the transports, seemingly in defeat.

It was all a tricky distraction to allow the Fourth Marines to come ashore unmolested at the White beaches. The understrength Fourth (which had lost 6,000 men on Roi-Namur and Saipan), along with the Second Marines, moved cautiously on Tinian, shunning an aggressive pace in the heat, humidity, and monsoons. But their two new young generals, Harry Schmidt and Clifford Cates (who had replaced Holland Smith), moved the men and equipment rapidly off the thin beaches. By nightfall, 15,600 marines were on Tinian, having lost 15 dead and 225 wounded. Commanding the Fourth Division, Cates brought barbed wire to secure the perimeter and called for nighttime bombardment from support vessels.

The Japanese garrison, split between navy and army personnel, had been established in the 1930s, in violation of the League of Nations Mandate not to fortify the Pacific islands. Nearly 9,000 men had joined Tinian's population of 16,000. The garrison's main army force had been transferred to Tinian from Manchuria in March 1944; it counted on a mountain artillery battalion, a company of 12 light tanks, and other support units. The navy unit included construction crews and also 7 aviation squadrons, but they had little to fly because U.S. bombing had either destroyed or rendered inoperable all aircraft. In addition, bad coordination and tension between the army and navy troops on the island added to the mistaken assumption that the Americans would land at Tinian Town. Yet even forty-three days of bombing before the invasion had not broken the defenders' spirit.

Indeed, the Japanese, under the command of Colonel Kiyoshi Ogata, pointed several thousand troops and tanks at the U.S. perimeter in a well-coordinated counterattack that hit the Americans hard, some defenders pushing through the perimeter and attacking from rear areas. Two marines manning a machine gun stood their ground as Japanese, yelling "banzai," charged them with guns and hand grenades. The next morning they were found dead, with 251 Japanese bodies around them. A group of nearly 600 Japanese fell victim to the 75-mm. howitzers. Meanwhile, a marine battalion came under attack from 600 naval troops, and the Americans were reduced to 30 men before being saved by medium tanks. Tinian was a vicious battle, fought at night and at close quarters. The marines proved overwhelming to the fanatical Japanese, however, and the perimeter held that first night. The Japanese dead numbered more than 1,500 (many had been hauled away from the scene before the marines counted them), whereas the marines had only 100 casualties. Cates recognized that his enemy was broken at long last, although only after being cut down to mere handfuls of soldiers.

By July 26, two days after the initial landing, the 2 marine divisions formed a skirmish line of infantry and tanks, wiped out the Japanese in the north with few losses, and drove south. Pursued by tanks and bombed by aircraft and navy gunships, the defenders fought a lost cause, despite a few instances in which they inflicted damage. On July 30 the Americans entered Tinian Town after sealing off surrounding caves with flamethrowers, took an airfield, and chased the remaining Japanese into the rugged southeastern corner of the island. Issuing a now common-place order, Major General Schmidt told the marines to massacre the enemy, a difficult task in the rocky and hilly area.

A fierce infantry and tank battle ensued, coupled with naval bom-bardment. At dusk on July 31 the Japanese initiated a probing attack, and that night they launched a massive banzai charge. Wave after wave rushed at a 37-mm. gun position; all were annihilated. "That gun just stacked up dead Japanese," recalled one gunner. Eight of the 10 marines on the gun were killed or wounded, but the shooters themselves were "nearly shoulder-high with dead Japanese in front of that weapon."[10] Those marines justifiably disagreed with later reports that called Tinian an easy campaign. Another banzai charge early the next morning further deci-mated the Japanese.

Schmidt sent his troops across the southeastern plateau to the sea, declaring Tinian secured. But that move was a bit premature, for hundreds of Japanese emerged from caves the next day. Most were killed or retreated. Civilians hiding in the southeast area also began surrendering by August 1, many of them children in terrible health. Four thousand civilians died on Tinian, but fewer committed suicide than on Saipan. Clad in colorful silk clothes, thousands surrendered when promised good treatment by the marines. Still, horrors occurred as parents threw children off cliffs, and the Japanese military rounded up civilians and blew them up with grenades. Mercifully, the killing ended shortly thereafter.

In nine days, Tinian had fallen, and the Mariana Islands were in U.S. hands. The V Amphibious Corps had suffered 2,355 casualties, with 328 killed. On August 14 the Fourth Marines left for Hawaii, and the Second hopped to Saipan to set up a base camp. For the Japanese the countable dead numbered 5,000, with hundreds more sealed in caves or underground defense works. Only 250 prisoners survived from the nearly 9,000-man garrison. The Japanese learned that they would have to change their defense tactics if they wished to inflict more casualties.

Tinian soon had monumental strategic importance, much larger than its size or the relative ease of its capture would indicate. For starters, the island operation inaugurated an innovation in American amphibious landings by maneuvering the marines at sea, instead of on land. This change effected a powerful thrust that did not lose momentum at the beachhead, as had been the case before. The battle also represented textbook amphibian warfare, revised and perfected since the hardships on Tarawa. Furthermore, the victory in Saipan shocked onlookers in Tokyo, prompting Tojo's resignation. Frantic over the loss of the Marianas, part of their inner defense line, Japanese officials began improving fortifications on their remaining Pacific holdings. They knew other American raids and invasions were imminent, and they resolved to make U.S. personnel suffer.

The greatest strategic significance of Tinian arose from the subsequent air war, as the island became the biggest base for the B-29 Superfortress. Just 1,200 miles from Japan, Tinian allowed bombing runs to Tokyo and other cities well within the 2,800-mile range of the B-29. Two wings of the Twentieth Air Force made their home on the island, and within three months of its capture they were bombing Japan itself. Superfortresses flew 29,000 missions out of the Marianas, dropping 157,000 tons of explosives over the next year (including the two atomic bombs). An estimated 260,000 Japanese people died in these sorties; 9,200,000 were left homeless; and 2,210,000 homes were destroyed. That devastation made the invasion of Tinian, proclaimed one marine, "a pretty good investment."[11]

The payoff came not only in the air but on land. The Marianas served as a crossroads in the Pacific, for the Americans used the island chain to hop southwest to the Palaus and the Philippines, as well as northwest toward the home islands. Entering the final year of the war, the U.S. military machine could roll forward in any direction, and Japan could only await the bloody onslaught that it had instigated.

Notes

1. D. Colt Denfeld, *Hold the Marianas: The Japanese Defense of the Mariana Islands* (Shippensburg, PA: White Mane Publishing Company, 1997), 8.

2. Alexander, *Storm Landings*, 70.

3. John C. Chapin, *Breaching the Marianas: The Battle for Saipan* (Washington, DC: Marine Corps Historical Center, 1994), 2–3.

4. William T. Y'Blood, *Red Sun Setting: The Battle of the Philippine Sea* (Annapolis, MD: Naval Institute Press, 1981), 211.

5. Willmott, *The Second World War in the East*, 146.

6. Chapin, *Breaching the Marianas*, 29.

7. Ibid., 32–33.

8. Carl W. Hoffman, *Saipan: The Beginning of the End* (Washington, DC: Marine Corps Historical Division Headquarters, 1950), 259–62.

9. Cyril J. O'Brien, *Liberation: Marines in the Recapture of Guam* (Washington, DC: Marine Corps Historical Center, 1994), 8.

10. Richard Harwood, *A Close Encounter: The Marine Landing on Tinian* (Washington, DC: Marine Corps Historical Center, 1994), 26.

11. Ibid., 32.

5

THE RETURN TO THE PHILIPPINES

In the last phase of the war the United States enjoyed the luxury of deciding where and when to go next. The fall of Saipan, Guam, and Tinian created choices: Douglas MacArthur itched to invade the Philippines, while the Joint Chiefs had long planned to take Formosa, off the China coast. When U.S. officials decided that Japan would have to be invaded, securing as much of the western Pacific as possible became imperative.

On July 26, 1944, President Roosevelt met with MacArthur and Chester Nimitz at Honolulu to decide on the next moves. Heading for reelection, FDR wanted to be seen with the popular MacArthur, and the egotistical general reveled in the fanfare. The two also talked strategy. In 1943 the Joint Chiefs had approved of securing the South China coast, Luzon in the Philippines, and Formosa—the China-Luzon-Formosa line —but now, a year later, only Admiral Ernest King and some of the other Joint Chiefs advised taking Formosa. Jiang Jeshi's obstructions, difficulties in India and Burma, and Japan's seizure of air bases in east China had ruled it out; besides, the Philippines were more alluring, for an invasion there had political, moral, and emotional appeal. American citizens since 1898, Filipinos sought liberation from Japan. MacArthur emphasized not only that Filipinos would never forgive the United States for failing to try to rescue them but that America's postwar image in Asia was at stake. The president implied that he wanted the Philippines re-taken. Both informally agreed on an attack on Luzon in return for the Republican general's support for FDR in the November 1944 election.

Peleliu

Critical decisions arose from intelligence findings. In early September 1944 the Third Fleet's aggressive and popular William "Bull" Halsey sent his fast carrier Task Force 38 snooping around the large southern Philippine island of Mindanao, Yap, and the Palau Islands to the west, near Formosa. Into October he attacked aircraft and merchant ships, destroying nearly 1,000 planes and 180 sea vessels, discovering such weaknesses in Japan's defense of the southern Philippines that he advised an ambitious thrust at Leyte, in the central Philippines. The Joint Chiefs approved a landing for October 20, and Admiral King finally came around. He assented to an assault on the large, northernmost island of Luzon, site of the capital of Manila and the infamous Bataan death march, rather than Formosa. Seeking revenge, the Americans called the shots.

As preparations got under way for the invasion of the Philippines, operations began in the Palau Islands, specifically against the large Japanese garrison on Peleliu. Admiral Nimitz planned to bomb all the way to the Ryukyus, south of Japan, as well as take the Palau Islands, which are about 800 miles west of the Philippines at the western edge of the Caroline Island chain. From the latter the Japanese could threaten MacArthur's invasion forces, so the general urged the navy to achieve air superiority over the Palaus, lamenting that his Seventh Fleet was inadequate to the task. The Japanese called the Palaus "the spigot of the oil barrel," for they lay at the entrance to their petroleum resources in the East Indies.[1] Yet not only did Peleliu turn out to be largely irrelevant to the liberation of the Philippines; it also proved to be one of the bloodiest places in the Pacific war.

An island merely 6 miles long by 2 miles wide, Peleliu held the main airfield in the Palaus. Led by the First Marines, the invasion would be relatively easy, erroneously believed the division's commander, General William Rupertus. He proceeded unimaginatively in the face of unexpected Japanese tactics, and his errors cost the marines dearly. Major General Roy Geiger, commander of the III Amphibious Corps that oversaw the operation, wisely sensed trouble. As the D-day landing of September 15, 1944, bogged down, he took a ride to the beach, noting that naval bombardment had missed the guns on the beaches, which hit and burned dozens of landing craft and vehicles in the shallows. Watching heavy artillery fire coming from a ridge well inland, he also realized that the Japanese would fight within Peleliu. This time around, the defenders had adapted to amphibious warfare, and the Americans' only salvation lay in showing no mercy as they rooted out the Japanese.

Having abandoned Truk after the Battle of the Philippine Sea, the Japanese had left the Palaus vulnerable to attack. As a result, Imperial Headquarters sent the experienced Fourteenth Division of the Kwantung Army (which dated back to the Sino-Japanese War of 1895) to the Palaus to slow the Americans. Distributed at sites throughout the islands, including the best air base on Peleliu, the Fourteenth was trained, seasoned, and well armed. The Second Infantry Regiment joined the Fourteenth in defense of Peleliu, under the command of the crafty Colonel Kunio Nakagawa.

Nakagawa concocted punishing defensive advantages. The rugged north coast contained coral ridges filled with natural caves, set in a maze of gorges. The Japanese blocked the cave entrances with concrete or oil drums, attached sliding steel doors to some, and gave all of them alternative exits. Some of the larger underground tunnel fortresses (incredibly, one had nine different levels), equipped with electric lights, ventilation systems, and telephone and radio communications, allowed troops to weather the U.S. bombardment. Although their aboveground installations and planes had been ruined, they waited below in the interlocked caves that faced each other and thus allowed for mutually supporting fire. The skilled architects of the defense had over 10,500 army and navy personnel at their disposal, as well as 1,500 on neighboring Angaur, who had learned harsh lessons from earlier U.S. amphibious assaults: namely the futility of guarding the beaches. Able commanders built deadly defense works on the beaches to impede the invaders, but they planned to do most of their damage "in depth," when the Americans were forced to expel them from the caves.

Because Geiger also had inadequate information about Peleliu's terrain, the north coast's novel cave configurations came as a surprise to

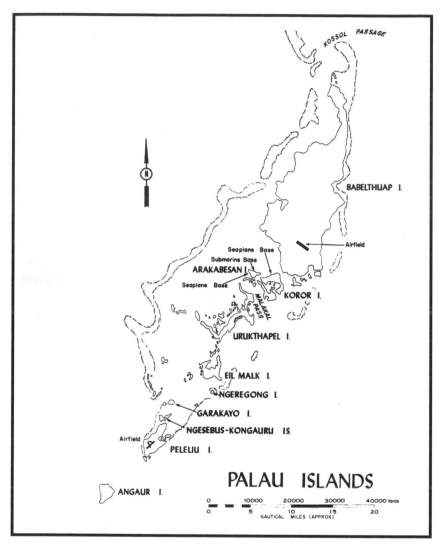

PALAU ISLANDS

Gordon D. Gayle, *Bloody Beaches: The Marines at Peleliu* (Washington, DC: Marine Corps Historical Center, 1996), 1. Reprinted by permission of the Marine Corps Historical Center.

the marines. Rupertus's First Marines, veterans of Guadalcanal and Cape Gloucester nicknamed the "Old Breed," came ashore after a bloody hour in which Japanese guns hit waves of amtracs, rubber-tired amphibious trucks, and other vehicles. Private Eugene Sledge, seeing his first action of the war, described the "assault into hell"—amtracs stalled and burning in the water, shells crashing around him, marines blown to bits: "The world was a nightmare of flashes, violent explosions, and snapping bullets." Stunned and terrified, he looked about him. "I asked God, 'Why, why, why?' I turned my face away and wished that I were imagining it all. I had tasted the bitterest essence of war, the sight of helpless comrades being slaughtered, and it filled me with disgust."[2]

Geiger held the Eighty-first Army Division in reserve, holding it for Agaur and Ulithi, or deployment to Peleliu if necessary—as it proved to be. Rupertus's optimism waned as his momentum inland was slowed by counterfire. Letting the amtracs land, Nakagawa directed his artillery at the Sherman tanks, but his guns lacked the velocity to inflict much damage on the big tanks. He also unleashed a charge of over 100 tanks that the Americans destroyed, although some did break through U.S. lines. Still, the Japanese stunned Geiger with their effective deadly defense. While the Seventh Marines struggled across the southern end of Peleliu, the Fifth Marines went up the center to the airfield. Despite carving out a modest beachhead on the first day, the Americans incurred over 1,100 casualties, including 200 dead, worse losses than the first day on Guam and Tinian (although fewer casualties than on Tarawa and Saipan). Still worse was yet to come, for the northern hills proved to be the place where "Bloody Peleliu" got its moniker.

From the second day through the next ten weeks, American troops fought a gory contest against the Japanese. Brutal conditions added to the rough terrain in the highlands. Temperatures reached 105 degrees the second day of the invasion and soared above that during the campaign; little shade and no breeze made matters worse. As heat prostration debilitated the troops, water supply was such a problem that the marines sickened themselves by drinking from old oil drums. As *Time* magazine correspondent Robert Martin conceded, "Peleliu is incomparably worse than Guam in its bloodiness, terror, climate and the incomprehensible tenacity of the Japanese. For sheer brutality and fatigue, I think it surpasses anything yet seen in the Pacific, and certainly from the standpoint of numbers of troops involved and the time taken to make the island secure."[3]

Beginning with an assault on "Bloody Nose Ridge" on the second day, the fighting was as savage as any in the war. Thinking the enemy were strung out along a perimeter on the highest ground, Rupertus sent the First Marines into a "final" offensive to break the line. They discovered that the forbidding landscape held the morass of defenses. The waves of hot wind, the craters and blistering coral rubble, along with Japanese fire, made Bloody Nose Ridge sheer hell. Private Sledge literally poured sweat out of each shoe.

In the first week on Peleliu, the marines sustained heavy losses. One battalion suffered 70 percent casualties. Geiger ordered ashore a regiment of the Eighty-first Army Infantry Division, nicknamed the "Wildcats," to relieve the First Division, while other units of the Eighty-first attacked Angaur and Ulithi Atoll. Angaur saw tough fighting, but by September 23 all of the 1,400 Japanese had succumbed, and the 321st Regimental Combat Team fighting on Angaur was transferred to Peleliu. Ulithi offered a deep lagoon for up to 600 warships—the fleet would be assembled there for the attacks on Iwo Jima and Okinawa—and it was taken at no cost, for not one of the Wildcats was lost. But the bloodbath on Peleliu dragged on.

Close air support helped the troops, but ten days after the initial landing the fighting remained vicious. Impenetrable coral plateaus, room-sized sinkholes, and jagged knobs and cliffs forced the troops to crawl and climb to protect their positions on the roads leading to and through the north. The troops advanced, not fully appreciating the vastness of the tunnel and cave networks they encountered. Air and naval gunfire, launches from the recently cleared tiny islets Ngesebus and Kongauru just to the north, and supporting tanks and amphibians, however, aided the flamethrowers, demolition teams, and troops. At the end of September, Geiger ordered the First Marines off Peleliu, Rupertus having lost over 5,000 casualties. The Wildcats replaced the Old Breed and spent another six weeks in battle.

In the Umurbrogol Pocket, a particularly well-fortified maze of caves and ridges suited to fanatical defense, the Japanese held on for eight days at the end of September, making sorties at night from their hideouts to counterattack. The ferocious siege continued into October, with some hills defended by deadly crossfire. Finally, American bulldozers and firepower reduced the cliffs to rubble, and napalm destroyed the vegetation and swept over human targets. Many of the dead on both sides lay unburied for hours and days, creating a gruesome scene of decay and stench. Into mid-October, Nakagawa's 700 or so soldiers fought until the Umurbrogol Pocket was reduced to an oval 800 by 500 yards, and then the Wildcats reduced it to nothing. Still, it took until November 27—a full seventy-three days—to grind down the Pocket. The stoic Japanese, refusing to surrender, burned or suffocated to death, for American troops took no pity.

Inside the caves the valiant defenders also suffered. They lacked sufficient water supplies; sanitation was abominable; food and ammunition were scarce; and some became so desperate underground that they chose suicidal night attacks. A handful were lucky to be captured. During the night of November 24, Colonel Nakagawa sent his final message to his commander on Koror, where the Japanese remained in strength. As even his last 56 men split into two groups to infiltrate U.S. lines—and most died—Nakagawa burned his regiment's flag and committed suicide. Incredibly, in March 1947 a U.S. Marine guard came across evidence of remaining soldiers, and a month later, informed by a Japanese rear admiral that the war had ended two and one-half years before, 27 survivors surrendered to the marines. That the Japanese would and did resist to the bitter end was never in dispute.

Declared secure on November 27, 1944, Peleliu went down in history as one of the worst, and most needless, battles of the war. It got scant press in the United States during the first five weeks, for the dramatic advances in the European theater overshadowed events in the Pacific. But the devastation in terms of human losses eventually drew attention to Peleliu, as did its dubious worth. *Life* magazine artist Tom Lea's haunting paintings dramatized the terror. Total marine and army casualties numbered 9,615 for Peleliu, Angaur, and Ngesebus, including 1,656 dead. The Japanese lost 10,900, almost all killed (of some 202 prisoners taken, all but 19 were laborers). For each defender killed, the Americans used 1,589 rounds of ammunition.

Because of the high casualty rate, commentators debate the worth of taking Peleliu, one historian calling it a "tragic triumph."[4] Most agree that the operations in the Palaus served little purpose other than exhibiting the most brutal effects of Japanese aggression. Nimitz might have canceled the assault (as Halsey had suggested) had he not been convinced, however wrongly, that the islands would serve as staging areas for invading Leyte in the Philippines. But the Palaus never did serve to guard MacArthur's right flank as he came up from New Guinea, and, contrary to earlier forecasts, Peleliu proved irrelevant to the seizure of Ulithi Atoll. Just as bad, the Americans—unlike their Japanese counterparts, who learned from their mistakes and applied new antiamphibious tactics—did not pass on the hard lessons of Peleliu to those U.S. troops who assaulted Iwo Jima. Future American invaders would suffer from the administrative oversight and petty infighting that led to this unconscionable result.

Still, the operation, though not crucial to winning the war, brought some benefits. It destroyed key military facilities, liquidated one of Japan's best divisions, the veteran Fourteenth, and isolated both the submarine base at Koror and the roughly 250,000 Japanese troops in the Carolines. In July 1945, 316 sailors from the torpedoed *Indianapolis* could thank Nimitz for the operation, for it was a patrol bomber flying out of Peleliu that sighted them after four days. The island also provided a convenient air and communications link between the Marianas and the Philippines; the western Carolines now served as a base for U.S. bombers; and Ulithi became a superb anchorage.

The chief value that can be placed on the operation came in the form of a warning: a foreboding of the determined and skilled Japanese resistance to come on Iwo Jima and Okinawa prompted the U.S. military and public to expect great hardship in the future. The battle also piqued philosophical pondering, as infantrymen such as Eugene Sledge lost their innocent faith that politicians made wise decisions when it came to starting wars. Peleliu served as a wake-up call throughout the ranks regarding the brutality of war, and leaders no longer lived under the illusion of easy conquest that had so undermined the efforts of General Rupertus.

Leyte

As the Peleliu operation continued on its bloody way, MacArthur and Nimitz moved up the timetable for the invasion of Leyte, in the central Philippines, to October 20. They would skip over Mindanao, using Leyte as a staging area to invade Luzon. Imperial Headquarters knew that the loss of the Philippines would interrupt supplies coming from Southeast Asia and thereby endanger Japan's survival. The Japanese Army, therefore, stationed several hundred thousand troops throughout the islands, while the Imperial Navy readied the Combined Fleet. The epic battle would be joined on and around Leyte.

A large island 110 miles long and 15 to 50 miles wide, Leyte had good landing beaches and easy access inland across coastal plains but also mountainous, cave-filled terrain ideal for defense. Its population of over 900,000 people had struggled against the Japanese occupiers. The Fourteenth Area Army, under General Tomoyuki Yamashita, oversaw the defense of the Philippines with a total of 432,000 troops, including air and construction units. They counted on support from the Fourth Air Army and First Air Fleet, and 884 aircraft on some 120 airfields (6 on Leyte) in the islands. The Combined Fleet promised 4 carriers, 7 battle ships, 2 battleship-carriers, 19 cruisers, and 33 destroyers out of Borneo and Formosa. Responsibility for defending Leyte fell on the 20,000 troops of the Sixteenth Division of the Thirty-fifth Army, under Lieutenant General Sosaku Suzuki.

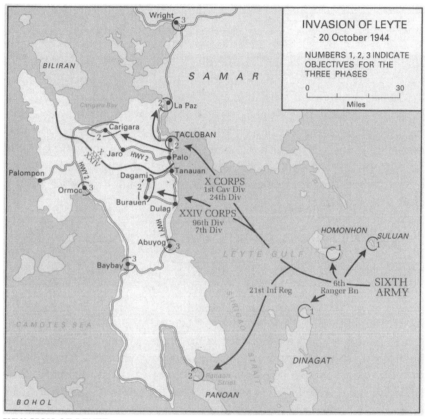

INVASION OF LEYTE

Charles R. Anderson, *The U.S. Army Campaigns of World War II: Leyte* (Washington, DC: Army Center of Military History, 1994), 11.

This largest U.S. amphibious operation to date in the Pacific relied on a convergence of the southwest and central Pacific Allied campaigns under MacArthur. American naval forces, composed mostly of the U.S. Seventh Fleet under Vice Admiral Thomas Kinkaid's 701 ships, would land and support 2 corps of the U.S. Sixth Army under Lieutenant General Walter Krueger, who commanded 202,500 ground troops; only

1 of the 6 infantry divisions had not seen combat. Added to them was the Sixth Infantry Ranger Battalion, ordered to secure outlying islands and guide forces to the beaches, as well as amphibious support groups, including 1,500 marines. The Seventh Fleet's planes provided air cover during the transport and amphibious operations, then transferred to the Allied Air Forces under Lieutenant General George Kenney. In addition, Halsey's Third Fleet and its 4 fast carrier task forces would patrol out at sea.

The preliminary phase of the invasion, code-named King Two, began at dawn on October 17, 1944. Minesweepers preceded the landing of the Sixth Rangers on three islands in Leyte Gulf. On two of these, Dinagat and Homonhon, no Japanese were discovered, and Saluan's defenders were quickly overrun. Demolition teams then cleared the beaches. After four hours of intense naval bombardment on "A-day," October 20, troops landed on Leyte between the provincial capital of Tacloban, which held the biggest Japanese airfield, and the Palo River. Another corps came ashore 15 miles to the south. Laboring through the swampy terrain, the army troops established beachheads and began moving inland. In only one sector did the Japanese mount resistance enough to compel landing craft to go elsewhere.

Even that sector was secure within hours, and thus MacArthur felt it safe to make his dramatic return to the Philippines. At one o'clock, with Japanese snipers still active in the Twenty-fourth Division's sector, the general and the new president of the Philippines boarded a landing craft—which took on too much water and had to stop short of the beach. At 1:30 P.M., sporting cap and sunglasses, MacArthur waded ashore and into history. In one of the most famous scenes of World War II, he played to the photographers as he marched up the beach, risking enemy fire. Stepping up to a microphone mounted on a weapons carrier, the general pronounced, "People of the Philippines, I have returned! By the grace of Almighty God, our forces stand again on Philippine soil." In a fit of interservice rivalry, the marines who came ashore as support afterward hung a sign that read "By the Grace of God and the Help of the Marines, MacArthur has returned to the Philippines."[5]

Americans had made the first move to liberate the islands, and by the next day a cavalry division had taken Tacloban, fighting a determined but unorganized enemy. Other troops pushed through the swamps to the south and seized key airfields. Two days after Tacloban fell, on October 23, MacArthur and President Sergio Osmena presided over the restoration of civil government to the Philippines. Allied forces cleared the strait between Leyte and Samar Island to the north and turned west to advance through Leyte. In the next five days the Nineteenth and Thirty-fourth Infantry Regiments killed over 800 Japanese on the way toward the northern port of Carigara. By early November they had wiped out another 3,000 defenders in overrunning the Leyte Valley. In the hot central highlands and the south, U.S. infantry and tanks destroyed enemy pillboxes and caves, captured more airfields, and killed hundreds more. At the town of Barauen, fanatical resisters charged out of spider holes to stop U.S. tanks by holding explosives to their hulls before being beaten back. At Buri Airfield, over 400 Japanese perished in senseless but fanatical defense of their territory. By late October the Army had occupied the east coast of Leyte and held Ormoc Bay, a major port, under observation. The fighting had been brutal.

Desperate, the Japanese mounted a counterattack on October 24. Approximately 200 Imperial aircraft headed for the U.S. ships off Leyte and toward American forces on the ground. Fifty U.S. planes took off from Leyte to meet them, and the Japanese aircraft, mostly bombers, went down in flames. Still, the counterattack continued for four days and nights, until the Japanese ran out of planes. Yet before that happened, they had another card to play. Mimicking the banzai suicide charges of their compatriots on land, a corps of pilots crashed their planes into American ships as astonished U.S. soldiers looked on.

These pilots were the kamikazes, named for the "divine wind" of two typhoons that had swept away Mongol invasion fleets off southern Japan in 1274 and 1281. Kamikaze pilots first aimed at the large transport vessels and then headed for the escort fleet in Leyte Gulf. They sank no capital ships and only one escort carrier, but they damaged many vessels and struck utter fear and loathing into the hearts of U.S. sailors. Scrambling on ships, the seamen realized that the end of the war would be fought, literally, to the death. As one recounted, the sky rained down airplane fragments, and the sea was on fire. On deck, "blood, guts, brains, tongues, scalps, hearts, arms, etc. from the Jap pilots" were scattered about before being hosed away.[6] The Japanese attacks arose from desperation and a fanatical commitment to the empire's cause. The Americans coupled this will to fight and die with an image of their enemy as crazed, nonhuman beasts to whom normal rules of behavior did not apply. Yet for all participants, the kamikazes also represented a tragedy, the pitiful plight of the defending combatants. To U.S. observers the Japanese seemed to lack reason, morality, and simple humanity, which made it all the more imperative to devastate them in all possible ways before they killed more Americans.

The Battle of Leyte Gulf

Farther out at sea the Americans had another problem, for the Combined Fleet, under Admiral Soemu Toyoda, was approaching for the long-awaited decisive encounter. After the Battle of the Philippine Sea the battered Japanese had pulled back toward the home islands and the Lingga Roads west of Borneo and south of Singapore. The Americans dominated the central Pacific; Japanese ships needed repairs, and the fleet and aircraft lacked fuel and ammunition. But Toyoda was defiant. Admiral Matome Ugaki, horror-struck but impressed by the mass suicides at Marpi Point in the Marianas, proclaimed that if the Japanese people and military stood united, they could yet fight the United States to victory.

That was an odd conclusion, especially after Halsey's Third Fleet had moved within the empire's defensive screen and repeatedly attacked Japanese air bases in the Philippines, destroying many aircraft on the ground. A return assault on Luzon, Okinawa, the Ryukyus, and Formosa on October 10 had denied the Japanese a staging area (Formosa was just 200 miles north of the Philippines), knocked out land-based aircraft, and diverted Japan's attention away from Leyte. The raids prompted a sustained counterattack for ten days, with few successes for the defenders. New recruits were called upon to fill out the Japanese air forces, and, not surprisingly, given their inexperience, over 500 planes were lost, as well as shipping and base facilities. The Americans had 2 cruisers damaged and fewer than 100 planes shot down.

Yet officials in Tokyo got a different story because the green pilots counted near misses as hits and hits as losses, thus claiming that they had shot down 1,200 U.S. aircraft and sunk 11 aircraft carriers. Senior naval officers grew suspicious, and Admiral Shigeru Fukudome wrote that "fighters were nothing but so many eggs thrown at the stone wall of the indomitable enemy formation."[7] But other top brass accepted the exaggeration of this "Victory of Taiwan" as the number of destroyed American carriers rose to 19. A Japanese task force sallied forth to sink the 2 crippled U.S. cruisers, but they quickly scurried home upon learning that Halsey's fleet was nearly intact. Regardless of the errors, the Imperial Navy longed for another battle like Guadalcanal. This time, however, Japan would add to the victory by using its huge battleships in a final showdown.

Weakened, the Japanese nonetheless gambled. Not only did they lack good pilots, but they could not replace the lost carrier air crews from the skirmish off Formosa. Furthermore, the Imperial Army reinforced the island, erroneously thinking U.S. airpower had disappeared. And Toyoda wanted to move hastily before the Americans had a secure base such as Leyte. To his credit, he still had most of his battleships and heavy cruisers, and thus he committed nearly his entire surface fleet to battle. Under the *Sho Ichi Go-1* (Operation Victory, or defense of the Philippines) plan, Ozawa's helpless aircraft carriers—4 of them with no planes on board— would serve as decoys to lure Halsey's Third Fleet northward, away from Leyte Gulf. Then, 2 groups of battleships and cruisers would converge on Leyte Gulf. One, under Vice Admiral Nishimura Shoji, would race through the Sirigao Strait, and the other, commanded by the stern and quiet warrior Vice Admiral Kurita Takeo, would approach through the San Bernardino Strait. Absent Halsey's protection, the Americans would be trapped. It is the consensus of historians that the plan was workable. Indeed, it succeeded, in that Halsey did take the bait.

So began the Battle of Leyte Gulf, the largest naval engagement in the history of warfare. Leyte Gulf involved 282 American, Japanese, and Australian vessels, thus dwarfing the Battle of Jutland in World War I. The Japanese force included the battleships *Yamato* and *Musashi*, the biggest surface warships ever constructed. These behemoths were 862 feet long and weighed 70,000 tons—134 feet longer and 30,000 tons heavier than the *Carolina*-class battleships, the closest U.S. vessels in size. Also enormous was the distance covered in the battle and the number of people involved: some 200,000 men fought in an area spanning over 100,000 square miles. Every type of vessel, weapon, and tactic available in naval warfare came into play, including submarines, airplanes, amphibians, surface exchanges, and the largest naval guns ever used. Kamikaze attacks, still a novelty, killed more Americans than any other Japanese weapon; thousands more died on the dozens of ships that were sunk or damaged. The first and last time a U.S. aircraft carrier was sunk by gunfire occurred during the Battle of Leyte Gulf, which was also the last engagement between old-style battleships.

The engagement has been shoved aside in history by the Battle of the Bulge and Iwo Jima, mainly because Americans believed that victory over Japan had become a given. But its significance was much more monumental than either of those conflicts; only the dropping of the atomic bombs had a greater impact. Leyte Gulf represented Japan's final, desperate hope to hold off the Allies, and the Imperial Navy never made another significant sortie after the conflict. At the very least, a U.S. loss might have slowed down the advance toward Japan. A Japanese victory at sea could have upset U.S. invasion efforts in the Philippines and might even have cost Roosevelt his reelection bid a few weeks later. Faced with a temporarily victorious enemy, one willing to go to any lengths to survive, a new president might have been willing to negotiate an end to the war on terms more favorable than the demand for unconditional surrender. Admiral Kurita thus told his men on the eve of the engagement, "You must remember that there are such things as miracles. What man can say that there is no chance for our fleet to turn the tide of war in a decisive battle?"[8]

The battle was also dramatic. On October 23, 2 U.S. submarines sighted Kurita's force as it approached Leyte; they sank two cruisers (including the flagship) and damaged a third. The next day, Halsey's force came under a three-wave attack from aircraft based on Luzon, but American Hellcats shot down most of them. Ace pilot David McCampbell knocked out 9 in one day, a record never duplicated. A Japanese plane crashed into the carrier *Princeton*, which eventually exploded near another vessel, causing casualties on both, yet another U.S. task force under Rear Admiral Gerald Bogan countered with an attack wave on Kurita, who had hoped for fighter protection from air bases in the Philippines. Bogan focused on the battleship *Musashi*, taking all day to sink the giant, on which over 1,100 sailors died. Incurring other damage, Kurita decided to retire beyond range of Halsey's carriers and await developments rather than sail through the narrow San Bernardino Strait and risk slaughter. It was not his last mistake, and certainly not fatal, but the lack of land-based airpower convinced him to withdraw when he might have inflicted significant harm to the U.S. Navy.

To the north, meanwhile, Ozawa's lure of aircraft carriers waited. After expending the remainder of his planes in the attack from Luzon, Ozawa went searching for Halsey, who finally spotted the Japanese admiral. Now the U.S. Navy had located all elements of the Combined Fleet—Kurita's San Bernardino group, Shoji Nishimura's Surigao Straits ships, and Ozawa. Kurita seemed to be withdrawing, and Kinkaid's Seventh Fleet prepared to intercept Nishimura, who had endured an air attack that morning. Halsey therefore decided to split his fleet. One group—Vice Admiral Willis Lee's Task Force 34—would guard the San Bernardino Strait with 4 battleships, 5 cruisers, and 14 destroyers in case Kurita should reverse course again and try to head back down the channel. The main group, comprising 3 carrier groups in the Third Fleet, would go north to engage the Japanese carrier fleet.

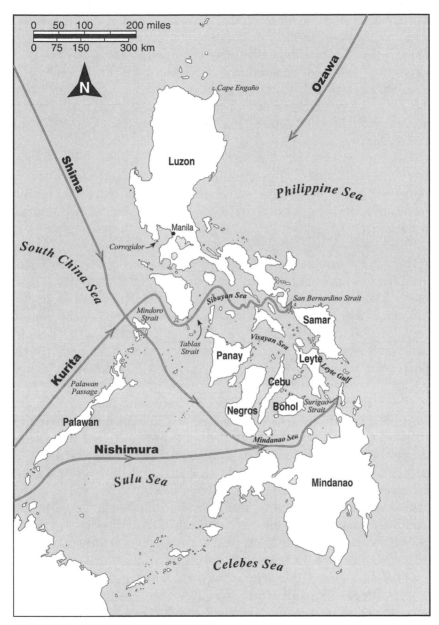

APPROACH OF THE JAPANESE FORCES
Map by Robert E. Schultz

At least that was the plan heard by Halsey's superiors and Kinkaid. Halsey, however, never actually formed Task Force 34. Instead, he took Willis and his ships north along with him, leaving the San Bernardino Strait undefended. Recalling the criticism of Spruance for letting Ozawa's carriers escape during the Battle of the Philippine Sea, Halsey resolved that caution would not undermine victory again. Nimitz had ordered the Japanese carrier fleet destroyed, should the opportunity arise, and Halsey planned to obey. Going after Ozawa's carriers with everything at his disposal, including the ships of Task Force 34, he steamed north—and thus fell for the Japanese decoy.

To the south, Kinkaid, who had risen to command the Seventh Fleet after successful battles in the Solomons and in Alaskan waters in 1943, waited with 6 old battleships, 8 cruisers, and 30 destroyers under the command of Rear Admiral Jesse Oldendorf. They blocked Nishimura's run through the Surigao Strait, confident that Task Force 34 was guarding their northern flank around the San Bernardino Strait. About 60 miles to the southwest in the Mindanao Sea, 39 tiny motor torpedo, or PT, boats of the Seventh Fleet were on alert for Nishimura. (These vessels had been made famous by MacArthur's departure from the Philippines in 1942 and by dashing figures such as Lieutenant John F. Kennedy, who had helped rescue marines on the island of Choiseul in early November 1943.) Just after midnight of October 24, the PT boats spotted the Japanese—4 destroyers followed by 2 battleships and a cruiser.

The PT boats attacked. Nishimura's oncoming fleet swept them aside, but the skirmish tipped off Kinkaid, who met the southern fleet in Surigao Strait. American destroyers coming down both sides of the strait let loose their torpedoes, and battleships and cruisers sitting broadside to them in the center—"capping the T"—unleashed their shells. In just 15 minutes only one Japanese cruiser and a destroyer escaped, and the former was hunted down and sunk. Arriving from the China coast, Vice Admiral Kiyohide Shima's force of 3 cruisers and 4 destroyers, which had followed behind Nishimura, also fled the strait. Oldendorf suffered no losses except for one ship caught in a crossfire. Kinkaid was satisfied.

The Americans had exposed their flank, however, for minus Task Force 34, the San Bernardino Strait was wide open to Kurita. He took full advantage of Halsey's error by going through it and down the coast of Samar into Leyte Gulf. There he engaged the Taffy 3, one of three groups of escort carriers and destroyers under Admiral Clifton Sprague that were supporting MacArthur's landing on Leyte. Sprague lacked armor and an ability to withstand or launch an attack on the Japanese ships. Taffy 2, under Admiral Felix Stump, and Taffy 1, commanded by Thomas Sprague (no relation to Clifton), were well to the south. Nonetheless, Clifton Sprague bluffed by sending his remaining planes toward Kurita in the running Battle of Samar, tricking Kurita into concluding that he had encountered Halsey's main carrier fleet. He therefore ordered a full attack in what he presumed was the decisive battle. Sprague's ships feinted, attacked, dodged, and harassed the Japanese battleships until bombers armed with torpedoes arrived, sinking 3 cruisers and damaging others.

Kurita charged onward, but Sprague's diversions caused chaos. One Japanese battleship went so far north to avoid torpedoes that it left the battle, while a destroyer squadron wasted its torpedoes by firing prematurely at a pestering U.S. destroyer. But Sprague, with Stump closing fast, could barely hold on. Several of his ships took hits, some went to the bottom, and the carnage on deck was gruesome. On the destroyer *Johnston* a 6-inch shell decapitated an officer; on the flying bridge, shrapnel hit a sailor's megaphone, breaking his teeth; and the captain had neck and chest wounds, his shirt and helmet blown off his body. The destroyer lost its steering, but like so many other outmatched U.S. vessels, it desperately fired away at the looming Japanese force. When the *Johnston* eventually sank, along with 2 escort carriers, a Japanese officer on a ship nearby saluted his worthy foe. Several hundred sailors were either dead or adrift in the shark-infested waters, waiting for rescue, as Sprague and Kinkaid frantically signaled for Halsey to return.

Mysteriously, although Halsey had been informed by others, including Rear Admiral Bogan, that Kurita had changed course and come through the San Bernardino Strait, he and his staff ignored the warnings. By the time Kinkaid and Sprague radioed in desperation, Marc Mitscher's planes had attacked Ozawa's sitting ducks, sinking two carriers and a destroyer. Yet heedless of the calls from the south for aid, Halsey refused to dispatch Task Force 34, focused as he was on destroying the Japanese Mobile Fleet. He did order a task group headed for Ulithi for rest to turn around and help Sprague, but by then—around 10:00 A.M. on October 25—Nimitz had intervened. Listening from Pearl Harbor, the commander of the Pacific Fleet asked Halsey, "Where is Task Force 34?" and then followed with the statement, "The World Wonders." This last part of the message was meant to confuse enemy code-breakers, yet it also insulted Halsey, who continued north for another hour before sending Task Force 34 and another carrier task group south to rescue Sprague's escort carriers. Kinkaid, meanwhile, was hurrying his old

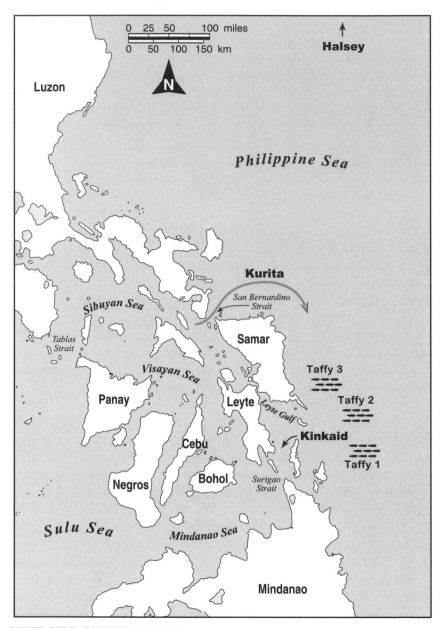

LEYTE GULF, OCTOBER 25, 1944
Map by Robert E. Schultz

battleships fresh from the Surigao Strait victory to Leyte Gulf. They were still three hours away.

Not only Sprague but Admiral Felix Stump's group of escort carriers were in deep trouble. Kurita's powerful force pushed them into Leyte Gulf, ostensibly ready to finish them off. Yet at 9:30 A.M., the Japanese suddenly left the scene, steaming off to the north. The Americans could not believe their eyes. Kurita, tired and worried that the U.S. carriers were about to overwhelm him, had decided to retreat. He knew that Nishimura's group was destroyed; he had not heard from Ozawa about the status of the *Sho* plan; his radios had intercepted Kinkaid's call for more battleships and cruisers, and Kurita feared that the Americans were rushing in to destroy his fleet. Just after noon, he informed Imperial Headquarters that he was heading for the San Bernardino Strait. In late afternoon, Halsey came south toward the strait with a small task force, having sunk all four of Ozawa's carriers but lacking enough fuel for all his ships. Kurita had escaped.

The Battle of Leyte Gulf was just about over, save for the kamikaze attacks. As a special suicide unit, the kamikazes had been created by Vice Admiral Onishi Takijiro of the First Air Fleet, who had abandoned hope that Japan, its planes and pilots outnumbered by battle-tested U.S. flyers, could fight by conventional means. Onishi explained to the first pilots as they prepared for takeoff on Luzon that Japanese air weakness could be overcome by organized suicide missions in which the greenest recruit could take part merely by crashing into an enemy vessel. Kamikazes were not skilled pilots or even warriors. Many college students, graduates, and even farmers flew these one-way missions out of obligation to family and nation, taking solace in the belief that they would die a noble death. Such terrorism in the air would also play well at home as an inspiration to the people: the Japanese warrior would undertake the ultimate sacrifice, unlike his American foe, showing the triumph of spirit over material superiority.

The kamikaze was used for the first time on a large scale at Leyte Gulf. Because coordination of the suicide missions proved difficult, they began as Kurita withdrew. Taking part in farewell ceremonies and then calmly boarding their planes after writing poems to loved ones, kamikaze pilots drank a glass of sake and headed for the American ships. Flying in groups of three, accompanied by fighters and an evaluation plane, they hit the southern escort carriers under Thomas Sprague. One crashed through the flight deck of the carrier *Santee*, and another opened a hole in the *Suwanee*. To the north, another group slammed into Clifton

Sprague's ships. One kamikaze destroyed the carrier *St. Lo* by going through the flight deck and igniting bombs and torpedoes. Sailors screamed at the Zeroes to pull out of their dives.

The Americans were stunned, alarmed, and angered. The kamikazes, soon organized into divisions of the Thunder Gods Corps, provoked the U.S. military into using every weapon at its disposal to destroy Japan. Americans were all the more convinced that the Japanese would go to any lengths to survive and that they lived under an impregnable illusion of coming victory. As historian Ronald Spector writes, the "fanaticism and contempt for life conveyed by kamikaze tactics may have contributed to American willingness to employ the atomic bomb as an alternative to confronting an entire nation of kamikazes in an invasion of Japan itself."[9] Using kamikazes was also the act of a desperate nation willing to sacrifice ordinary people. That scary thought incited Americans to grind out this war to its bitter end.

Thus ended the epic Battle of Leyte Gulf. Halsey came under criticism for leaving the San Bernardino Strait unguarded and not coming to the rescue fast enough, but he retorted that his orders were to destroy Ozawa's carrier fleet. Even though it turned out to be a decoy, he went to his grave convinced he had done the right thing. Nimitz realized that Halsey had erred but left him in command. After all, "Bull" Halsey had done as much as any leader to stoke confidence during the gloomy months after Pearl Harbor by his colorful talk and bold, morale-boosting strikes in the Marshalls and against Tokyo in early 1942. He had almost singlehandedly turned the tide at Guadalcanal after replacing a failed commander, but then he had been frustrated when a debilitating skin rash laid him up during the critical battle of Midway. Thus, Leyte Gulf was Halsey's big chance, at long last, to engage the Japanese fleet. In his defense, regardless of the disappearance of Task Force 34, Japanese naval power had been destroyed. Halsey's mistakes paled when compared with the staggering implications of Imperial Japan's rout.

For routed the Japanese were, despite their usual bravery and maniacal behavior. Kurita made tactical errors, especially by failing to press home his advantage during the skirmish with Clifton Sprague. The loss column had grown large by October 26: the Combined Fleet lost all 4 of its carriers, 3 battleships, 6 heavy and 4 light cruisers, 9 destroyers, 2 amphibious ships, and 1 submarine, in addition to 500 planes and 10,500 sailors and airmen—placing Japan at a tremendous disparity relative to U.S. power. The Americans suffered 2,800 dead and 1,000 wounded, but paid a relatively cheap price of 6 ships (2 escort carriers, a light carrier, 2 destroyers, and a destroyer escort). Nimitz now had a huge edge: 46 carriers to Japan's 4; 12 battleships to 9; 162 destroyers to 35; 56 cruisers to 20; 29 submarines to none, and nearly as many oilers as Japan had had in 1941. By the end of November 1944, Japan had lost another 50 warships in U.S. mopping-up operations, as well as 48 service ships and merchantmen.

In short, Japanese naval power and effectiveness had ceased to exist by November 1944, just one year after the initial U.S. offensives across the Pacific had begun. As Ozawa testified, "Japanese surface forces became strictly auxiliary, so we relied on land forces, [kamikaze] attacks, and air power."[10] Indeed, only the huge *Yamato*, among all elements of the fleet, ventured out again for a meeting with the Americans. The Japanese had just 10 fleet units left after Leyte, having committed—and lost—almost everything they had.

The Japanese would defend to the death, but their war was lost. Leyte Gulf represented the last time the empire would not fight out of sheer desperation. Nimitz later claimed that "the Battle of Leyte Gulf was the Trafalgar of World War II. Halsey and Kinkaid in 1944, like Nelson in 1805, had finally wiped out the Japanese fleet as an effective fighting force. There would be no more stand-up battles at sea in this war."[11] The defeat meant that Japan would stake all on holding the Philippines but that its position in the islands was untenable in the long run. Even the reinforcement of Leyte was difficult, for at least 3,250 soldiers died en route to the island, victims of pinpoint intelligence sent to prowling U.S. submarines.

The stranglehold that the Americans placed on Japan after November 1943 had assured victory, but the Battle of Leyte Gulf in October 1944 brought all elements of Japan's defeat together. The nation was overpowered decisively on the seas, as well as on land and in the air, and as thousands of tons of shipping went to the bottom, it was no longer able to mobilize sufficiently its industry, finances, and trade. Japan was also losing the appeal to Asians to fight against the West, and its military was faltering in Burma and China. In short, the empire was essentially helpless to fend off the United States. Its Navy reduced to "coastguard status," its major weapon suicide attacks, its cities soon prone to relentless bombing, Japan was defeated.[12] How long the nation could hold out and when it would decide to surrender were the only questions. That it would not surrender meant the sacrifice of thousands upon thousands more lives, on both sides, and the complete wrath of massive American firepower.

Curiously, the Japanese believed that the Battle of Leyte Gulf had given them a victory by destroying the U.S. carrier force, an illusion that led Imperial Headquarters to conclude that MacArthur's forces were now stranded on Leyte. Thus, the Japanese decided to reinforce the garrison there and chase MacArthur out of the Philippines. Even during the Battle of Leyte Gulf, Japanese units were convoyed ashore at Ormoc, and more arrived through November and into December 1944. MacArthur thought the convoys were evacuating troops until ULTRA intercepts showed him his mistake. Although the U.S. Navy sent dozens of transports and merchant ships to the bottom, the Imperial Army amazingly managed to add 34,000 more troops to the 20,000 already on Leyte. A major ground battle awaited both sides.

 Notes

1. Alexander, *Storm Landings*, 108.

2. E. B. Sledge, *With the Old Breed: At Peleliu and Okinawa* (New York: Oxford University Press, 1981), 59, 60.

3. Gordon D. Gayle, *Bloody Beaches: The Marines at Peleliu* (Washington, DC: Marine Corps Historical Center, 1996), 15.

4. Bill D. Ross, *Peleliu, Tragic Triumph: The Untold Story of the Pacific War's Forgotten Battle* (New York: Random House, 1991).

5. Charles R. Anderson, *The U.S. Army Campaigns of World War II: Leyte* (Washington, DC: Army Center of Military History, 1994), 12; John Chapin, *And a Few Marines: Marines in the Liberation of the Philippines* (Washington, DC: Marine Corps Historical Center, 1997), 3.

6. Samuel Hynes, *The Soldier's Tale: Bearing Witness to Modern War* (New York: Viking Penguin, 1997), 171, 172.

7. Thomas J. Cutler, *The Battle of Leyte Gulf: 23–26 October 1944* (New York: HarperCollins, 1994), 70.

8. Ibid., 93.

9. Spector, *Eagle against the Sun*, 441.

10. Adrian Stewart, *The Battle of Leyte Gulf* (New York: Charles Scribner's Sons, 1980), 210.

11. Ibid., 211.

12. Willmott, *The Second World War in the East*, 169.

6

LIBERATION

Over the six months after the American return to the western Pacific in October 1944, the Allies would push the Japanese out of the Philippines and Burma, control Imperial forces in the sideshow of China, recapture the Dutch East Indies (and thus deny Japan oil resources), and launch bombing campaigns and island-hopping assaults ever closer to Tokyo. Those last actions proved decisive, yet although they captured the most attention, the liberation of the Philippines was paramount. Into the summer of 1945 the Allies' inexorable pressure broke Japan's hold in the islands and added to the disintegration of the empire, despite the dogged resistance of the occupiers. By taking the Philippines the Allies undermined what little remained of Japan's earlier conquests—but not without a vicious fight.

The Final Phase on Leyte

Despite the Battle of Leyte Gulf, Japanese convoys managed to trickle reinforcements into the western port of Ormoc on Leyte. The Americans had taken all of the island except for the port and surrounding areas, but by December 1944 they faced enemy troops that had more than tripled in number (to 65,000) since October. The U.S. Army and U.S. Marine artillery support no longer feared a naval attack from the rear, given the victory at Leyte Gulf, but the heavy rains of the monsoon season made forward movement difficult and turned newly captured airfields into muddy tracts. Most of the airfields on Leyte were eventually abandoned, yet the Japanese ominously brought in aircraft from Formosa and Japan, a signal that Imperial Headquarters was still staking a claim to the island.

In actuality, Japan's only real hope on Leyte had been lost when Kurita failed to lay waste the Sixth Army's support vessels after Halsey rushed away north. Still, the defenders stocked Leyte with arms and men. They took heart from observing that the naval battle off Samar had damaged or sunk a number of U.S. escort carriers, with kamikazes taking their toll. Halsey also lacked fuel and supplies. Furthermore, his big carriers were expected off Iwo Jima, scheduled for attack in February 1945, although MacArthur got Nimitz's approval for Halsey's fast carrier task forces to return to the Philippines after refueling. In November the carriers launched air strikes on convoys which destroyed ships carrying 10,000 men. Still, Japanese soldiers continued to land on the island, sent from Luzon, which both sides knew was the ultimate prize for the Americans in the Philippines.

In early November, General Krueger prepared to move Major General Frank Sibert's X Corps up from the south and Major General John R. Hodge's XXIV Corps down from the north in a pincer movement to capture the Ormoc Valley in the west. Both would come through rugged mountainous terrain in which their enemy had readied typically effective defenses. Hodges had to clear ridges that ran along the coast of Carigari Bay before turning south toward X Corps. On November 4 the Twenty-first Infantry, moving along Highway 2 just a half-mile from the coast, met fierce resistance from the fresh, elite Japanese First Division at "Breakneck Ridge." This spot included trench lines connected by heavy logs, camouflaged gun emplacements, and spider holes.

The Americans slugged away, slowed by a three-day monsoon that lashed the troops with driving rain and wind, and also hindered by Krueger's cautious fear of a counterattack from the sea. The Twenty-first was soon joined by the Nineteenth Infantry on the right flank, while the Thirty-fourth Infantry looped around the Japanese left flank to approach Kilay Ridge. Nonetheless, on November 13 the defenders held as the Americans struggled in the mud, suffering logistical shortages. Breakneck

Ridge proved to be the bloodiest battle on Leyte; it took U.S. troops until December 2, nearly a month after beginning this part of the operation, to capture two ridges that overlooked Highway 2. The Twenty-fourth Division finally severed Japanese communication and supply lines, but Carigari Bay and the Ormoc Valley were not secure for another two weeks, which cost the Americans 26 dead and 101 wounded. Over 900 Japanese perished.

Meanwhile, the X Corps labored from the south, targeting the town of Ormoc. In mid-November the Thirty-second Infantry occupied the western part of Leyte, while the remainder of the units had to secure Barauen to the east. Scarcity of supplies hampered the Americans, but so did the formidable defenses and counterattacks of the Japanese. Krueger hoped to land troops at Ormoc by the sort of amphibious jump around the mountains that MacArthur had used on New Guinea. With transports lacking, MacArthur postponed the landing on Mindoro for ten days to help out Krueger. As U.S. troops fought their way inland in intense battles, Amphibious Group 9 took the Seventy-seventh Division from Dulag on the east coast around to Ormoc Bay on December 6.

That same day, however, 350 Japanese paratroopers launched their own offensive to recapture the Leyte airstrips in the central Burauen area. Poorly coordinated, the attacks had little effect on the Leyte operation, yet the indefatigable Japanese seized some abandoned weapons and destroyed supply dumps and aircraft. The assault on the Buri Airstrip was the most terrifying: Japanese paratroopers ran from the jungles, throwing grenades and bayoneting sleeping U.S. engineer and supply troops. Thrown into confusion, the Americans suffered from friendly fire as well as their attackers. Krueger rushed reinforcements to the airstrips and beat back the enemy on December 11.

Meanwhile, the Seventy-seventh Division landed uncontested just 3 miles south of Ormoc. The troops moved rapidly inland, but the task force that had carried them by sea to the landing encountered kamikaze air attacks—which the Japanese began perfecting in the waning days of the Leyte campaign—that sank a destroyer and destroyer escort. Empire convoys, however, were chased far to the north and out of the action. By the end of December the marines and army had lost 34 planes and 9 pilots killed but had routed Japanese airpower. Hearing of the Seventy-seventh's landing, General Sasaki Suzuki pulled his forces away from the Burauen airfields and sent them across the mountains to defend the Ormoc Valley. The effort was in vain. A contingent of 1,740 soldiers, sailors, and paratroopers at old Camp Downes put up the most resistance, but the Seventy-seventh marched through to Ormoc on December 10, within three days of landing, aided by artillery, rocket, mortar bombardment, and a big edge in personnel. The division suffered 123 dead, 13 missing, and 329 injured but took only 7 prisoners and accounted for 1,506 Japanese lives.

Now the XXIV and X Corps stood 16 miles apart and sought to link up. The Seventy-seventh moved northward from Ormoc, siezed a key airfield, and on December 18 met up with elements of X Corps. Most of Sibert's units engaged in heavy fighting with flamethrowers, grenades, rifles, and bayonets, literally inching forward until they had finally cleared out the defenders by December 21, and the pincer closed around the Ormoc Valley. Airborne units pushed into Ormoc Town a day later, and after seven weeks of struggle, Leyte was liberated. It took until early May 1945 to rid the island of the remaining stragglers, however, and until July 1 to call the island secure.

Supply, weather, and terrain problems had plagued the Americans, as had Krueger's decision to wait on the north coast of Leyte in anticipation of a Japanese amphibious landing rather than to head immediately south. His delay gave the defenders two more days to strengthen their fortifications on Breakneck Ridge and also exposed U.S. troops to the typhoon, thereby causing more casualties. Yet the American reconquest of the Philippines had begun in decisive fashion. U.S. casualties numbered 15,584, of whom 3,504 were killed, whereas the Japanese lost over 49,000 troops and additional air and naval support. These setbacks were so devastating that although General Yamashita still had 250,000 troops on Luzon, he was forced to fight a mainly defensive battle. Other than the sea battle, the Leyte defenders never mounted a serious counter-attack, despite the numbers of paratroopers and infantry they used. Losing Leyte meant that the Philippines were lost, and the Japanese knew it. The Americans did, too, but they still had to fight a grueling campaign for the big prize of Luzon.

Luzon

In mid-December, as the Leyte operation wound down, General Mac-Arthur began the invasion of Luzon. This northernmost island in the Philippines, the political and cultural center of the island chain, was the heart of Japanese land defenses. The general had staked his reputation on liberating Luzon, but his subordinates were less sanguine about taking the island after the intense defense of Leyte. MacArthur wanted Vice Admiral Thomas Kinkaid's Seventh Fleet and the air forces under George Kenney to secure air bases around Lingayan Gulf, from which they could then move on Manila, the capital city. Fearing kamikaze reprisals, both doubted that they could attain air superiority over Luzon. Kamikazes had been so effective in an October 30 mission against Task Force 38 that Halsey had suspended operations and sought refuge on Ulithi. Kinkaid and Kenney asked MacArthur to attack Mindoro to the south of Luzon, instead, and to postpone the Luzon campaign until mid-January 1945.

Unhappily acquiescing to this request, MacArthur acted sensibly, for he knew that even with Leyte in the bag, the island was too far from Luzon to serve as much more than a staging area, and it also lacked suitable airstrips. Mindoro, meanwhile, was lightly defended and possessed airfields from which aircraft could protect the Luzon operation, plus bases for ships and transports. Still, because of Mindoro's inclement weather, a landing posed a risk. As well, only the embattled U.S. escort carrier fleet, victorious yet beleaguered from combat in Leyte Gulf, would provide air support.

Krueger's Sixth Army took Mindoro with relative ease, the threat coming from land-based kamikaze missions against the small American fleet. In anticipation, the navy had refitted the carrier air groups by adding a fighter squadron and Marine Corps F4U Corsairs for protection, reducing scout-bombers and torpedo planes and replacing many 20-mm. guns with 40-mm. rapid-fire antiaircraft cannon. The Japanese still inflicted considerable damage, hitting the light cruiser *Nashville*, killing 133 and injuring over 200, including the commander of the landing force, William Dunkel. Three landing vessels went to the bottom, as did 5 cargo ships. Yet U.S. forces destroyed over 700 Japanese planes, and just as humbling, the army air corps and navy PT boats repelled an attack by 2 cruisers and 6 destroyers.

By the end of the first day of the invasion, on December 15, Allied engineers began readying airfields on Mindoro, and two became operational by December 24 for the assault on Luzon. MacArthur was impatient, however. He wanted Manila in U.S. hands by his sixty-fifth birthday, on January 26. He considered replacing the cautious Krueger, turning to Generals Charles Willoughby and Courtney Whitney, who were eager to please him. So hasty were their preparations for the invasion of Luzon that they underestimated Japanese troop strength on the island by 94,000, working from Krueger's figures. Japanese commander

Tomoyuki Yamashita would make MacArthur pay for his ego and miscalculations.

MacArthur intended to use 2 armies of 10 divisions, 5 regimental combat teams, and support to seize Luzon from General Yamashita's 267,000 underequipped troops. Eventually, 16 divisions entered the Philippines, making the islands' liberation the first large-scale campaign by the U.S. Army in the Pacific War. The Philippines engaged more U.S. soldiers than the operations in North Africa, Italy, and southern France combined. Supported from Mindoro, MacArthur planned to land on the accessible beaches of Lingayen Gulf, up the western coast, and then move across the central plains to Manila and down to the Bataan Peninsula.

Yamashita obliged him. Because his air support and best troops on Leyte were lost, the Japanese commander realistically decided to fight a battle of attrition. Since kamikazes could do no more than slow U.S. supply operations, Yamashita withdrew his troops to three remote mountain areas and determined to hold out as long as possible. The Shobu Group, the largest unit, numbering 152,000 troops under Yamashita's command, occupied northern Luzon. The Kembu Group of 30,000 held the bases of the Clark Airfield complex and the Bataan Peninsula and Corregidor. A third force, the 80,000 men of the Shimbu Group, moved into southern Luzon, including the Bicol Peninsula and the mountains east of Manila, which allowed them to control reservoirs and the capital's water supply. A collection of naval base forces and remnants of crews who had survived the Leyte operation occupied Manila, trying to render the city's port facilities useless before they joined the other groups in the mountains. Japan eventually lost Luzon, but not before inflicting tremendous punishment. MacArthur's eagerness to liberate the capital played into Yamashita's hands. Conceding the landing, the Japanese would wait for the Americans in Manila—brilliant defensive tactics which so humbled MacArthur that the American general hanged Yamashita after the war.

In the week before the landing day of January 9, 1945, a bombardment force under Jesse Oldendorf had arrived from Leyte Gulf, after a kamikaze attack. Unknown to them, they faced a determined enemy. With a mere 200 aircraft left from Halsey's latest strike, the Japanese incredibly mustered enough firepower against the invading troops to sink the escort carrier *Ommaney Bay* and damage four other vessels. As the bombardment began, waves of kamikazes swept over the U.S. force in Lingayen Gulf. American combat air patrol and antiaircraft guns shot

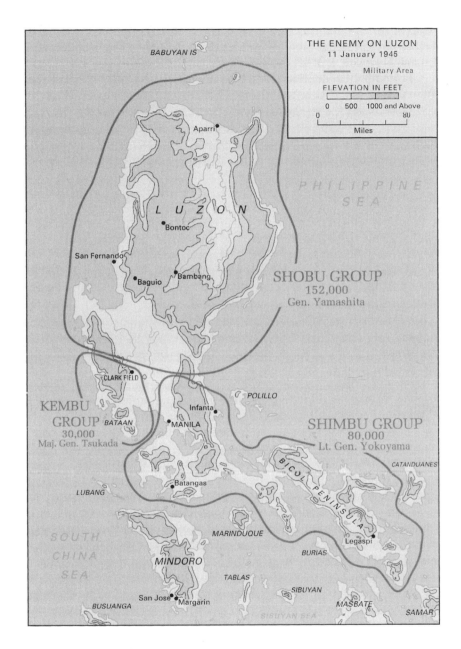

THE ENEMY ON LUZON

Dale Andrade, *The U.S. Army Campaigns of World War II: Luzon* (Washington, DC: Army Center of Military History, 1996), 9.

down many, but others made it through the defensive screen by flying close to land, thus preventing the Americans from discerning which ships the suicide fighters were headed for. Two battleships, 3 cruisers, and several smaller vessels were harmed, and a destroyer escort went to the bottom. One kamikaze came close to MacArthur's flagship, and another killed senior officers on the bridge of the battleship *New Mexico*. All told, 25 of Oldendorf's ships had taken hits by the time the Japanese ran out of aircraft. Then, turning to suicide speedboats, the defenders damaged or sank 9 amphibious landing craft before they were entirely spent. The havoc the Japanese had wreaked in these desperate actions signaled that taking Luzon would be costly.

In a few days, 175,000 men of the U.S. Sixth Army were ashore on a 20-mile-long beachhead. Impatient to get to Manila, MacArthur urged Krueger on. The XIV Corps was headed toward Clark Field and Manila, but Krueger preferred to await the I Corps, which was driving north and east to secure key junctions and guard his flanks. This advance stalled when I Corps encountered linked caves and tunnels in the hills above the major Damortis road. MacArthur erupted in anger at the delay, arguing that the Japanese lacked the power to attack the XIV Corps's rear or flanks. Driving up and down the lines, he gave orders directly to division commanders to advance on Clark Field and not await I Corps.

Krueger reluctantly moved again on January 18, meeting little resistance on his march south as the Shobu Group evacuated the central plains. Five days later his XIV Corps reached the outer perimeter of the Kembu Group guarding the Clark air base. On February 2, XIV Corps left the Fortieth Division behind to occupy the Clark area and continued on to Manila. MacArthur would have it no other way, for even though his birthday had come and gone, the capital was still not in his hands. He ripped into Krueger on January 30, criticizing "the noticeable lack of drive and aggressive initiative" of the Thirty-seventh Division. He then told the recently arrived commander of the First Cavalry Division to "go to Manila, go around the Nips, bounce off the Nips, but go to Manila."[1] The First Cavalry dashed off.

The race to Manila had begun. MacArthur had bolstered the attack by launching a second amphibious assault 45 miles southwest of the city on January 15. Two weeks later, two divisions of the Eighth Army under Lieutenant General Robert Eichelberger came ashore at Bataan and below Manila Bay. Paratroopers of the Eleventh Airborne Division swooped down on the unsuspecting Japanese, taking a key bridge before the defenders could demolish it, and then sped north toward the capital.

On February 3 the 511th Regiment, coming up from the south, discovered 50 Japanese huddled in a thick-walled, old building impervious to bombing in the hamlet of Imus. Technical Sergeant Robert Steel climbed on the roof, cut out a hole, and dropped in gasoline and a grenade. The fleeing defenders were gunned down. Yet the next day the 511th's advance from the south was stalled at the Paranague River, just 4 miles from Manila, by heavy rifle and machine-gun fire coming from the camouflaged steel and concrete pillboxes of the city's main southern line of defense, as well as from Nichols Field. The Eleventh Airborne ground to a halt.

With the southern entryway shut off, the Thirty-seventh Division and the First Cavalry Division, which had flown down the gravel roads to the capital at a clip of 50 miles per hour, arrived from the north, competing for the honor of reaching Manila first. The ponderous Thirty-seventh, with its tanks and heavy artillery, was no match for the First Cavalry. Near Talipapa, just a few miles northeast of the capital, the Americans roared past a stunned Japanese convoy, obliterating it as they headed for the gorge of the Tuliahan River on the city's outskirts. One bridge over the steep ravine remained. The Japanese had just lit the long fuse running to dynamite that would demolish the bridge when a squadron of the Eighth Cavalry arrived, and Lieutenant James P. Sutton, a navy demolitions expert, bravely ran through enemy fire and cut the fuse. Within a few hours the Eighth Cavalry whipped through the northern suburbs and into Manila itself, but the First Cavalry had won the race. That night, a U.S. tank rammed through the walls of Santo Tomas University, freeing 4,000 civilian prisoners and cutting down the Japanese guards.

Manila was still far from liberated. In this city of 800,000 the Japanese occupied numerous strong points within the old Spanish stone fortresses and the large public buildings designed to survive earthquakes. Yamashita deemed the city too big to defend, so he ordered Shimbu Group commander General Yokoyama Shizuo to destroy the bridges over the Pasig River that separated north and south Manila, then to blow up other vital installations, and withdraw. Yokoyama ignored the requests. The group of naval forces in Manila under Rear Admiral Iwabachi Sanji also remained, even though the sailors had little experience in street fighting. Yokoyama added his 3 battalions of army troops to Iwabachi's 16,000 men, and the defenders salvaged a naval cannon from the harbor, converted antiaircraft guns, and stacked up their automatic weapons. Setting fire to the wooden buildings around him, Iwabachi pulled back across the Pasig River and entrenched his troops in southern Manila, well armed and resolved to fight to the last man.

This was "the Pacific War's most severe slide into savagery," as one historian puts it.[2] MacArthur announced a victory parade for the day of the breakthrough into the city, on February 4, but his plan was premature. The Americans immediately met stiff Japanese defenses, for Iwabachi had ordered his men to pay for their deaths with enemy lives. Drunk on liquor pillaged from stores, the Japanese went on a rampage of burning, raping, killing, and torturing civilians—including babies, old women, and hospital patients—until brutally reined in by U.S. forces. It took nearly a month of fierce combat to secure Manila, with fighting taking place by street, block, and building. To protect civilians, MacArthur prohibited air attacks, yet both sides used heavy artillery, and Filipinos were caught in the crossfire. A shocking 100,000 civilians died in the siege of Manila, six times the number of military personnel. Once more, Japanese barbarism had necessitated vicious tactics on America's part.

The defenders prevented U.S. encroachment into southern parts of the city by blowing up the only bridge left across the Pasig River, and in the north, residential districts went up in flames. The Thirty-seventh Division and First Cavalry worked their way through the city, the former incurring its heaviest losses on the industrial Provisor Island, where less than half of a Japanese battalion held them off until February 11. The First Cavalry, meanwhile, had quicker success in the eastern suburbs, although it, too, fought ferocious battles over water supply installations north of Manila.

By February 10 the XIV Corps had established two bridgeheads on the banks of the Pasig River and was moving to clean up the south. The Eleventh Airborne Division, after a week of entrenched fighting, finally captured Nichols Field. Encircling the defenders, the Americans spent February mopping up in repeatedly bloody battles until March 4, when U.S. troops captured the Finance Building in the city center, and the capital was finally freed from Japanese tyranny. Its destruction was virtually complete, however. Manila experienced more devastation than Cologne, Hamburg, or London, coming second only to Warsaw in World War II. Over 1,000 U.S. soldiers died, and 5,600 were wounded in the street fighting; some 16,000 Japanese had perished. The terror continued to the end. In one case, raging Japanese soldiers took 3,000 Filipinos into the buildings of the inner city and killed a third of them. Other defenders took to the sewers, where they died from gasoline and grenades. Not surprisingly, Americans present at the siege of Manila pondered with foreboding the likely carnage of future campaigns as they neared Japan's homeland.

U.S. troops move into Manila on February 12, 1945. The battle for the city was one of the most destructive of the Pacific war, and the loss of military and civilian life high. U.S. Army, *United States Army in World War II: Pictorial Record: The War Against Japan* (Washington, DC: Department of the Army, 1952), 345.

On February 27, 1945, General MacArthur assembled Filipino officials at Malacanan Palace and declared the reestablishment of the Commonwealth of the Philippines after its cruel punishment at the hands of the Japanese. Cruelty was the right word, for the destruction was so enormous that Manila was a dead shell of its former self.

Overcome by the holocaust, MacArthur could not complete his speech, uttering the Lord's Prayer instead to end the ceremony.

Nevertheless, the fall of Manila was critical to the liberation of the Philippines. Its capture provided a psychological boost to the Allied powers, secured stable supply lines throughout Luzon, and gave the Americans a superb harbor. But because the harbor could not be used until the Japanese were cleared from the Bataan Peninsula, on Manila Bay's western side, and from Corregidor, the island fortress at the peninsula's southern tip, MacArthur sent the Sixth Army and the XI Corps from Leyte to the area. Landing 35,000 troops unopposed, the Americans took the Subic Bay area and suffered only 1 casualty the first day—when a bull gored a soldier. Filipino guerrillas had already taken a key airstrip.

On January 29 the XI Corps landed 25 miles northwest of Bataan. Moving eastward, the Americans ran into resistance in the mountainous northern base of Bataan, which they called ZigZag Pass. Yamashita had placed only 4,000 troops of the Kembu Group on Bataan; nonetheless, the main defensive force, a regiment of the Tenth Division under Colonel Nagayoshi Sanenobu, was supplied for an extended battle. His line was only 2,000 yards long, which could be easily outflanked, but Nogayoshi held out for two weeks in a network of foxholes and trenches. The bloody struggle for ZigZag Pass ended on February 8 only after U.S. air support destroyed the defenders. Nogayoshi lost 2,400 men before he escaped south with 300 troops, only to be routed a week later. The rest of Bataan fell more easily by the end of the month.

On tiny Corregidor, which was less important in the Japanese defensive scheme than Bataan, MacArthur expected high casualties. The island, barely 5 square miles, could hardly accommodate the paratroop assault that landed, unexpectedly for the Japanese, on a hilltop: while a battalion of the Thirty-fourth Infantry came ashore on February 16, the 503d Parachute Regimental Combat Team dropped out of the sky. The Japanese nearly managed to knock the Americans off their hilltop foothold, but after nine days of fighting, Allied forces prevailed. The defenders either accidentally or purposely set off their ammunition stores in the tunnels, killing hundreds of soldiers on both sides in rock slides and flying debris. On March 4, MacArthur returned to Corregidor, from which he had fled in shame three years earlier.

Despite their losses, the Kembu, Shimbu, and Shobu Groups understood Yamashita's charge of dragging out the fighting on Luzon. The Kembu Group perished on Bataan, but the well-supplied Shimbu Group under Yokoyama posed the greatest threat. Leaving 20,000 men along the narrow Bicol Peninsula to the southwest, Yamashita had moved about 30,000 of these regular army troops into the mountains east and south of Manila. These proved the biggest challenge to U.S. forces as they dug in around reservoirs, dams to the northeast along the Angat and Marikina Rivers, and aqueducts. In order to make Manila a logistical base for other operations, Krueger and MacArthur decided that the Shimbu force had to be eliminated, but MacArthur made the Sixth Army's task difficult by constantly detaching units from Krueger and sending them to fight in the central and southern Philippines. Nonetheless, by February 20 the XIV Corps was ready to move east into the hills against the Shimbu Group's positions around the water supply areas.

Krueger made two errors that led to an unfortunately protracted campaign. First, he targeted the Wawa Dam, not knowing it had been abandoned since 1938, and bypassing the dam could have saved two months of hard fighting. Of course, the delay delighted Yamashita, who waited in northern Luzon. Second, Krueger's intelligence estimated 20,000 Japanese troops east of Manila, where there were really 30,000. The defenders were strung from Antipolo in the south to the northern Ipo Dam, which had replaced Wawa as the key source of Manila's water supply, and they also occupied the high ground east of the capital. In the Marikina Valley they built underground strongholds and covered all points by machine guns. It took until March 4, fully two weeks into the operation, for the Americans to reach Antipolo, at times advancing a mere few yards a day. The Second Cavalry incurred nearly 60 dead and 315 wounded, including its commander.

To the north, the Sixth Infantry Division gained a foothold on Mount Pacawagan above Wawa Dam, but the Japanese held Mount Mataba to the north. Yokoyama launched a bold but unwise counter-attack on March 12. Lacking enough artillery and sophisticated communications to pull off the surprise, the 3 battalions were so feeble that the Americans hardly knew they were under attack, and Yokoyama's forces failed miserably. The general fell back on his original, more effective tactics, realizing that the Shimbu Group could only "trade lives for terrain and time."[3] Thus, from March 13, the defenders engaged the Americans in a bitter contest for Mount Mataba. The XIV Corps lost 300 dead and over 1,000 injured in a month of fighting, while the dual offensives against Mounts Pacawagan and Mataba killed 3,350 Japanese troops.

By March 27 the Japanese had withdrawn into the Sierra Madre mountains, where they died of starvation and disease over the remainder of the war. U.S. forces destroyed the Shimbu Group's left flank. On May 17 the Forty-third Division and guerrilla fighters, aided by the heaviest concentration of napalm ever used in the southwest Pacific area, routed the enemy from the Ipo Dam. Manila's water supply was thus open and secure (the useless Wawa Dam fell into U.S. hands on May 28). The Shimbu Group's most effective defenses, east of Manila, had disintegrated, and its remaining units were also cleared out along the Bicol Peninsula by the XIV Corps. Enveloped by the First Cavalry Division and the Eleventh Airborne Division by April 19, the remnants of naval service and support troops could neither occupy any towns nor evacuate. It did not matter, for southern Luzon was in U.S. hands by May 31, 1945.

The Shobu Group in the northern part of the island remained under General Yamashita, occupying a large region between Lingayen Gulf in the west and the Sierra Madre range to the east. Luzon's rice bowl and its key supply depot, the Cagayan Valley, were in the center. The Japanese outnumbered the American I Corps, under General Innis Swift, but they also faced vengeful Filipino reinforcements, numbering 60,000, who included survivors of the 1942 Japanese invasion and postwar leaders such as Ramon Magsaysay. Yamashita cleverly fought a passive holding action rather than an aggressive, suicidal operation. I Corps's probes discovered heavily guarded roads approaching the town of Baguio, Shobu Group headquarters. Not until mid-March could the Americans move up the coast to capture Bauang, and they then came at Baguio from the north. Drawing on an additional division, guerrilla fighters, and air attacks, the offensive destroyed Yamashita's supply lines. By the end of the month, Yamashita had relocated east to Bambang, and after a six-day stand in a gorge on the Irisan River, Baguio fell on April 27.

Yamashita was not done, even though one of the three legs of his defenses had been overrun. In fact, the Sixth Army fought the Japanese in northern Luzon until the end of the war, as the defenders slowed and harassed them and, in the case of the Thirty-second Division, inflicted heavy losses as they approached Bambang. The Shobu Group suffered major casualties from fighting, starvation, and disease, but Yamashita held out in the monsoon-drenched north-central Sierra Madres until he and 50,500 men surrendered on August 15, 1945. The Eighth Army had relieved Krueger on June 30 with the Allies in control of key areas of Luzon. Still, 115,000 Japanese remained at large on the island and in the southern Philippines, tying down three U.S. Army divisions.

MacArthur had reconquered Luzon, but not without criticism. The focus on Iwo Jima and Okinawa, as well as the death of Roosevelt in April 1945, distracted attention from the brutal liberation of Manila and Luzon, but the U.S. Army paid a high price for the costly Luzon campaign, which was not as critical to winning the war as were the central Pacific operations. Yamashita had refused to fight an aggressive defense, preferring a war of attrition that resulted in a drawn-out but ultimately pointless battle for survival. Yet his prolonged slugfests slowed the Americans and caused staggering casualties on both sides. And had Yamashita taken a more active stand, MacArthur might have walked into a shorter, but more intense disaster.

Even the passive war of attrition cost the American Sixth and Eighth Armies 10,380 deaths and 36,550 wounded, and noncombat casualties—mostly from disease on Luzon—numbered a stunning 93,400, including 260 deaths. The Philippines came second only to the Africa–Middle East theater in the numbers of hospitalizations and outpatient treatments. The American divisions on Luzon were battle tested, and their experience, along with superior weapons, equipment, and supplies plus easier terrain than on Leyte, led to the containment of the Japanese—but only after considerable time, effort, and casualties. At the end of the Luzon operation, 380,000 defenders were isolated, and 230,000 troops lay dead or wounded, and by summer 1945, 9 of Japan's best divisions had been destroyed, and another 6 had been rendered useless. Although faced with the U.S. losses the new president, Harry Truman, who despised MacArthur, saw no reason to criticize the arrogant general in the midst of the war. Yet the New Guinea and Philippines campaigns, to those who studied them, brought into question MacArthur's status as a hero.

Significantly, the conquest of Leyte and Luzon showed U.S. forces what lay ahead. The battle for Luzon represented the first time the Japanese had been pushed out of a strategic area that they had captured, and the effort had consumed months. With their air power minimized, the defenders had relied on fatalistic tactics of destruction. The prison camps liberated on Luzon showed the horror inflicted on civilians and the sacrifices that Imperial Headquarters might force on the Japanese people. A marine flyer who was shot down in the southern Philippines recounted how the Japanese had tortured and killed about fifty Filipinos and their families for not turning him in—just one instance of the horrifying developments in the war's endgame.

Southern Philippines

A major reason why MacArthur's high marks as a commander deserve special scrutiny is that unknown, at first, to the Joint Chiefs, he ordered Eichelberger's Eighth Army to liberate the rest of the Philippine Islands, even though he had no directive from Washington to do so. In February 1945, at the Yalta Conference, Army Chief of Staff General George C. Marshall told the British that a small number of U.S. forces would supplement Australian and Filipino troops to reconquer the rest of the archipelago, but he gave no orders for the use of large numbers of American troops beyond taking Luzon. Yet MacArthur arrogantly held that as the theater commander in the southwest Pacific, he could deploy his forces however he wished. This he did in an operation that endured until the end of the war. Though obscured by the more dramatic events leading to the use of atomic bombs, the campaign in the southern Philippines was nevertheless massive and difficult.

MacArthur bullied onward, arguing that on humanitarian grounds, the subject Filipinos should be liberated quickly: the battle for Manila showed Japanese brutality, and earlier, the defenders had killed 140 U.S. and Filipino prisoners on Palawan. But such considerations had not driven American policy before, either in the Pacific or in Nazi-run Europe. In addition, continued MacArthur, the islands held cities, airfields, and ports that could serve as bases to interdict shipping and communications from the Netherlands East Indies into the South China Sea and on to Japan. They could serve as a staging area not only for invading the East Indies but also for preparing the final assault on the home islands. The Australians were planning to liberate Palawan, the Sulu Archipelago, and North Borneo, and taking the rest of the Philippine chain would provide cover for them. Yet realistically, Japan was already cut off from resources in southeast Asia. Furthermore, Australia would merely be restoring Dutch and British colonial power in the campaign for Borneo.

Nonetheless, MacArthur reasoned that neither the Eighth Army nor the Seventh Fleet was needed elsewhere in early 1945. But herein lay the problem. Even as the tremendous battle for Manila was under way, MacArthur had sent parts of the Eighth and Sixth Armies to other areas of Luzon and shipped out Eichelberger's forces for amphibious landings south of Leyte. Perhaps MacArthur did so to take attention away from the laborious campaign on Luzon, needing to redeem his prestige and elevate his standing so that the Joint Chiefs would choose him to com-

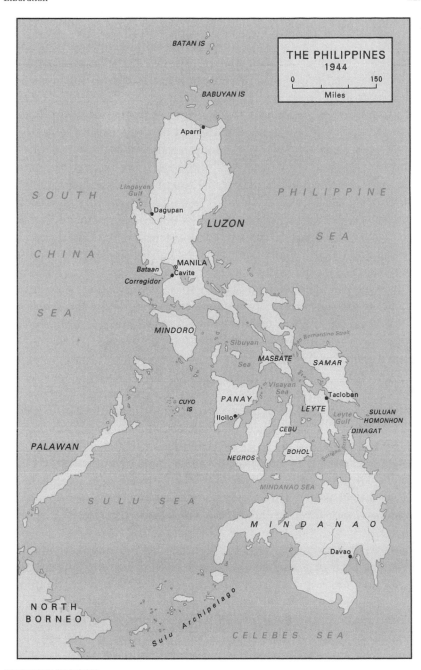

THE PHILIPPINES

Charles R. Anderson, *The U.S. Army Campaigns of World War II: Leyte* (Washington, DC: Army Center of Military History, 1994), 6.

mand the final invasion of Japan. But the upshot was that Krueger's depleted forces on Luzon could count on few reinforcements. Yamashita had taken advantage of the shortfall by prolonging the Luzon campaign for months. In sum, in the grand strategic scheme of defeating Japan, the southern Philippines campaign was a waste of effort. For MacArthur's purposes, however, freeing captive people, brushing over the Luzon quagmire, and helping his own career—it was a necessity.

Beyond Luzon and Leyte to the south lay the thousands of small isles that made up most of the southern Philippines. Lying between Mindanao in the extreme south and Luzon at the top of the archipelago were the Visayan islands of Bohol, Cebu, Negros, and Panay. Also of strategic significance was Palawan Island farther south and Mindanao's Zamboanga Peninsula, both of which stretched toward Borneo. The terrain on all was diverse and difficult, containing mangrove swamps, rain forests, mountains, and steep ravines that gave the Japanese excellent conditions for defenses. The defenders had built garrisons throughout the islands, usually around ports and coastal towns. Disease, long distances without reliable logistical support, and the launching of simultaneous operations throughout the southern islands awaited Eichelberger's well-trained Eighth Army.

Eichelberger's tactic of organizing small units that could move efficiently proved critical. Lieutenant General Sasaki Suzuki's Thirty-fifth Army of 100,000 men was scattered throughout the archipelago, with his best troops, the Thirtieth Infantry Division, on Mindanao. But he had moved half of the troops to Leyte, and now only about 30,000 of his soldiers had been trained in combat. The strongest defenses were at Cebu City and around Davao City, on Mindanao. Sasaki, who would die in mid-April 1945 as he sailed from Cebu to Mindanao, did not expect large contests on every island, yet he spread out his units just in case U.S. forces attacked.

MacArthur decided to send the Eighth Army to Palawan, then move up the Zamboanga Peninsula on Mindanao and the Sulu Archipelago, thereby isolating the Visayas. In total, there were 14 major and 24 minor landings in the southern Philippines, most meeting scant resistance on the beaches but encountering tough defenses inland. Off Palawan, as it would do repeatedly in the campaign, Kinkaid's Seventh Fleet lent naval support: cruisers and destroyers provided cover while the fleet's component VII Amphibious Force, under Rear Admiral Daniel Barbey, landed the troops. Marine flyers and special engineer brigades assisted. The southern Philippines campaign showed America's domination, for the

Japanese could only wait, fight, and then withdraw, to be hunted down another day.

On February 28, 1945, after two days of air and naval bombardment, Eichelberger's forces moved ashore on Palawan, an island in whose inland mountain forests the Japanese had dug in. Moving into the interior, the Americans took a key port and were pursuing the Japanese into the hills when, to their horror, they discovered the bodies of U.S. and Filipino prisoners of war killed in December when the defenders mistakenly believed that Palawan was about to be invaded. The Japanese had placed the POWs in air-raid shelters which they set on fire and then shot any who fled. Yet a few had amazingly survived, protected by natives, to tell the story to the enraged Eighth Army. American troops spent five days of vicious combat rooting the defenders from their strongholds. Some escaped deeper into the jungles, to be pursued and killed, and many more fell victim to mopping-up operations that lasted until late April.

That pattern of destroying pockets of Japanese, then methodically stalking the remainder, repeated itself throughout the southern Philippines campaign, as did the unbalanced casualties. The Americans suffered 12 dead and 56 wounded on Palawan, whereas half of the island's Japanese garrison, or nearly 900 men, perished. By mid-April 1945 the small islands north and south of Palawan had been liberated, and an existing airfield was under use even before that. Engineers struggled in the swampy soil to construct a large airstrip for the heavy bombers that supported the Australians in Borneo. (That campaign, led by Australian ground troops with Allied air and naval support, continued from May until the end of the war. Fewer than 600 Australians died in liberating the island; the Japanese lost ten times that number but they had also killed more than 3,500 Allied prisoners and civilians on forced marches.)

At the same time as the Palawan operation, the Americans moved on Zamboanga, a city that 9,000 Japanese had surrounded with strong defenses. Filipino guerrillas advanced toward an airstrip 145 miles north of the city, and a week before the Eighth Army landed on Mindanao on March 10, 6 marines flew behind enemy lines to help the guerrillas secure the field. After three days of air and sea bombardment, Zamboanga City was captured. The Japanese then fought doggedly from the hills above the coastal plains until March 23, when their lines of deep trenches, barbed wire, minefields, and booby traps in rugged terrain gave way under intense firepower from marine flyers and naval guns. They withdrew up the Zamboanga Peninsula, sniped at by Allied forces, who mopped up for months. Denuding wooded areas, waves of marine flyers torched foxholes and ravines. The 6,400 Japanese dead outpaced the U.S. Army's 220 deaths. Engineers built new airfields on Zamboanga to support operations on other islands.

Elsewhere, U.S. and guerrilla forces enjoyed similar successes. They advanced in the Sulu Archipelago, the battle for Jolo proving the most difficult affair. The Japanese garrison of 3,900 had built defenses around Mount Daho, situated in the middle of the island. Hard fighting began on April 9, and thirteen days later, Allied forces overwhelmed the defenders. Some fled to the western reaches of the island and held out for two months more. By mid-June, 2,000 Japanese had died, while the Americans suffered 40 killed and 125 wounded. Sulu Archipelago airfields were extended and ready for use against the East Indies.

In mid-March, operations began to capture the Visayan Islands, which were now isolated because of the other campaigns. Filipino guerrillas controlled most of the countryside on these four islands, but 30,000 Japanese still held Cebu City and Iloilo on Panay. These coastal cities were the second and third biggest metropolitan areas in the Philippines, offering MacArthur the opportunity to liberate thousands of people. Moreover, the Joint Chiefs had ordered MacArthur to find staging areas for 22 divisions, which would arrive by November 1945 in preparation for the invasion of Japan. Cebu City and Iloilo, with their large ports, would fill this bill.

Two weeks of air attacks on the Japanese preceded the invasion of Panay on March 18. Numbering 23,000, guerrillas had already taken most of the island, and they, along with the Americans, attacked 2,750 defenders around Iloilo. It took two days to capture the city, with a loss of 80 Japanese and 20 American dead. The remaining occupiers fled to the mountain jungles, where 1,500 surrendered at war's end.

With Panay captured, Eichelberger next aimed at northwestern Negros. There, 13,500 Japanese were headquartered at the capital of Bacolod and positioned along the coast and around several airstrips. The key was the seizure of a bridge over the Bago River, for if the defenders blew it up, they could derail the Negros operation. Eichelberger decided on surprise rather than on bombing. The 185th Regimental Combat Team slipped ashore before the main landing, took the bridge, and held it until reinforcements arrived several hours later. On March 30, Bacolod fell, and by early April most of the coastal plain was in Allied hands. The Japanese now fortified their positions in the rugged interior mountains, harassing U.S. forces at night until Eighth Army units slowly cleared them out. By early June the Japanese had withdrawn into the deepest interior. Eight weeks of defense had cost them 4,000 lives. At the end of the war, 6,000 surrendered, but 3,300 more perished from starvation and disease in the jungle, while the Americans sacrificed 370 lives and sustained 1,025 injuries.

Next up were Cebu, Bohol, and the southeastern Negros islands. Occupying Cebu were 14,500 Japanese, 2,000 of whom were pinned down in the northern part of the island by 8,500 Filipino guerrillas. One-third of these combat troops defended Cebu City on the eastern coast. They had constructed 3 defensive lines, stretching from the harbor 2 1/2 miles inland and stacked one behind the other, consisting of concrete pillboxes, caves, and tunnels overgrown with vegetation. Barriers, anti-tank ditches, and minefields littered the beaches. On the morning of March 26, after a one-hour naval bombardment, the Americans landed and encountered trouble. Ten of their first 15 tracked landing vehicles were destroyed by the mines, and then waves of invaders piled up behind one another, bogging down the advance. Fortunately, the Japanese did not fire artillery into this mess. The next day, Eighth Army units entered Cebu City, which had suffered major destruction. The defenders moved to their outer defensive line, and the following day the Americans ran into it. After ferocious fighting, U.S. troops eventually seized two hills on the line, but not before the Japanese blew up an ammunition dump, killing or wounding 50 Americans.

The end came slowly. Inexorably, after the constant pounding of the Seventh Fleet and the retorts of Japanese mortars and machine-gun fire, U.S. troops ground through the defenses. Their commander, Major General William Arnold, secreted his troops around the defense line by night marches, attacking on April 13. Three days later they compelled the defenders to evacuate, and Arnold's troops, along with guerrillas, pursued the Japanese into the remote northern mountains, where about 8,500 Imperial troops survived until war's end. U.S. combat casualties numbered 410 dead and 1,700 wounded, with another 8,000 hospitalized by infectious hepatitis, while the Japanese suffered 5,500 killed. Cebu City served as a harbor and storage facility for the Allies.

Smaller garrisons of Japanese on Bohol and southeastern Negros gave way to guerrillas and U.S. troops in a matter of weeks in April. MacArthur lauded the speedy Eichelberger, in contrast to the ponderous Krueger, for liberating the Vasayas quickly. Mindanao was next. Except for Luzon, this large island held the last remaining big concentration of enemy combat forces, and it also had all the elements familiar in the

Residents of Cebu City welcome American infantry and armored troops as they occupy a key location in the southern Philippine campaign. U.S. Army, *United States Army in World War II: Pictorial Record: The War Against Japan* (Washington, DC: Department of the Army, 1952), 383.

southwest Pacific: mountains, swamps, rivers full of crocodiles, and dense rain forest. Only the largely east-west Highway 1, in southern Mindanao, and the Sayre Highway in the north were useful roads. The Japanese had fortified the coastal area around Davao City, the island's key urban area, with mine, artillery, and antiaircraft impediments; 43,000 troops under Lieutenant General Gyosaku Morozumi were dug in to a depth of 12 miles around the city and held positions in the island's center and north as well. They lacked weapons, communications equipment, and vehicles, however, and to make matters worse for them, a 1942 escapee from Bataan, Colonel Wendell Fertig, harassed them with 24,000 guerrillas.

On April 17 the U.S. Navy moved troops toward Malabang, which the guerrilla force had already secured, and landed the Twenty-fourth Division unopposed at Parang. The Twenty-fourth sped along Highway 1, joined by an engineering brigade that had used the Mindanao River to travel inland. Stunned Japanese garrisons fled north and west at the sight of the gunboats when they reached Kabacan, a town situated at a road junction critical to the capture of the island. The Twenty-fourth Division routed the Japanese outside of Davao City, then entered the town on May 3, traveling 115 miles in just over two weeks.

After the fall of the city, however, the American campaign for Mindanao proved to be a most punishing one. Conditions were arduous on the island. Tall, closely bunched abaca trees, grown on vast plantation fields for hemp, surrounded Davao City, and dense jungle provided excellent cover for the tenacious Japanese, who hid in spider holes. The Americans, struggling in the prostrating heat, crept along in an offensive that lasted two months after Davao City was in their hands. The U.S. Twenty-first Infantry came under attack from three sides at one point, but Private James Diamond, on patrol with Company D, saved the day by drawing enemy fire. He died en route to an aid station. The Twenty-fourth incurred 350 dead and 1,615 wounded; the defenders suffered 4,500 killed, and more would die in mopping-up operations that lasted until mid-July 1945. In the southern Philippines the Americans learned they could not bypass isolated pockets of Japanese but instead had to wipe them out or disperse them into the mountains.

The Sayre Highway and the area north of Kabacan remained under Japanese control. The highway was really an unfinished muddy road that crossed dozens of bridges in need of repair. The Thirty-first Division labored up it from Kabacan, thrusting aside a unit of Japanese headed south, and on May 3 the troops reached Kibawe, the head of a supposed enemy supply trail to the south and Davao City. The Americans pursued the Japanese down the Talomo Trail to their headquarters at Pinamola, killing 400 but losing 80 of their own. The 124th Infantry then began its toughest fight yet on Mindanao. Slowed by ruined bridges, rain, and unforgiving terrain, lacking adequate artillery, and facing a combat-ready battalion at Maramag, U.S. troops fought for six days coming up from

Kibawe. "One of the many brutal struggles in the Pacific theater that never made any headlines," writes one historian, the battle of Colgan Woods (named after a chaplain killed while aiding wounded soldiers) involved rooting out the defenders from interconnected spider holes and camouflaged pillboxes.[4] The Japanese troops chose death rather than retreat, and twice they launched banzai charges. During the night of May 14–15 the last one ended the battle, as 73 defenders died in machine-gun fire. The 124th Infantry had 69 men killed and 177 injured.

By May 23, U.S. troops linked with the 108th Infantry were heading down the Sayre Highway. It had taken the 108th four days to overwhelm the Japanese in a steep river canyon, but now the entire route was in American hands. Airstrips were operable around Maramag and Maly-balay to bring in supplies, and Japanese units withdrew into the mountains to the east. Some engaged the U.S. Thirty-first Division on June 5, but more disappeared into the jungle. In late June the U.S. First Battalion, 155th Infantry, landed along the Agusan River valley on search-and-destroy missions, remaining there as both they and the surviving Japanese battled swamps, torrents of rain, and reptiles. In similar hardship, U.S. units pursued the Japanese into the interior at the southern tip of Mindanao. MacArthur declared Mindanao secure on June 30, although pockets of Japanese popped up until the end of hostilities on August 15, when 22,000 surrendered. Their 18,000 unfortunate comrades, dead in combat or from starvation or disease, lay on Mindanao along with 820 American soldiers; 2,880 Americans were wounded.

The severe campaign for the southern Philippines continued until Japan surrendered officially in early September 1945. The Eighth Army lost 2,100 dead and 6,990 hurt, but compared to other operations in the war, and considering the vast territory taken, the sacrifice was minimal. The Japanese Thirty-fifth Army, meanwhile, was destroyed. With that loss added to the toll on Leyte and Luzon, nearly 400,000 Japanese were killed in the Philippines. As an omen of their impending defeat, the defenders could do little more than await the Americans, either to be pulverized or to flee into the wilderness and try to survive at great odds against starvation and sickness.

Eichelberger ran an efficient, well-planned campaign backed by abundant resources and soldiers who patrolled in small groups, exposing themselves dangerously to their enemy. Most telling in the comparison of American and Japanese power were the simultaneous offensives conducted in the Philippines that brought the archipelago under U.S. control. Eichelberger's many operations, in tandem with Krueger's slow progress on Luzon, showed that the United States, with its 16 divisions, could act at will and in an overwhelming fashion. By V-J day the Americans in the Philippines were preparing to link with the Australians on Borneo. Operations in the Philippines may not have been necessary to win the war (except to MacArthur), but the massive campaign did facilitate American victory. Above all, it showed the vast capability of the United States to defeat Japan on a variety of fronts.

 Notes

1. Dale Andrade, *The U.S. Army Campaigns of World War II: Luzon* (Washington, DC: Army Center of Military History, 1996), 11.

2. Gerald F. Linderman, *The World within War: America's Combat Experience in World War II* (New York: Free Press, 1997), 176, 177.

3. Andrade, *Luzon*, 23.

4. Stephen J. Lofgren, *The U.S. Army Campaigns of World War II: Southern Philippines* (Washington, DC: Army Center of Military History, 1996), 31.

7

THE INNER RING

By the last year of the war, in 1945, the United States occupied much of the southern, central, and western Pacific, completely controlled the seas and air, and were denying Japanese civilians consumer goods, shelter, and safety. The Imperial war machine retained but a facade of its former glory. It was time to decide how, exactly, to complete Japan's defeat. Admiral Ernest King floated the idea of invading Formosa as a step to entering the home islands, but with MacArthur engaged in the Philippines, ground troops were lacking. Chester Nimitz suggested assaults on the islands of Iwo Jima and Okinawa as the initial moves to taking out Japanese air defenses and thus clearing the way to Tokyo. The Joint Chiefs had agreed with him in October 1944, and even MacArthur consented in order to avoid a campaign in Formosa that might detract from the Philippines. Marines and infantry, backed by the Third Fleet, would launch epic battles for Iwo Jima and Okinawa, their efforts—coupled with the fanatical resistance of the defenders—initiating the final round of violence of the war. Most ominously for Japan, the capture of the two islands brought the heart of the empire within range of the most destructive weapons of the war and the sheer force of American power.

B-29s and Bombing

On March 4, 1945, at the end of the Americans' second week on Iwo Jima, a huge silver bomber appeared through the overcast sky over the island. This 65-ton Boeing B-29 Superfortress, called *Dinah Might*, came down with a bump and roar on Iwo Jima's main airfield, clipped a telephone pole, and rolled to a stop just feet from the end of the strip. The plane had suffered damage during an air raid over Tokyo, and the island was the closest friendly place to land. Fearful of an attack, the crew made repairs in a half-hour, then climbed through enemy fire toward their base on Tinian. The event indicated the stark reality that the United States could level Japan with impunity.

First delivered to the army air forces in early 1944, the B-29, with its long range and large payload, was well suited for use against Japan. In June 1944, Superfortresses were based in China, targeting Manchuria's raw materials facilities and Japan's factories, assembly plants, harbors, and frightened people. They boosted Jiang's morale as interest in China waned. Under the command of the Twentieth Air Force, squadrons of seven B-29s, each with a crew of 5 officers and 6 enlisted men, first attacked railyards at Bangkok on a trial run. A few days later, 60 bombers struck Japan for the first time, hitting the Yawata iron and steel works on Kyushu Island. Most of the mills survived the bombing because of a citywide blackout, but the attack's psychological value was considerable. In Washington, Congress celebrated news of this initial direct hit on the home islands.

The B-29s encountered mechanical problems and lacked sufficient supplies of fuel, but the appointment of Major General Curtis LeMay as commander of the Twentieth Air Force brought better results. A veteran of B-17 missions in Europe, LeMay improved aircraft and crews by practice, more accurate radar bombing, and larger bomber formations. Effective operations on Hankow in November and December 1944 helped slow the Japanese offensive in China, and massive doses of napalm burned the city's docks and warehouses, despite the fact that only 40 percent of the bombs hit their targets (many of them fell on Chinese civilians). The raid also represented the last major B-29 operation from bases in China. Because the planes required 15 percent of the fuel tonnage flown over the Hump, Stilwell, Jiang, Claire Chennault, and Wedemeyer sought their removal.

Leaving from a base on Guam for a strategic bombing mission, these B-29s proved critical to the destruction of Japan's military installations and industry. The capture of the Mariana Islands gave the Superfortress forward bases from which to attack Japan. U.S. Army, *United States Army in World War II: Pictorial Record: The War Against Japan* (Washington, DC: Department of the Army, 1952), 325.

Consequently, the Twentieth Air Force transferred to the Mariana Islands in February and March 1945, and joined the new Twenty-first Bomber Command already operating from Saipan, Tinian, and Guam. They met the disapproval of navy officials, who viewed the Marianas as their terrain and looked skeptically on the effectiveness of long-range bombing for the defeat of Japan. But the new bomber commander, the experienced army strategist Brigadier General Haywood Hansell, launched the first large-scale series of air raids designed to destroy the empire's aircraft production. Given cloud cover and winds that forced them to rely on radar rather than sight, pilot inexperience, and the fact that the planes consumed so much of their fuel in their long flights that they could not focus on their targets, the bombardiers inflicted little damage on the factories. Out went Hansell, and in came LeMay again. He did not do much better, and worse, the Japanese shot down or crippled bombers at an alarming rate.

One answer to the snafus was to shorten the distance to Japan. Iwo Jima, which lay between Saipan and Japan, would provide a refueling stop as well as give the navy support for its invasion of the home islands. Thus, Iwo Jima's significance was as a safe haven, and by the end of the war the island had given refuge to thousands of airmen. Bombers made approximately 2,400 emergency landings on its airstrips. Estimates showed that the number of airmen saved—even though many would likely have survived crashes in the ocean—exceeded the number of marines killed taking Iwo Jima. This made the difficult campaign for the island worth the effort.

As the Iwo Jima invasion stretched into March 1945, B-29 attacks rolled over Japan. Pilots abandoned precision bombing for incendiary campaigns with napalm and other explosives. The bombing of Japan increased eleven times in March alone, as U.S. military planners recognized the futility of solely targeting plants. Both sides knew that Japan's paper and wood cities would burn easily; therefore, intelligence analysts recommended mass bomber runs using incendiaries to destroy urban areas and thus disrupt factory production. A trial over Nagoya had not been impressive, but on February 4 the Twenty-first Bomber Command had attacked Kobe, the sixth largest city in Japan and a major port, using only incendiary bombs dropped from high altitudes. Five key factories were damaged, and a shipyard's production halved. Three weeks later, LeMay firebombed Tokyo, igniting 28,000 structures and leveling a square mile of the city.

Area bombing worked well, especially when deteriorating weather led bombers to descend to lower altitudes. That tactic risked damage from flak; indeed, the *Dinah Might*, forced to land on Iwo Jima, was one such victim. But area bombing augmented the terror and destruction. On March 8, LeMay sent 334 bombers swooping over Tokyo, some at just

4,900 feet, a dangerously low altitude that scared many U.S. pilots. Caught by surprise, and too optimistic after the bombing failure over Nagoya, the Japanese suffered. Nearly 16 square miles of the city were burned, including 267,000 buildings, in "the most destructive single bombing raid in history—more destructive than the Moscow fire of 1812, the great Chicago fire of 1871, or the San Francisco earthquake," writes a Pacific war expert.[1] Inadequately equipped and trained fire-fighters could not stop the holocaust, which boiled water in canals and charred 83,000 people, injured another 41,000, and rendered 1,008,005 homeless. The carnage was the result of technological superiority and years of hatred toward Japanese aggression. Area bombing represented satisfying yet chilling payback for Imperial brutality.

Attacks of a magnitude never before witnessed in bombing campaigns were repeated over other industrial centers such as Nagoya, Kobe, Osaka, Yokohama, and Kawasaki. Low-level area bombing, combined with the high population density, flammable construction, and lack of roads and parks for escape, had burned out 40 percent of these cities by June 1945. The 600 bombers then ranged over smaller cities, gutting about fifty of them. When these forays were added to the Twenty-first Command's mining of Japanese shipping lanes through the Inland Sea, which cut tonnage into Kobe to one-eighth its normal wartime level, the impact was awesome. In the five months from LeMay's first massive incendiary bombing in March 1945, precisely 43.46 percent of Japan's sixty-three major cities had been ruined and 42 percent of the nation's industrial capacity; 22 million people had been killed, hurt, or made homeless. So total was the campaign that LeMay was soon announcing his targets to the Japanese by dropping leaflets before raids. The psychological impact was decisive, for while just 2 percent of the population in 1944 thought the war was lost, by July of 1945, 68 percent had abandoned hope. The Americans had become omnipotent, destroyers of Japan itself.

Iwo Jima

The air war over Japan, it was thought, would justify fierce combat on Iwo Jima, the most heavily fortified island that the United States invaded during the Second World War. For LeMay's bombers to be effective, the American military had to knock out Iwo Jima's early warning radar, which pinpointed B-29s for Imperial fighter planes and thus forced the

Americans to fly a circuitous dog-leg around the island that reduced their payloads and fuel and made them sitting ducks to attack planes from Honshu. Furthermore, Japan's medium bombers based on Iwo Jima hit U.S. airfields on Saipan and Tinian, destroying more B-29s on the ground than had been downed in the air. The island, therefore, had to be taken to safeguard the strategic bombing campaign. In addition, Iwo Jima would serve as the advance troops and supply base to take Okinawa in the Ryukyu Islands, which itself was the final step to the home islands.

The battle for Iwo Jima represented the largest and bloodiest conflict in the 169-year history of the U.S. Marine Corps. It was a rushed affair, for MacArthur's slow seizure of Luzon delayed the campaign twice by holding up the transfer of naval support and landing craft. The operation waited under the command of Raymond Spruance and his Fifth Fleet team of Mark Mitscher of the Fast Carrier Task Force, Richmond Kelly Turner of the Expeditionary Forces, Harry Hill, who led the Attack Force, and William Blandy of the Amphibious Support Forces, charged with minesweeping, demolitions, and preliminary bombardment. These seasoned veterans of amphibious missions would have to act fast, however. From Iwo Jima they would need to reposition their forces for the Okinawa invasion by April 1, at the latest, to avoid the summer monsoons.

General Harry Schmidt, joined by Holland Smith—invited along for one last campaign—guided the landing force of the V Amphibious Corps, comprising the battle-tested Third and Fourth Marine Divisions and the new but well-trained Fifth Division. It was the largest force of marines ever sent into a single battle, numbering 80,000, half of whom had already seen action in the Pacific. Iwo Jima was the fourth landing in thirteen months for the Fourth Marines; the Third had succeeded on Bougainville and Guam; and the Fifth contained former Raiders and paratroopers with combat time in the Solomons. The V Amphibious Corps was a proficient force, a fortunate trait because it faced a formidable enemy on difficult terrain. The results bore out harsh predictions, for the Americans emerged victorious from the battle by, notably and shockingly, incurring more casualties than the Japanese. Iwo Jima was the only invasion that reversed the normal Japanese edge in the casualty column.

Iwo Jima, Japanese for Sulphur Island, has been likened to a pear, with the volcanic Mount Suribachi as the stem and gradually rising terraces and plateaus filling out the bulk of the fruit. An ugly outcropping of volcanic sand and rock about 4 miles long and 2 miles wide, usually wrapped in sulphuric-smelling steam, and lacking water, it piqued the imagination as a scene from the moon or Dante's *Inferno*. In the north, the largest part of the pear, caves permeated the broken stone landscape. A large central plateau held two airstrips and the beginnings of a third. For Japan, Iwo Jima was a critical outpost, but in actuality it fell within the "Inner Vital Defense Zone," being just three hours' flight time from Tokyo. Said a Japanese officer, "Iwo Jima is the doorkeeper to the Imperial capital."[2]

For that reason, it was defended to the end by Lieutenant General Kuribayashi Tadamichi, who turned out to be a most worthy and dangerous foe. Experienced in combat, innovative, and determined to resist the Americans, this fifty-three-year-old former cavalry officer had also been posted to embassies in Canada and America and had seen action in Manchuria against the Chinese. Kuribayashi knew that no help would be coming from Tokyo; thus, as a realist who coldly assessed weaknesses and made adjustments, he would defend Iwo Jima at all costs. He even left his samurai sword with his family, acknowledging that he would never return. Although Kuribayashi had never faced the Americans, he had studied the central Pacific campaigns. To the dismay of other senior officers and strategists, he abandoned water-edge defense and banzai tactics and instead prepared for a drawn-out battle, adopting tactics from Biak, Peleliu, Angaur, and Luzon, where the Japanese had prolonged the seizure of territory in bloody conflicts. Kuribayashi would do the same, but on a larger scale, on Iwo Jima. His tactics earned him grudging compliments from U.S. commanders, yet they also steeled American intentions to wipe the Japanese off the island.

Kuribayashi fortified Iwo Jima's interior. Engineers built underground, interconnecting tunnels and rooms with multiple entrances, exits, and ventilation tubes; one installation on Mount Suribachi was seven stories deep. Blockhouses protruded on the outside, and hidden guns gave the defenders interlocking fields of fire. The Japanese found that a mix of volcanic sand and cement proved such a sturdy substance for constructing the subterranean installations that men and matériel were able to go underground when the Americans began daily bombing in early December 1944. Kuribayashi also had time to prepare, for he had been on Iwo Jima since mid-June, and in the ensuing months until the U.S. assault began in February 1945, he had taken over a chaotic garrison and received reinforcements from Saipan. These soldiers were tough veterans, hungry for revenge for their nation's losses and ready to die. More troops and equipment followed to build the garrison to 21,000 soldiers. Eventually, 361 artillery pieces, 65 mortars, 33 large naval guns, and nearly 100 large-caliber antiaircraft guns were placed in bunkers, blockhouses, and caves.

Kuribayashi would unleash his firepower once the Americans came ashore, hitting them from carefully assigned and protected emplacements. If he could not win, perhaps he could make battle so horrific that the American public might balk at an invasion of the home islands. Thus, he evacuated all civilians from the island, put the garrison on half rations of water months before the invasion, and concentrated his defenses in the central tablelands and northern highlands. His troops would not defend the beaches or charge in suicide attacks; instead, they would either set ambushes or prowl at night in small groups to search and destroy. A stalwart and resourceful defense backed by keen marksmanship and night infiltration would punish the U.S. troops. As he received word that Kelly Turner's expeditionary force had left Ulithi and Saipan in a fleet of 495 ships, including 125 amphibious craft and 75 seagoing landing vessels, Kuribayashi sent his men to their bunkers. He told them they would die for the emperor with glory.

The Americans headed for D-day were concerned about the landing in Iwo Jima, with good reason. Preliminary bombardment of the island lasted just three days, even though Schmidt's marine command asked for ten. The navy preferred to send Mitscher's carriers, along with all 8 Marine Corps fighter squadrons, against Honshu, guard against a counterattack at sea, and preserve large-caliber shells for the invasion of Okinawa. Iwo Jima also competed with the campaign in the Philippines, so there was less navy to go around, and Admiral Spruance's insistence on the big B-29 attack on Tokyo and other cities took away additional support. Spruance argued that three days of intense bombardment, added to the previous two months of aerial attacks, would amply prepare the way for the marines. Schmidt rightly disagreed, demanding a week more and countering that only sustained bombardment would be able to reduce Japanese strongholds. Indeed, Schmidt proved right, as most of Kuribayashi's positions in the north survived the bombardment. That the Japanese protected their underground assets in the face of Blandy's shelling, which was four times as large as the Tarawa bombardment and one and one-half times that of the bigger Saipan, revealed the impregnability of Kuribayashi's defense.

The drama escalated as D-day neared. Kuribayashi made one major error at this point. Two days before the landing, 100 navy and marine demolition experts approached the eastern beaches, backed by landing vehicles firing their rockets and guns. There was no sneaking in under cover as in the Marshalls, Marianas, and Palaus. But when the frogmen went in in broad daylight, Kuribayashi, thinking they led the main invasion force, let loose his batteries located on Mount Suribachi and along the rock quarry on the right flank. They hit their marks, sinking a vessel, damaging others, and causing over 200 casualties, but U.S. battleships and cruisers rushed over to bombard the Japanese guns into submission. Spruance had now located the Japanese batteries.

The Americans next had to figure out how to cut down on congestion on the exposed beaches once the landing occurred and how to limit the expected large number of casualties. The marines soon wished that the admirals *had* postponed the landing in lieu of further bombardment, because most of Kuribayashi's major defenses remained inland. Many were hidden and out of reach, but some had been identified and could have been taken out by prolonged naval bombing. No other Pacific assault began with so many Japanese positions left intact, and the Americans would pay for their haste. On the eve of D-day, General Holland Smith shocked those present at a press briefing by predicting as many as 15,000 American casualties.

At dawn on February 19, 1945, ideally clear weather developed for the landing. Blandy's battleships came as close as 2,000 yards offshore to blast away at selected targets, and his rolling barrage, timed and guided from the air, regulated the pace of the invasion to ensure that the bottlenecks of Tarawa would not be repeated. There were also no reefs, deadly tides, or Japanese at the shoreline, so the amphibians shot to the beaches in just thirty minutes. The navy kept up its barrage, and Mitscher's task force reappeared from its raids on Honshu to aid the landing, his marine aviators bringing cheers from the landing force as they strafed the beaches.

The barrage moved 400 yards ahead of the landing vehicles, the product of good planning and experience gleaned from months of storm landings. Vessels brought 8,000 marines to shore in the first minutes as the V Amphibious flotilla came over the horizon. The Fourth Marines aimed for beaches designated "Green" and "Red" on the left flank, their mission to head northeast toward the southernmost airfield, while the Fifth headed for the flat expanse on the right of "Yellow" and "Blue" beaches, intending to sever the small stem of the pear from the rest of the island and take Mount Suribachi. Troops were laden with 50 to 100 pounds of equipment. Demolition squads carried explosives, rocket-firing bazookas, and flamethrowers behind armored amphibious tractors, backed by gunboats, which led the way. Waves of amtracs followed at 2-minute intervals. Despite immobilization in the violent surf and soft sand, Schmidt had landed 30,000 men and their tank battalions and field artillery within ninety minutes. Japanese observers on Mount Suribachi watched in awe.

The marines unload on the black beach of Iwo Jima, later meeting heavy fire from automatic weapons, mortars, and artillery. U.S. Army, *United States Army in World War II: Pictorial Record: The War Against Japan* (Washington, DC: Department of the Army, 1952), 390.

So ended the easy times for the Americans on Iwo Jima, however. As they attempted to move out of the landing zones, U.S. troops came under increased fire from the interior strongholds that overlooked the beaches. As the Twenty-eighth Marines of the Fourth Division cut off the bottom of Iwo Jima and Mount Suribachi from the larger pear, they awakened Japanese mortar positions. The 700 yards that the Twenty-eighth traveled across Green beach represented the deepest penetration made that day. The other three regiments moved up the sand terraces and into an open bowl, a shooting gallery exposed to Suribachi on the left and the tablelands to the right.

Kuribayashi turned the area into hell. His gunners in the highlands patiently aimed at beaches clogged with enemy troops and vehicles, and just after ten o'clock in the morning they let loose a barrage. Lacking cover, the invaders found themselves caught in a vicious crossfire from the large-caliber coastal and antiaircraft guns. They were pinned down by mortars, artillery, and machine guns with nowhere to hide. Caught in the "deadly scissors" of the big guns, marines stumbled over the terraces, only to be mowed down in a "buzz-saw" of automatic weapons fire. Recalled one regiment commander, "It was one of the worst blood-lettings of the war. They rolled those artillery barrages up and down the beach—I just didn't see how anybody could live through such heavy fire barrages."[3]

Many did not, but the veteran troops did not panic. Aerial spotters helped the navy locate and destroy some of the exposed Japanese guns, and fighter planes dropped napalm. The defenders continued their bombardment, but it would never again be as overwhelming as in the first hour of the invasion. Pockets of marines stumbled forward, capturing the quarry cliffs, regrouping in a shell hole at the base of Mount Suribachi, crawling ashore under withering fire. Journalist Robert Sherrod, who came ashore late in the afternoon, reported that "nowhere in the Pacific had I seen such badly mangled bodies. Many were cut squarely in half. Legs and arms lay fifty feet from the nearest cluster of dead."[4]

The marines counted 2,420 casualties (501 killed) the first day—a rate of 8 percent—comparable to the V Corps losses on Omaha Beach at Normandy but less than the first nights on Tarawa and Saipan. On Iwo Jima that night, Kuribayashi's bands of prowling wolves probed the lines, while bombardment from the highlands persisted. A barge of defenders even tried to land on the western beaches. The Americans survived all these assaults and completely eliminated the last. As the dawn came on the second day, the marines were still dug in. Under intense attack, they began clearing the beaches of debris and digging up the deadly rows of antitanks and antiboat mines at beach exits—the strongest minefield defenses yet encountered by the Americans in the Pacific war.

The marines moved on Mount Suribachi at the southern tip the next day, for the looming rock had to be seized before the advance north could succeed. Kuribayashi's garrison of 2,000 soldiers on Suribachi manned nests of machine guns, observation sites, big-gun positions, and a network of tunnels, pillboxes, and bunkers. Recognizing that the 556-foot-high mountain would be isolated from the main defenses, Kuribayashi wanted the garrison to hold out for ten days. The marines took it in four, but every yard up was sheer murder. About 70 camouflaged blockhouses protected the approaches to Suribachi, and 50 more dotted its slopes. Only tanks could knock them out as Japanese mortars blasted away at them.

A patrol led by Lieutenant Harold Schrier reached the summit on the fourth day, February 23. The men planted a small U.S. flag on a 20-foot piece of pipe found at the top. But the marines thought this flag was too small, so they retrieved a larger one from a landing craft and took it up Suribachi. Joe Rosenthal of the Associated Press stumbled on this scene, snapping his famous photograph from atop a pile of stones. The photo, one of eighteen he took that day, was delivered and processed in Guam, ahead of the photo of the first flag. For Rosenthal, the picture honored a bloody campaign led by the bravest of men, who cheered with gusto as the flag was driven into the ground by, among others, Ira Hayes, a Pima Indian from Arizona.

The dramatic capture of Mount Suribachi was a blow to Kuribayashi, but he knew that the central and northern plateaus were where Iwo Jima could be defended. As the battle for Suribachi began, the advance to the north was joined by the Fourth and Fifth Marines, along with most of the Third Division, which had opened the southern beaches. Navy Seabees then rebuilt the island's airfields while antiaircraft guns came ashore in anticipation of an air strike from the home islands. The only real threat on this score came two days after D-day when 50 kamikazes from the Katori Air Base near Yokosuka made their way through the Third Fleet's screen. All were shot down but one sank the escort carrier *Bismarck Sea*, and another damaged the *Saratoga*. On Iwo Jima, attack from the air was minimal, and even the Combined Fleet was silent except for a launch of "human torpedo" subs that never made it to the island. Thus, Spruance ordered Mitscher's task force out of the area to strike at Honshu and Okinawa, leaving naval and air support for the marines to pilots flying off the 10 remaining escort carriers. His order slowed the advance on the island.

On the ninth day of the battle the Americans discovered that Kuribayashi was on the island, and that he had several thousand more troops
than had been believed and still occupied a position of strength. One of
his caves had an 800-foot tunnel with fourteen exits. He had at his
disposal 8 infantry battalions, a tank regiment, 2 artillery and 3 heavy
mortar battalions, and 5,000 naval infantry, and he launched spoiling
attacks with small groups of men to disrupt the U.S. advance. Traps of
antipersonnel mines were set on a scale never before witnessed in the war,
and Japanese firepower, at times, outgunned the Americans. Kuribayashi
picked his battles, forcing the marines to expend lives and tanks as they
moved forward, while his own resolute nature instilled calm and
determination in his troops. With few exceptions they never panicked,
and they rarely exposed themselves, which frustrated the marines. The
defenders often moved underground as the Americans moved above
them.

The capture of hills, gorges, and caves involved bloody fighting, now
becoming commonplace at the end of this merciless war. The Twenty-
sixth Marines' day-long battle for a hill in early March cost them 500
casualties, while the Twenty-eighth lost 200 men, including Lieutenant
Colonel Chandler Johnson, a hero of Suribachi's capture. Nearly two
weeks into the invasion, and the same day the *Dinah Might* landed for
repairs, Kuribayashi was forced to move his command post to a northern
cave. Schmidt ordered a general stand-down the next day to relieve his
exhausted forces, but thereafter, the drive north continued with increased
difficulty. High, craggy, twisted gorges and hills lay ahead, and sniper fire
from excellent marksmen in that highland terrain became more lethal
than shrapnel from explosives. Marines now drew on a deep base of
support. Medical teams saved lives, Navajo code-talkers stymied the
enemy, and a semblance of air power kept the Japanese at bay. Yet even
when they reached the northeast coast on March 9, the Americans
encountered intense resistance. One battalion reported a 70 percent
casualty rate, and commanders warned of imminent exhaustion.

The end came violently, for both sides. Mopping-up never occurred,
for all the pitched battles on Iwo Jima involved fights against small
pockets of Japanese. By March 16, Schmidt declared victory, but the
killing continued. Kuribayashi readied for his final defense in his command center deep inside a cave within a gorge aptly nicknamed Death
Valley, and it took nine days of cave-by-cave fighting, and thousands of
tons of explosives, to destroy his fortifications. Ignoring pleas to

surrender, he sent his final message to Tokyo. Ironically, Imperial Headquarters informed him of his promotion to full general, but he never replied, for he committed suicide during the night of March 25–26. The logical option left for his troops was surrender, but his legacy lived on: that night, an organized group of 300 men left their caves and infiltrated sleeping U.S. troops down the island, achieving total surprise before being obliterated in a counterattack. They took 100 pilots, Seabees, and marines with them and wounded 200 others. Two months later, U.S. troops had killed another 1,602 Japanese and captured 867 prisoners.

The capture of Iwo Jima took thirty-six days. During that time, airfields were rebuilt and enlarged to accommodate the Superfortress, but Iwo Jima never became the offensive base once deemed necessary, for the B-29s had turned to night raids, and Japanese airpower was weakening. A number of pilots used its airstrips for emergency landings, but the human toll outweighed the usefulness of the island's airstrips.

About 22,000 Japanese died on the island, and only a few hundred wounded survived. For the marines, 6,821 lay dead and nearly 20,000 were injured. One of every 3 corpsmen who landed became a casualty, and about 700 died for each square mile of Iwo Jima. Five times the number of Americans who died on Guadalcanal or Tarawa perished there. Kuribayashi inflicted more casualties than he had lost, having decimated whole companies of marines. The 133-man Company I, Third Battalion, Twenty-fourth Marines, ended up with 9 survivors, while only 17 of the original 250 men of Company D, First Battalion, Twenty-sixth Marines, remained in the ranks. So depleted was this unit that when it merged with another company, a lowly private first class was serving as a platoon commander. The outcry at home was considerable, this time aided by journalists who reported the losses even as the fighting con-tinued. Iwo Jima yielded a wartime record twenty-seven Medals of Honor, thirteen bestowed posthumously.

American commanders had obviously perfected the storm landing tactic, but controversy erupted over the necessity of so many sacrifices, over the loss of V Amphibious Corps veterans, over the lack of extended preliminary bombardment, over the piecemeal replacements for fighting units during the battle. Still, Iwo Jima was a possible strategic gain amid great loss. The Japanese were now more sober and most significant, had lost one of their key inner strongholds to Americans, who appeared just as willing as Imperial troops to sacrifice their lives for victory. The Americans had learned once again that the closer they came to Japan, the more savagely their enemy would fight, but they were prepared to match Japanese ferocity with their own if need be.

Okinawa

By spring 1945, Japan was a "wounded, wild animal, enraged, cornered, and desperate" but ready to defend the home islands, states one account.[5] That continued resistance in the face of American omnipotence made the invasion of Okinawa an ordeal equal to that of Iwo Jima. The largest of the Ryukyu Islands, Okinawa lay equidistant from the China coast, Formosa, and the home island of Kyushu, just 350 miles to the northeast. Japan considered the 60-mile-long island, a distant prefecture since 1879, the doorstep to Tokyo. This once peaceful island, before July 1944 ignored by Imperial Headquarters because it lacked surplus food and industry, became the site of the biggest and costliest single operation of the Pacific war. The battle for Okinawa involved over 1 million combatants (including island natives), rivaled the Normandy invasion in scale, and claimed an average of 3,000 lives for each of the eighty-two days of fighting. Both sides paid dearly as the Americans climbed over the inner wall that guarded the sanctuary of Japan proper.

The previous October the Joint Chiefs had issued a final strategic directive for MacArthur to take Luzon and for Nimitz to move on Iwo Jima and, ultimately, Okinawa. There was no more talk of attacking Formosa. Taking Okinawa posed the biggest challenge of the war, for it required a huge amphibious task force vulnerable to the unrelenting assault of kamikazes, coordination of the armed services as they executed an assault on this large and now well-defended island, and suppression of counterattacks from a large population of hostile enemy combatants and a half-million civilians—all in the midst of the demanding campaigns on Iwo Jima and the Philippines. But Okinawa was a prize worth the sacrifice. It fell within medium-bomber and fighter-escort range of Japan's heartland and contained ports, airfields, anchorages, and training areas for troops. Okinawa could be a staging area for the final assault on the home islands and the ultimate defeat of Japan.

Raymond Spruance's Fifth Fleet, with Turner again commanding the amphibious landing, moved on from Iwo Jima to prepare for the assault. The Tenth Army expeditionary force, swelled after Iwo Jima to the size of a field army of 182,000 assault troops, was led by Army Lieutenant General Simon Bolivar Buckner Jr., the son of a Confederate general, who had commanded the Aleutians campaign. A multiservice command, the Tenth Army marshaled four army (the XXIV Corps's Seventh, Seventy-seventh, Ninety-sixth, and Eighty-first Infantry) and two marine (First and Sixth) divisions of 116,000 men, reinforced by tank and tractor battalions, attached service units, the Tactical Air Force, and an additional reserve of two divisions (the Twenty-seventh Infantry and Second Marines), which floated offshore. Three divisions had landed on Saipan and Iwo Jima; Okinawa would involve eight. The troops would be amply provisioned, too. The medical supplies alone for the Tenth Army's initial assault numbered 25,000 litters, 50,000 blankets, 100,000 cans of foot powder, 100,000 iodine swabs, 30 million vitamin pills, and 7 billion units of penicillin.

This force reflected America's enormous power, especially considering that other divisions were still on Iwo Jima and in the Philippines. Buckner and the senior marine commander, Roy Geiger, worked well together, and thus there was no interservice tension at the top. But they would be landing with a handicap: because constant cloud cover prevented photo reconnaissance, and also because of Japanese ingenuity at disguising their defenses, many of them underground, they lacked accurate knowledge of the numbers of enemy troops and weapons, and their placement. In comparison with the Americans, the Japanese were starving, yet they fought on with the elements of surprise and determination as their weapons.

After the fall of Saipan in July 1944, Imperial Headquarters had reinforced and fortified Okinawa. The Thirty-second Army was heavily armed, and additional troops arrived from the Asian mainland and the home islands. In August the Thirty-second's command fell to Lieutenant General Mitsuru Ushijima, who, like Buckner, was the head of his national military academy and who, also like his American counterpart, would tragically die on Okinawa. Ushijima had at his disposal a large quantity of field artillery and heavy mortars but had lost his most valuable force of men, the experienced Ninth Division, which had been sent to Formosa in November 1944 in expectation of the main U.S. assault there. He was thus left with 110,000 troops, including 20,000 island conscripts, and 1,700 Okinawan boys fourteen years of age or older who served as volunteers—not enough to guard Okinawa's long coastline. So, Ushijima set his troops to work, and like Kuribayashi on Iwo Jima, he produced a masterpiece of defense.

With airfields, ports, and anchorages concentrated in the southern third of the island, Ushijima decided to focus there by building a ring of fortifications around the ancient Shuri Castle. He conceded the Kadena and Yontan airfields on the East China Sea, but he would fight for the port of Naha from his stronghold at Shuri. In just seven months and using hand tools (no bulldozers were available), the Thirty-second Army dug a maze of underground tunnels, caves, and positions. These, added to the natural caves and ridges in the southern part of the island, resulted in a honeycombed defense system ideal for a protracted battle of attrition. The caves contained hospitals, barracks, command posts, supply rooms, and ammunition storage areas where Ushijima cached his huge number of heavy weapons.

The Japanese would await the Americans around Shuri Castle, deny them Naha, slow and halt their advance, make them bleed, and ultimately provide time for Imperial Army and Navy kamikazes to destroy Spruance's Fifth Fleet. The U.S. Navy expected suicide missions, but the Japanese introduced a more expansive version at Okinawa: hundreds of kamikaze planes, in ten separate waves called *kikusui*, or "floating chrysanthemums," targeted U.S. ships, in tandem with conventional air strikes and other tactical attacks. ULTRA intercepts failed to detect these offensives or uncover Ushijima's formidable fortifications.

The Americans expected L-day (Love Day, to avoid confusion with Iwo Jima's D-day) to follow the pattern of earlier amphibious attacks: namely, with resistance on the beaches. On April 1, Easter Sunday, they moved ashore from an armada so large that it covered the horizon. Seizing the outlying island of Kerama Retto, the troops stumbled on the main fleet of 300 suicide boats. They then placed a battery of 155-mm. guns on a barren spit of sand, which added to the 25,000 rounds of 5-inch shelling off Okinawa that had preceded the landing for a week.

L-day casualties were predicted to run as high as 85 percent, yet the landing was uncontested, relative to other islands. Storming across the reefs and over the seawalls, 16,000 infantry and marines came ashore in the first hour of combat, and by evening some 50,000 troops were on land along an 8-mile long, 2-mile deep beachhead. Roy Geiger's First and Sixth Marines landed at the northern end of the Hagushi beaches while John Hodge's Seventh and Ninety-sixth Infantry took the southern end. They met just occasional sniper, mortar, and machine-gun fire, but both were aided by the decoy Second Marines, who pulled off a Tinian-style feint to divert attention from the main landing. Ushijima bit by directing a group of kamikazes toward the Second Marines, and the suicide flyers inflicted 100 casualties on a tractor battalion and sailors on a troop ship. Still, L-day resulted in just 28 Americans killed, 104 wounded, and 27 missing.

The Americans took the Yontan and Kadena airfields, and they then moved the Tactical Air Force to these bases, cleared the beaches, and broke out from the beachhead in chase of small guerrilla units of defenders. The Seventh Division arrived on the east coast during the second day, and the First Marine Division took the Katchin Peninsula, cutting the island in two. The XXIV Corps's momentum seemed unstoppable. Infantry were struck by the pastoral beauty of Okinawa as they marched through the countryside. By April 7 the Sixth Marines had taken Nago, the largest town in northern Okinawa, and twelve days after the landing a company reached the opposite end of the island from the Hagushi beaches, 55 miles to the south.

The honeymoon ended abruptly. Northwest of Nago, on the Motobu Peninsula, a garrison of 2,000 seasoned defenders armed with cannons and heavy weapons in caves engaged the Americans around Mount Yae Take in a 5-day battle. April 15 saw three U.S. commanders in one company become casualties. Support from the battleship *Tennessee* and marine aviators helped secure the peninsula on April 20, but the Sixth Marines suffered 207 deaths and 757 injured. Just off the peninsula, marines seized some tiny islets for battery positions, but Ie Shima, holding 5,000 Japanese, required six days and 1,100 U.S. casualties to overrun. Popular war journalist Ernie Pyle died there, shot in the head by a machine gunner, and his death on April 16, following President Roosevelt's the week before, caused much grieving among the troops.

In the south the Tenth Army found Ushijima's defenses during the first week on Okinawa, when Hodge's infantry met the first sustained enemy resistance on April 5 as his XXIV Corps turned south. Hand-to-hand combat ensued five miles north of the Shuri Line until U.S. troops, incurring 1,500 casualties, cleared the area. Kakazu Ridge was next, where well-prepared defenders held the two hills and their connecting saddle. The tenacious Japanese stalled the Ninety-sixth Division's assault on April 9, then launched their own counterattack three days later. American casualties were already heavy when the Japanese mounted another assault on April 14. After ten more days of fighting, the Americans' continuing vulnerability to night infiltration was evident. Still, the defenders decided to withdraw from the ridge in the face of superior firepower.

Meanwhile, Buckner organized a 3-division offensive on the Shuri Castle complex. On April 18 he opened the "ungodliest preliminary

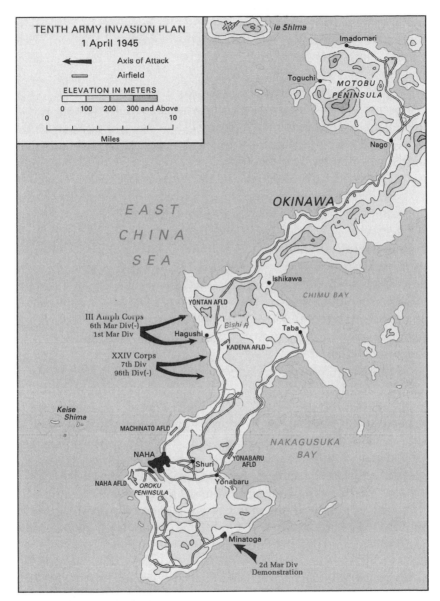

TENTH ARMY INVASION PLAN

Arnold G. Fisch, Jr., *The U.S. Army Campaigns of World War II: Ryukyus* (Washington, DC: Government Printing Office, 1995), 10.

bombardment of the ground war, a virtual 'typhoon of steel' delivered from 27 artillery batteries, 18 ships, and 650 aircraft," writes one historian.[6] Despite this barrage from the largest concentration of artillery pieces in the Pacific war, the defenders just burrowed farther underground, waiting for the bombing to end and the Americans to advance deeper into their main defensive lair.

The XXIV Corps moved forward a day later, gaining ground, then getting thrown back by a major counterattack. Again, fighting was at close quarters. The disciplined Japanese held, cleverly digging in on the reverse slopes of the ridgelines to minimize artillery fire and then emerging from their caves to hit the climbing Americans with mortars and grenades. Flamethrowing tanks cleared several caves but failed to break the defenses. The Japanese actually separated the tanks from their supporting infantry around Kakazu Ridge and then destroyed 22 of the 30 Shermans. They also attempted to wend their way around the Americans by an amphibious landing, but U.S. artillery killed 6,000 men. As the American casualty total reached 702, Buckner realized that the Tenth Army was in for a long struggle on Okinawa. In part, his offensive suffered from unimaginative, World War I–style tactics of assault, but in the main, he faced enemy troops so protected and committed to their cause that only burning, bombing, and blasting them out—yard by yard—would make them yield.

Meanwhile, the struggle was merciless off the coast. The Japanese had spent much of April assaulting the Fifth Fleet with the kamikaze special attack units, as inexperienced pilots flew planes from bases in Formosa and Japan that the Americans had not reached. To be sure, many of the 2,373 suicide missions never reached Okinawa, but those that did make it through the defensive screen of the U.S. fleet inflicted great damage. The first attacks came on April 6, the last on June 22. The first sank 3 destroyers, a landing craft, and 2 ammunition ships. Then 10 *kikusui* waves numbering as many as 350 planes, plus nightly raids by small groups of planes, disrupted Spruance's operations. By the end of the Okinawa campaign the Fifth Fleet had lost 34 ships and other craft and had 368 damaged, while nearly 10,000 sailors were recorded as casualties, half of them dead. These figures represented the largest losses ever for the U.S. Navy in a single battle. For their part, the Japanese lost 1,500 men and aircraft among the kamikazes and escort carriers.

The Americans survived the ordeal with a combination of British assistance, sheer heroism, and a Japanese temerity that bordered on folly. A British Royal Navy task force, along with U.S. carrier-based planes, counterattacked against kamikaze bases in the southern Ryukyus and Formosa. (The British had become targets of suicide bombers, too, but because their carriers had more protective armor—at the price of carrying fewer planes than the Americans'—they incurred fewer losses.) In addition, U.S. naval firefighting training, begun on an intensive scale in late 1942, saved many lives and ships. Marines and infantry also landed on islets to establish early-warning and directional systems, and LeMay's B-29s continued to hit Kyushu. The Japanese neutralized some of the Anglo-American raids on their kamikaze bases, and they had well over 100 concealed airfields, which made pinpointing the kamikazes difficult. Japan also developed a new weapon called the *Ohka*, or "cherry blossom." Nicknamed *Baka*, or "foolish," by the Americans, this inhumane weapon was a manned, solid-fuel rocket—packing 4,400 pounds of explosives— launched from a bomber. These human missiles mostly missed their mark, being too fast for their green pilots to steer, yet one did obliterate a destroyer.

Special missions also indicated the determined ferocity, and desperation, of the Japanese. Most famously, the Imperial Navy dispatched the giant battleship *Yamato* on its final voyage. This last great dreadnought sailed at the heart of a task force, carrying only enough fuel for a one-way trip. After distracting U.S. carriers away from a wave of *kikusui* fighters, the *Yamato* was to head for Okinawa's west coast, beach itself, and pulverize the landing force with its huge 18.1-inch guns. The mission was doomed to failure because of U.S. airpower. Submarines picked up the battleship as it exited the Inland Sea, and on April 7 nearly 300 of Mitscher's planes intercepted the *Yamato* 100 miles from Okinawa. Sent to the bottom along with the behemoth was a new cruiser, 4 destroyers, and about 3,600 men. In addition to this bizarre event, the Japanese tried other, more effective tactics. On the night of May 24–25, one of 6 transport planes packed with commandos made it through the U.S. gunnery protecting the Yontan air base; the commandos destroyed 8 aircraft and damaged double that number, burned 70,000 gallons of aviation fuel, and caused chaos on the base for twelve hours before being killed.

Reading inflated damage reports, Imperial Headquarters wistfully believed it had destroyed the Fifth Fleet. In part, Tokyo could not be blamed for the error because kamikazes had, indeed, ruined several small ships as well as the carriers *Bunker Hill, Franklin, Enterprise*, and the new *Wasp* and *Yorktown*. The Japanese, moreover, still had many planes to sacrifice for the home islands. Nor did the loss of the *Yamato* mean the demise of the Imperial Navy, which, although offensive maneuvers were impossible, still had cruisers, battleships, carriers, and destroyers. Moreover, the kamikazes had indeed frayed the nerves of American sailors. "The strain of waiting, the anticipated terror, made vivid from past experience, sent some men into hysteria, insanity, breakdown," reported a journalist.[7]

In reality, the invasion of Okinawa was not deterred by the Japanese aerial assault. On the contrary, the disparity between American and Japanese power grew greater. The Japanese had lost 3,000 aircraft in the Philippines and lost another 7,000 over Okinawa. Thus, regardless of their successes, the kamikazes drained the strength of the empire. In addition, U.S. pilots flew 90,662 missions off carriers during the Okinawa operation between March 14 and June 8, as the carrier task force remained at sea continuously for an amazing 92 days, while food and other supplies poured into the war zone. There were even enough cigarettes for every man to have twenty a day for eight months. While the Japanese scraped for roots and subsisted in caves, the U.S. quartermaster general learned that American infantry divisions were receiving "too much Barbasol brushless shaving cream," throwing away about a quarter of it.[8] Hospitals on Saipan and Guam could accommodate the sick and injured of two armies. Naval forces received more petroleum, oil, and lubricants than the entire nation of Japan imported in 1944. Despite the kamikaze attacks the Americans readied 14,000 aircraft and 100 carriers for the invasion of Honshu. Off Okinawa, the U.S. Navy absorbed the punishing blows of *kikusui* attacks while it continued to support the troops on the island and progressed toward Japan's inner defenses.

The offensive on Okinawa had clearly bogged down, however, and General Buckner came under increasing pressure to break the Shuri line by launching an attack on the Japanese left flank. As the invasion dragged into May a concerned Admiral Nimitz met with Buckner, urging him to speed up the attack in order to save U.S. ships from kamikazes. Buckner had available the Second Marines for an amphibious assault, but he worried about the logistical problems of opening a second front after failing to dislodge the Japanese on three fronts in April. The careful general, unfamiliar with amphibious tactics, would be criticized for a lack of imagination and failure to conclude the operation in a timely fashion. But Buckner correctly stated that regardless of the number of offensives, the Japanese would still have to be rooted out from their underground strongholds by "blowtorch and corkscrew" tactics.[9]

In late April, Ushijima gathered his commanders deep under Shuri Castle to discuss a change in tactics. Although holing up on land and letting the kamikazes loose at sea had inflicted great losses on the Americans, his impetuous chief of staff, Lieutenant General Isamu Cho, was tired of this defensive war of attrition. He ill-advisedly persuaded Ushijima to launch an offensive, including an amphibian landing to encircle Buckner, which predictably failed miserably on May 5. After the Japanese lost 6,000 top troops and 59 artillery pieces, Ushijima returned to his previous methods of deadly defense, which prolonged the Okinawa conflict for six more weeks.

Fighting heavy rains and entrenched, camouflaged, and well-supplied enemy forces, the Americans inched forward on the stalemated fronts. It took a week to clear the Awacha Pocket, at great loss to both sides, by May 10. U.S. troops received word of Germany's surrender, but they hardly cared, mired as they were in mud and Japanese crossfire. Then, on May 11, Buckner ordered the Tenth Army to attack the Shuri defenses. The III Amphibious Corps's Sixth and First Marine Divisions moved to the west, the Seventy-seventh and Ninety-sixth Infantry of the XXIV Corps went eastward; and the Seventh Division held the center.

The Seventh was occupied for three weeks on Dakeshi Ridge, to the south of the Awacha Pocket. Commanded by veterans who had seen action on Guadalcanal, Bougainville, and Peleliu, the Seventh advanced to the crest, withdrew under swarms of counterattackers, then retook the ridge after eliminating the Japanese but lost 700 men in the process. From Dakeshi they gazed across the tortured terrain of Wana Draw, which was surrounded by caves from which the Japanese Sixty-second Infantry division laid down deadly interlocking fire until the marines killed them to a man. But the 1,200 yards across the draw to Wana Ridge took eighteen days of intense tank fire, a run across the gorge in the face of enemy fire, then the manhandling of drums of napalm up the north side of the ridge to be tumbled down toward the cave complexes. The defenders replenished themselves at night and punished the Seventh Division, which lost 200 marines for every 100 yards it gained.

Meanwhile, to the west, the Sixth Marines advanced to a low, steep hill called Sugar Loaf, which joined two other hills in a defensive complex anchoring the western end of the Shuri line. None of the hills were higher than 230 feet, but the placement of the reinforced, reverse-slope mortar, antitank, and machine-gun positions gave the Japanese a great advantage (as did heavy rains that turned the ground to slop). They could hit the

Americans from any one of the three hills. An eight-day pitched battle for Sugar Loaf ensued, in which Corporal James Day, a squad leader, held a position on the hill's western shoulder for several days with a few men while marines tried to reinforce him. Tanks, artillery, and mortars gathered on May 16 to pound the ridge from the north, but Japanese reinforcements won the day. The marines were then called off the hill, and a thundering air, naval, and artillery bombardment began. Yet a new ground attack also failed to dislodge the defenders until tanks and infantry penetrated Sugar Loaf on May 18. Marine riflemen, bayonets drawn, beat back a counterattack, and finally, U.S. troops held an end of the Shuri line. At the eastern end the Ninety-sixth succeeded after weeks of tough fighting. To top it all, the Sixth Marines marched into Naha, the capital, on May 23–24.

At this point, Ushijima wisely pulled his forces from Shuri Castle, now outflanked on two sides. He had cost the Americans 26,000 casualties, the most of any Pacific war battle, but the Japanese themselves lost 64,000 killed or wounded around Shuri as his 3 main combat units were being eaten away. On May 23, Ushijima moved to the southeast corner of Okinawa along an 8-mile coral outcropping, the Yuza Dake and Yaeju Dake escarpment, to mount a secondary defense. Each defender carried a twenty-day ration and strained under equipment. Six days later the U.S. flag flew over Shuri Castle, but the enemy remained as dangerous as ever.

The pursuit and defeat of Ushijima's relocated forces cost another three weeks and more casualties. The Tenth Army used 3,000 tons of ammunition a day in its artillery bombardment—totaling 2,046,930 rounds —as well as 707,500 rockets, mortars, and 5-inch or larger shells from the navy offshore. While Buckner relied on artillery, the Sixth Marines made another amphibious assault, this time on the Oroku Peninsula in the southwest, which yielded the Naha airfield. Admiral Minoru Ota fought savagely for ten days, causing 1,608 casualties and destroying 30 American tanks, until marines took the peninsula on June 14. Ota and 5,000 of his sailors lay dead; the naval base force was destroyed. The bloody six-day seizure of Kunishi Ridge, which included night attacks that infuriated the Japanese, led to the capture of the southwestern part of the island. The Thirty-second Army had nearly withered away.

Once the Sixth Marines reached the sea, and much-needed supplies, they could assess the fury of war on Okinawa. As they rested, they noted how blasts had uncovered the dead, as the ridges were often "stinking compost piles." Those unfortunate enough to slide down the muddy slopes often reached the bottom vomiting, with maggots pouring out of

their pockets. "We didn't talk about such things," noted Private Eugene
Sledge. "They were too horrible and obscene even for hardened veterans.
The conditions taxed the toughest I knew almost to the point of screaming." On a ridge taken earlier he was distracted by the sight of a marine
killed days before. The soldier was sitting up in a crater, his "half-gone
face" smiling up every time Sledge gazed down at him from his foxhole,
seemingly "mocking our pitiful efforts to hang on to life in the face of the
constant violent death that had cut him down."[10]

A flame-throwing medium tank fires into a cave on southern Okinawa. U.S. Army,
United States Army in World War II: Pictorial Record: The War Against Japan
(Washington, DC: Department of the Army, 1952), 405.

On June 18, U.S. forces swept from the Oroku Peninsula toward
Ushijima's escarpment, led by the newly assigned Eighth Marines.
General Buckner climbed up on an observation post to watch them
advance along the valley, but Japanese gunners spotted his party and fired
shells in his direction. One splintered some nearby coral, which shot into
his chest, and the general died ten minutes later, one of the highest-
ranking U.S. officers killed in World War II. Geiger, the only marine and
only aviator ever to command a field army, took over the Tenth Army for
five days until General Joseph Stilwell relieved him. But by then, on June
21, Ushijima and Cho had committed ritual suicide, along with their
troops. Geiger had secured Okinawa.

The battle's cost was nearly unfathomable. Although 7,400 Japanese
surrendered on the island (perhaps an indication that the once fanatical
defenders had begun for the first time to think resistance was futile), an
enormous number perished: the result of devotion to the emperor, the

total Japanese dead came to 110,000, including kamikazes and sailors. Native Okinawans suffered greatly as well. Although figures are uncertain (because many people fled into caves where they were later entombed by bombing), tragically, from one-tenth to one-quarter of the inhabitants died—at the lowest estimate, 42,000 people. Some Okinawans even turned on their own family members, bludgeoning them or slitting their arteries rather than allowing their surrender to the supposedly demonic Americans. For their part, Tenth Army combat casualties numbered almost 40,000, including over 7,000 killed; nonbattle casualties—mostly combat fatigue—ran to 26,000 men. In total, U.S. Army, Marine, and Navy losses in the Okinawa operation climbed to 49,151, of which 12,520 were deaths, the highest U.S. casualty rate for any Pacific campaign.

Many aspects of the Okinawa campaign stand out, but none more so than the nature of the fighting and what it presaged for Americans in the endgame of the war. Along with Iwo Jima, the battle for Okinawa involved mostly small groups of platoons or squads, and in many instances, individual soldiers played the critical role in victory. Such developments, writes one expert, "ominously showed how difficult the final conquest of the Japanese home islands might be."[11] Indeed, Spruance spoke of Okinawa as "a bloody, hellish prelude to the invasion of Japan."[12] Now, the Okinawan invading force prepared for a landing on the main home island of Honshu, and veterans of Iwo Jima and Luzon readied for Kyushu. All guessed that the landings in Japan itself would provoke the worst savagery of the war. With these terrifying thoughts in mind, the soldiers soon learned that President Harry Truman had revealed a secret weapon designed to save the troops from the burden of that nightmare.

 Notes

1. Spector, *Eagle against the Sun*, 505.

2. Joseph H. Alexander, *Closing In: Marines in the Seizure of Iwo Jima* (Washington, DC: Marine Corps Historical Center, 1994), 3.

3. Ibid., 15.

4. Alexander, *Storm Landings*, 142.

5. Joseph H. Alexander, *The Final Campaign: Marines in the Victory on Okinawa* (Washington, DC: Marine Corps Historical Center, 1996), 2.

6. Ibid., 20.

7. Spector, *Eagle against the Sun*, 539.

8. Schrijvers, *The GI War*, 231.

9. Alexander, *Storm Landings*, 166.

10. Sledge, *With the Old Breed*, 270.

11. Arnold G. Gisch Jr., *The U.S. Army Campaigns of World War II: Ryukyus* (Washington, DC: Government Printing Office, 1995), 31.

12. Alexander, *The Final Campaign*, 51.

8

UNCONDITIONAL DEFEAT

In September 1944, Franklin Roosevelt and Winston Churchill met in Quebec, where they called for a blockade of Japan, intensive bombardment, and the destruction of Japanese naval and air strength as a prelude to forcing the empire's unconditional surrender. The Joint Chiefs had formulated this total war strategy, called Downfall, months before, and then spent months debating which of the home islands would be the first target. They settled on Kyushu, from which the Allies would move to Honshu and across the Kondo Plain to Tokyo. Douglas MacArthur and Chester Nimitz were charged with drawing up plans for the Kyushu operation, code-named Olympic, to begin on November 1, 1945. The Honshu landing, called Coronet, would follow on March 1, 1946. Given primary responsibility for Olympic, MacArthur would command all army personnel, while Nimitz would oversee naval and amphibious forces. The invading forces would number over 5 million troops, most of them American, and constitute the two largest amphibious assaults in history to bring Japan to its knees and end the Pacific War.

The Americans actually rushed the timetable, for troops landed on the two home islands in late August and September 1945. Given the complete U.S. domination of the land, sea, and air, while diplomatic initiatives also left Japan no way out but surrender, the Japanese could only buy time, hoping that America would sue for peace once faced with the terrifying prospect of invading the home islands. Or, perhaps, the Allied coalition might crumble, or a typhoon would once again bring salvation from seemingly omnipotent invaders. But none of the miracles occurred. Instead, the immediate cause of the rapid end of the war was the advent of the nuclear age, which poised Japan on the very brink of annihilation. After carnage wrought from the skies, the United States entered the home islands not as invaders but as occupiers, a reflection of its growing ability since late 1943 to bring Japan to its knees.

Defense and Diplomacy

Intelligence reports, and experience in the war's increasingly ferocious battles since November 1943, indicated that the Japanese—even in their depleted state—could mount a lethal defense of the home islands. To be sure, bombing had leveled several small cities, devastated most of the larger ones, and undermined morale and hopes for victory. From spring 1945 to the war's end the ruined factories idled homefront production, already reduced by the long-time dearth of raw materials. The people faced starvation by winter, and even the military realized that it was spent. Yet if the Americans could be convinced that an invasion would cost them casualties well beyond the recent numbers on Luzon, Iwo Jima, and Okinawa, then perhaps the Japanese could come away with a negotiated settlement. The war could end with minimal loss of territory and life, or it could end in vast carnage.

Thus, Imperial Headquarters prepared for the landing on Kyushu. ULTRA intercepts in April 1945 led to estimates, based on the number of vessels involved in moving a combat unit from Manchuria, that the Japanese would have 30,000 to 60,000 additional soldiers on the island, bringing Kyushu's complement to 246,000, with another four divisions totaling 100,000 men expected by November 1, 1945, when Olympic would begin. Troops were being mobilized for the final stand.

Incredibly, ULTRA also revealed optimism among Japanese leaders. Studying the damage off Okinawa, Imperial Navy strategists claimed that they could neutralize up to half the U.S. fleet with kamikazes. As for ground warfare, the Thirty-second Army had held out for over 100 days on Okinawa with less than 3 divisions, even though they were cut off from reinforcements and supplies as well as bombarded. Kyushu would have more support and men, a number of troops equivalent to Krueger's force. The island had terrain similar to the mountains and gorges on Luzon and Okinawa, and heavy artillery coverage from caves would blanket the beach approaches. Commanders assigned large groups of soldiers and civilian volunteers to attacks on tanks, using armor-piercing explosives, asking "all able-bodied Japanese, regardless of sex" to "be prepared to sacrifice his [sic] life in suicide attacks on enemy armored forces."[1] The Japanese lacked good leadership, adequately reinforced fortifications, and fuel but they were prepared to make a stand to the bitter, bloody end.

President Truman heard this assessment on June 18, 1945, and he responded to the Joint Chiefs that he feared another Okinawa (then reaching its end) but on an even larger scale. The president therefore asked for more information to help him decide whether isolation, blockade, bombardment, or invasion would defeat Japan with the least loss of American lives. He did not care about time or money, impressed as he was or, rather, sickened and horrified by the Japanese will to barbarism and fatalism. Truman instead focused on saving the lives of U.S. soldiers. Admiral William Leahy, head of the Joint Chiefs and the president's chief of staff, predicted that there would be 35 percent casualties on Kyushu, similar to the losses on Okinawa. With 766,500 men in the landing force, that judgment meant 268,000 killed, wounded, and missing in action. MacArthur gave lower estimates, but despite claims that the U.S. Navy would deny access to the island, Truman worried that the enemy could reinforce Kyushu. The president approved Olympic, leaving a decision on the Honshu invasion for later when he could gauge the impact of the Kyushu campaign and Soviet entry into the Asian war.

He had more worries, though, as he sailed to Europe to attend to European peace matters at the Potsdam Conference in July 1945. The estimates of Japanese troop levels on Kyushu had been confirmed, and worse, they had been increased by 2 new divisions and were expecting another 4. Regardless of overstretched resources, Imperial Headquarters had instituted an ambitious plan using several divisions, as well as mixed and armored brigades, which would "fight to the finish" on Kyushu and perhaps even launch a "full scale offense" intended to destroy Allied forces at sea and on the beaches.[2] By August 2, as Truman headed home,

Kyushu's manpower had climbed to 600,000 personnel, and ULTRA decrypts hinted at even more. U.S. military planners now estimated 11 divisions on the island (with 2 more en route), or over double the number Truman had been told at his June meeting with the Joint Chiefs. The landing in southern Kyushu would encounter 320,000 of these forces. As well, intelligence discovered that 18 hidden bases were being built to launch 940 suicide aircraft and torpedoes. Planners prudently recommended a review and reexamination of Olympic.

To be sure, neither Truman nor his top advisers knew of these fresh estimates, but they did expect a large number of casualties. Historians still contest how many U.S. troops would have died (and how many Truman was told would die) in invasions of Kyushu and Honshu. The Joint Chiefs made no mention of casualty estimates at the June 18 meeting because Truman might have panicked, but figures ran from 250,000 to 500,000 killed or injured. The latter number seemed high to those who noted that campaigns for the Philippines, Iwo Jima, and Okinawa had yielded 133,000 casualties, and that losses in Europe from D-day at Normandy through the next eight weeks or so totaled 63,360. Also, administration officials often confused casualty with death figures.

Nonetheless, with the experience of Tarawa, Saipan, Iwo Jima, Okinawa, and other battles of annihilation in mind, and especially considering the vicious style of fighting, officials held that the invasion of Japan would be more deadly than the landing in France. On Kyushu the Japanese would benefit from shorter lines of communications and supplies than anywhere else the Americans had confronted them. With the Japanese government whipping up patriotism and civic duty by beginning a program called "The Glorious Death of One Hundred Million," American commanders talked of canceling the invasion altogether and relying instead on fire-bombing and blockade.[3] The most conservative estimates of the Joint Chiefs called for 60,000 casualties during the first two months on Kyushu, one-quarter of them killed in action.

The Joint Chiefs closely examined the situation in mid-July 1945, and they found both weaknesses and worries regarding Japan's position. Imperial forces were in retreat in Manchuria and China; their communication and transportation lines from Southeast Asia and China were practically severed; sea traffic between China, Korea, and Japan was limited to hazardous coastal runs; even the relatively short shipping lane across the Sea of Japan was increasingly risky. Sea and air operations had nearly destroyed all naval and air capabilities, while blockade and air attacks were reducing the existing defenses. Bombing had undermined morale and economic activity at home. Japan simply could not hold on. Yet despite the bleak assessment, the Joint Chiefs "saw no prospect of surrender until the army leaders acknowledged defeat" either through actual defeat or the realization that the military's survival was at stake.[4]

Although the Allies could invade the home islands, Korea, or the central China coast from their forward bases on Okinawa and elsewhere, perhaps diplomacy could better end the war. Intelligence reports informed policymakers that the Japanese, or at least a cadre of diplomats and military leaders in the government, had been searching for peace. The inability to advocate peace in public handicapped them, as fanatical militarists marked for assassination anyone willing to surrender. The population would be torn because of its complete allegiance to the emperor, for whom they had fought and died, but even the emperor's closest political adviser, the Lord Privy Seal Marquis Kido Koichi, was pushing for diplomacy. He joined members of General Koiso Kuniaki's cabinet (which had succeeded the Tojo government after the Marianas debacle in July 1944), some former prime ministers, and other elites to consider the peace option. Their efforts took on particular urgency after defeat in the Philippines in spring 1945.

The major peace initiative focused on the Soviet Union. Koiso sent out feelers to Soviet leader Josef Stalin, but the dictator had promised FDR that he would declare war on Japan in early August, three months after the European war ended. With the fall of Okinawa came the demise of Koiso's government, yet the new prime minister, Admiral Suzuki Kantaro, continued the effort to woo the Russians. Stalin brushed aside the entreaties by refusing to renew his neutrality pact with Japan. Suzuki countered with offers of generous territorial and economic concessions, but the Soviets knew full well that with Japan on the brink of defeat, they would get the booty anyway. Stalin held to his Yalta agreement with Roosevelt, and the Japanese peace effort came to naught.

American diplomats also considered their terms of peace. The key element—and an enduring point of controversy among scholars—hinged on the retention of the emperor. At the Casablanca Conference in 1943 the Allies had decided to insist on the unconditional surrender of Japan, which put the Imperial structure at risk. Critics argued that the Japanese would fight harder to defend their spiritual and national leader, Emperor Hirohito, but polls showed that few Americans wanted Hirohito to stay, and many more sought his execution after the brutal conflict fought in his name. The State Department leaned away from unconditional surrender, diplomats reasoning that if the emperor remained, he would actually enhance postwar stability, as long as Japan adopted a truly democratic constitutional monarchy. British Prime Minister Winston Churchill, Army Chief of Staff Marshall, and William Leahy of the Joint Chiefs of Staff agreed, and in 1945 they pushed for retaining the emperor, if need be. A high-level committee appointed by Truman and consisting of Secretary of War Henry Stimson, Secretary of the Navy James Forrestal, and Undersecretary of State Joseph Grew also sided with the moderates. The president took their new surrender terms to Potsdam in July, but his new secretary of state, James Byrnes, a longtime congressional leader and former governor of South Carolina, urged Truman to return to unconditional surrender; if not, he warned, there would be hell to pay with the voters.

The Potsdam Declaration of July 26, 1945, thus represented a compromise, in Truman's eyes at least. This pronouncement did not mention the emperor, but it demanded the creation of a peaceful and responsible government endorsed freely by the Japanese people. Stimson and his partners hoped that the Japanese peace advocates would take heart from these terms, for the wording allowed for the retention of the emperor. Meanwhile, Byrnes had Truman protected at home, because the record still demanded unconditional surrender. Truman issued a statement that revealed his unease with Byrnes. On May 8, the day Germany stopped fighting, the president pledged to pound the empire until it unconditionally surrendered, a term that he interpreted as meaning the elimination of Japanese militarism without "the extermination or enslavement of the Japanese people."[5]

In sum, America required Japan's complete capitulation, but Hirohito's status was negotiable. The Japanese target did not get that message, however; in fact, Tokyo was encouraged by the Potsdam Declaration, since its conditions for surrender seemed to demand less than total submission. But translations and interpretations so tortured the Potsdam Declaration that Tokyo rejected it. Moreover, Foreign Minister Togo Shegenori, despite being the most senior critic of the war, persuaded the cabinet to stall for time, and Soviet help. Intercepted messages revealed that the Japanese would not accept unconditional surrender because they feared the emperor was at peril; absent Soviet intervention, the empire determined to fight on. Newspapers in Japan therefore received a censored version of the Allied surrender demands; in general, the government remained silent. It was a tactical blunder, leading the Americans to conclude that Japan had refused the surrender terms.

The Atomic Bombs

Japanese reticence rendered the impact of scientific testing all the more significant for the Truman administration. The president received word at Potsdam on July 16 that the costly, complex, and secretive Manhattan Project had come to fruition. Five days later a detailed report arrived from the project's chief, General Leslie Groves, and U.S. leaders sent out instructions to drop the atomic bomb on Japan after August 3, weather permitting. Truman authorized the mission, to be launched from Tinian sometime after he had left Potsdam on August 2 and a few days before intelligence confirmed that the Japanese had raised their troop strength on Kyushu to 11 divisions. Thus, it is clear that he and his advisers had decided before Potsdam to use the atomic weapon. Whether its use was justified, or what factors ultimately motivated the administration to drop the bomb, are matters of contention. But undoubtedly, this devastating weapon would add to the ferocious and overwhelming U.S. response to years of Japanese aggression and cruelty.

A product of discoveries in physics, fear that Germany would make such a bomb first, and huge federal outlays and organization on a scale never before mounted for a single project, the atomic bombs provoked controversy and trepidation even though leaders hoped to speed Japanese surrender by dropping them. Developed on a swift timetable throughout the war, the Manhattan Project was testimony to the scientific skills of the Allied powers. The U.S. contributions were numerous, the nation's productive scale proving most critical. Working in thirty-seven facilities in nineteen states and Canada, more than 120,000 people were funded by over $2 billion in government finances. The scientists achieved success on July 16, 1945, at Alamogordo Air Force Base in New Mexico, beating the Germans (and a meager Japanese project) into the nuclear age. Those watching the explosion realized the bomb's awesome, and terrifying, implications.

The science, government, and industry leaders in the Manhattan Project, along with political advisers, had met under the guidance of Secretary of War Stimson well before the test to make recommendations on the bomb's use. This Interim Committee advised Truman to drop the bomb without warning, and as soon as possible, on a Japanese military-industrial target. The advice had its dissenters, however, and debate continued through June and July 1945 regarding the need first to provide a warning by demonstrating the bomb's potential destructiveness. Some scientists not on the Interim Committee urged that the weapon not be used at all. Truman and his advisers had no intention of listening to them.

Contemporaries and historians would accuse the administration of an exercise of atomic diplomacy against the Soviet Union as the rationale for dropping the two bombs on Japan. That is, a quick end to the war would prevent the Soviets from restoring their hold in Manchuria and annexing the southern half of Sakhalin Island and the Kurile Islands. The bomb might also persuade Stalin to negotiate a peace in Europe amenable to American interests. Indeed, Truman's advisers believed that the atomic bomb made Soviet entry into the Asian war unnecessary, and even troublesome. Playing the peacemaker at Potsdam, Truman did inform Stalin of the successful bomb test, but perhaps he also meant to imply that Russian help against Japan was no longer needed. Stalin held to his Yalta pledge, however, and declared war on Japan on August 8.

Debate in July focused on suitable Japanese targets for the bomb, but solid evidence of atomic diplomacy does exist. The Soviet issue, indeed, occupied some discussion time in the Interim Committee, and postwar tension over America's control of atomic weapons bears out historical interpretations claiming that some administration officials sought to use the bomb as a trump card in a brewing Cold War poker game. Furthermore, Interim Committee records reveal no mention of the increase in Japanese troops in the home islands. Thus, atomic diplomacy against the Soviets is a greater suspect as a motivation in the bomb's use. Yet it is just as true that Truman, and his advisers, remained focused above all on finishing off the Japanese rather than on postwar strategy. The context of the ongoing Pacific war, and the objective of finally crushing an implacable foe, overrode considerations of U.S.-Soviet diplomacy at this time.

Deciphering with certainty the motivations in the decision to use the bomb is challenging, but the argument that Truman viewed this weapon as the quickest way to end the war, even without knowledge of the larger forces on Kyushu, is most compelling. The recent history of the Pacific war, stretching back to Tarawa but highlighted by the Philippines, Iwo Jima, and Okinawa, simply convinced U.S. leaders that the bomb would save American lives. With luck, the Manhattan Project might even avoid altogether the need for an invasion of the home islands. In early August the military reported that the Japanese had engaged in a buildup of divisions on Kyushu. As one close reader of the situation has written, this disclosure "reinforced the belief that the decision to use the bomb was the path of least resistance."[6]

Historians have also presented myriad "what if" scenarios, or alternatives that might have brought peace without resort to nuclear bombs. What if a demonstration bomb had been dropped in Tokyo Bay with Imperial leaders as onlookers? What if the Americans had merely proceeded with the invasion of Kyushu under Operation Olympic, or delayed the invasion a bit to allow for more pounding from the air? What if a blockade and bombing strategy had been allowed to run its course? What if the unconditional surrender terms had been modified to permit the emperor to remain, thus meeting the demands of Japanese civilian leadership? What if Truman had waited for the advance of Soviet military power? Or how about some combination of these alternatives? They are all interesting but ultimately fruitless avenues of exploration, for debate boils down to a guessing game and interpretation.

It is clear that no American at the time would lament the devastation of Japan. Imperial forces had a gruesome record of mistreatment of prisoners, involving death marches, experimental surgery, fatal slave labor, massacres of incarcerated combatants and indigenous people, and such perverse acts as cannibalism and crucifixions. Biological testing on adults and children, and forced prostitution, shocked the public. The Japanese had also engaged in the slaughter of hundreds of thousands of people throughout Asia, in addition to having mounted a sustained, punishing defense against the Allies. Although some U.S. personnel killed indiscriminately, contemptuously butchered and degraded corpses, and took trophies of body parts of their enemy, these atrocities paled in comparison with Japanese butchery. The vicious Pacific war, in which racial prejudices intensified the will to kill, made rational thinking regarding alternatives to the bomb extremely difficult. Americans were clear about one thing: the Japanese politicians and militarists were the savages. Their ice-cold, fanatical, and systematically barbaric behavior required their total destruction by U.S. troops, and America had the technological and industrial wherewithal to bring this about.

In the end, Truman simply did not await discussion over alternatives. It was not that he took his decision lightly. As his private journal indicated, Truman thought the bomb was a terrible weapon that placed him in a moral dilemma of seeking peace while unleashing terror on the world. Nonetheless, America had to force Japan to surrender. Therefore, in late July the U.S. Navy brought two bombs to Tinian after the president ordered the Twentieth Air Force to pick one of four cities when the weather was right. Truman and Stimson decided to pass over Kyoto, a city with vast cultural treasures, even though air force planners recommended it. General Curtis LeMay, in command of the special unit of B-29s of the 509th Composite Group, selected Japan's eighth largest city, Hiroshima, since it had military value, a bridge that provided a target, and, purportedly, no POW camps.

Located in southwestern Honshu, Hiroshima had a population of 350,000 when the war began but more than that by 1945, with the addition of Korean and Japanese workers. A commercial and agricultural hub, and a manufacturing center possessing shipyards, engineering facilities, textile and light industry, the city also headquartered the Fifty-ninth Army and several divisions and brigades. Situated in a flat area surrounded by hills, it was purposely left untouched by fire-bombing so that the atomic bomb's effects might be magnified.

The 509th had made numerous practice runs over Japan, even dropping simulated atomic bombs that the population soon ignored. But the real thing arrived on August 6, 1945, as Colonel Paul Tibbetts, commanding a B-29 named after his mother, *Enola Gay*, dropped a uranium device called *Little Boy* on the center of Hiroshima from an altitude of 8,500 yards. The bomb, roughly 9 feet long and weighing 4 tons, exploded 590 yards above the city at 8:15 A.M. Its force reached an equivalent of 13,000 tons of TNT. Two escort bombers photographed and gauged its impact as Tibbetts banked his plane away.

The survivors described a ghastly scene of carnage. One resident wrote that "the sky filled with black smoke and glowing sparks. Flames rose and the heat set currents of air in motion. The streets were deserted except for the dead. Hiroshima was no longer a city but a burnt-over prairie. How small Hiroshima was with its houses gone."[7] A doctor saw reservoirs full of people who had been boiled alive, and another passed soldiers whose flesh was "wet and mushy where the skin peeled, and they had no faces! Their eyes, noses and mouths had been burned away, and it looked like their ears had melted off."[8] A photographer who witnessed people trapped under wreckage thought that it was just as well for them to die there, because they could not have outrun the flames if they had escaped. The corpses "were still burning from below and the fat of the bodies was bubbling up and sputtering as it burned. That was the only time I've seen humans roasting."[9]

Nearly 100,000 people perished instantly as a fireball of several thousand degrees ignited the city. Within hours, thousands more died, a third of these military, along with 20,000 Korean laborers and factory workers and about a dozen U.S. prisoners of war. Intense thermal radiation burst from the fireball for ten seconds after the explosion, killing several thousands more in the days to come.

Burned, shocked, irradiated, the citizens of Hiroshima suffered in ways novel to the Pacific war. A half-mile from the epicenter, heat annihilated people and ruptured their internal organs; 2 miles away, people, clothes, and houses burned. A pillar of smoke and debris rose 9,000 yards into the sky within eight minutes, forming a mushroom-shaped cloud, and the explosive wind that followed the blast tore clothing and skin and sent shards of objects into people and buildings. Wooden buildings nearly 2 miles from the epicenter were destroyed, and concrete structures near the point of detonation were leveled. Within a minute of the explosion, gamma rays and neutrons shot from the blast. Those a half-mile or closer to the site received intense doses, but people as far as 1 1/2 miles away were radiated. Residual radiation lasted for over four days, and radioactive dust and rain felled or damaged living organisms for years afterward.

More such horror lay in store. Two days later, dealing a military and psychological blow, the Soviets declared war on Japan and sent 1.6 million soldiers into Manchuria. American pilots dropped millions of leaflets with a stark warning that more atomic bombs were on the way unless Japan surrendered. Washington wanted a response from Imperial Headquarters, but when none arrived, the United States made good on its threat.

On August 9, at 11:00 A.M., three days after Hiroshima, a B-29 called *Bock's Car,* commanded by Major Charles Sweeney (who had piloted one of the escort B-29s over Hiroshima), dropped the plutonium *Fat Man* on the city of Nagasaki. The primary target had been Kokura, but overcast skies forced Sweeney to his secondary target. Nagasaki was a major port and industrial city in western Kyushu, with extensive steelworks and shipyards, an army base, and a thriving fishing and coal-mining center. About one-third of the city was ruined, and 65,000–75,000 died or were fatally wounded. Whether the Nagasaki bomb was necessary or not is another bone of contention among scholars, for Hiroshima seemed to provide enough of a message to an incapacitated Japan, and war leaders in Tokyo had gathered to discuss the surrender before the second bomb fell.

The second atomic bomb fell on Nagasaki, on August 9, 1945. U.S. Army, *United States Army in World War II: Pictorial Record: The War Against Japan* (Washington, DC: Department of the Army, 1952), 451.

Surrender

The Hiroshima bomb had the desired effect of mobilizing Japan's Supreme Council for the Direction of the War. On August 9, leaders pondered anew the Potsdam Declaration, but even the news of Nagasaki could not budge the adamant hardliners. During a morning meeting,

1 admiral and 2 generals pushed for continuing the war, while 2 admirals and Foreign Minister Togo urged negotiations. Prime Minister Suzuki then invited his entire cabinet to give opinions. Deadlock persisted. Upon hearing of the Nagasaki disaster, and consistent with their practice of fanatical persistence in the face of certain doom, the minister of war and a handful of supporters demanded even further resistance.

Desperate for a resolution, the prime minister called another conference for that evening, inviting Emperor Hirohito and his advisers to decide between the two courses. The impressionable Hirohito, who had neither welcomed war nor tried to avoid it, now tossed his lot with the peace faction. But the debate continued into the early morning hours of August 10 before he finally gave his verdict, declaring that "if we let matters stand and did not act, the Japanese race would perish and I would be unable to protect my subjects."[10] Hirohito accepted the terms of the Potsdam Declaration, with the caveat that the emperor would remain the representative of the Japanese people.

Digesting this proviso, the Truman administration decided to accept Japan's surrender. Secretary of War Stimson counseled that retaining the emperor would avoid more rabid fighting in Asia; Hirohito was the only person who could persuade Japanese troops to lay down their arms. By ending the war quickly, the surrender would deny territory and a greater role at the peace table to the Soviet Union, as Stalin recognized. On August 12 the Allies agreed to let the emperor remain, though holding him responsible for helping with the surrender and reminding him that the Japanese people must ultimately determine their form of government.

For a few days, however, the Japanese were unable to accept their own terms. On August 12, 8 captured U.S. airmen were executed by military fanatics, and 8 more tragically perished three days later. Debate continued to rage in the war council even after the American response arrived, the military demanding more protection for the government, the Foreign Office urging acceptance of the U.S. terms, and Prime Minister Suzuki vacillating. Finally, on August 14, Hirohito agreed to meet again with government leaders, and a shocked and sad cabinet heard him order that Allied conditions be accepted. He made a vocal recording of an Imperial Rescript to that effect for dissemination, to ensure the failure of an attempted coup by right-wing military and nationalists: they would be unable to claim that surrender was not the true wish of the emperor.

Yet the lengths to which determined resisters would go, even at this late date when continued struggle was hopeless, reflected the nature of the beast that Americans had long confronted on the battlefield. Indeed,

Aftereffects of the atomic bombing in Nagasaki. The only buildings left standing were usually made of reinforced concrete, such as the Ohashi Gas Works (3,200 feet north of ground zero) at bottom center and the Yamazato School (2,300 feet north of the impact point of the bomb). U.S. Army, *United States Army in World War II: Pictorial Record: The War Against Japan* (Washington, DC: Department of the Army, 1952), 453.

before the public heard the Imperial proclamation, a group of junior army officers tried to overthrow the government. During the night of August 14 they seized the Imperial Guards Division in Tokyo and killed its commander, who became the last Japanese killed in the Pacific war before the surrender—and this by persons on his own side. The fanatics broke into the palace in search of the emperor's recordings, hoping to destroy them and thus prevent the surrender, but they could not find the tapes. The coup was aborted when senior officers refused to join the rebels, but rather than hear the emperor's words, the minister of war and the army chief of staff committed suicide and urged other officers to do likewise. Suzuki and other leaders then dodged a superpatriot assassin's bullets, and that same night a massive U.S. bomber raid of 1,014 aircraft flew the grand finale over Tokyo, not losing a single plane amid the devastation of an already ravaged capital city.

Then, for the first time, the Japanese heard the emperor's voice. The people had no illusions about victory, but they had anticipated a demand for new sacrifices or a declaration of war on the Soviet Union. What they heard, however, in the emperor's solemn words, came as a shock: Japan would accept its defeat and surrender. Hirohito counseled them to lay down their arms and bravely consent to an unbearable fate as a disgraced nation. They had no other choice, he warned, for "the enemy has begun to employ a new and most cruel bomb, the power of which to do damage is indeed incalculable, taking the toll of many innocent lives. Should we continue to fight it would not only result in the ultimate collapse and obliteration of the Japanese nation, but also it would lead to the total extinction of human civilization."[11] The atomic bombs had persuaded Japan to end its war.

The surrender process locked into gear. Members of the Imperial family went abroad to persuade military commanders to give up. A new government under the younger brother of the emperor assumed power on August 15, a move designed to protect the civilian leadership. Some in Japan were relieved, but others committed suicide upon hearing the proclamation. President Truman merely acknowledged that Japan had surrendered on U.S. terms on August 14, 1945. Bombers returned from the last raid to hear the news.

The relief and joy felt by American military personnel readying for the Olympic operation was intense. Typical was Stanley Frankel, a soldier in the Philippines when the *Enola Gay* flew over Hiroshima: "The A-bomb was a surprise to all of us, and, I confess, a pleasant one. It was only in later years that I realized the full horror of atomic weapons. The dropping of the second bomb on Nagasaki was an equally happy read although we didn't quite understand the implications. We figured if two were needed, then perhaps more would be dropped every week. We still expected the Japanese to continue the war until we had invaded and captured their islands."[12]

The surrender a few days later brought the same outpouring of happiness and relief. Troops welcomed the invasion that never was, parading and dancing on bases or seeking to confirm that this was not another ploy by the insidious Japanese. On August 27, Japanese emissaries boarded the USS *Missouri*, Halsey's flagship, to provide information on minefields and shipping channels. The next day, elements of Rear Admiral Oscar Badger's Task Force 31, part of the U.S. Third Fleet, moved into the outer reaches of Tokyo Bay, anchoring off the Yokosuka air and naval base. Other task forces stood by in case of need as carrier planes swept over to discourage treachery. Encountering British prisoners of war, Chester Nimitz ordered special rescue teams to liberate nearby camps. Charged with the occupation, Douglas MacArthur had ordered the navy to await the army before going ashore, but Nimitz had felt obliged to help the prisoners. Over the next two weeks, some 19,000 POWS were freed from mostly inhumane conditions.

After a typhoon postponed their landing in Japan, the Fourth Marines went ashore on August 30. The Americans had finally landed in the Japanese home islands. Both Nimitz and MacArthur came ashore that day as well, the former at Yokosuka to inspect the naval base, and the latter by air into the Atsugi airfield. MacArthur then moved to temporary headquarters in the Grand Hotel in Yokohama as Allied personnel spread throughout Japan. Incidents of violence toward the local population ensued, as did some corruption in a developing black market, yet on the whole the Americans focused on demilitarization and demobilization. Meanwhile, in Manchuria, Korea, China, Southeast Asia, and the East Indies, Japanese soldiers laid down their arms.

In Tokyo Bay, aboard the *Missouri* on September 2, 1945, General MacArthur accepted the formal surrender of the empire of Japan. The new foreign minister, Shigemitsu Mamaori, led a delegation of nine military and foreign ministry officers, who silently signed the surrender documents just after nine o'clock in the morning. Admiral Nimitz signed for the United States; MacArthur spoke eloquently about returning Japan to the community of peaceful nations. The war in the Pacific and Asia was over. The Allied Occupation of Japan had begun.

The War with Japan

In all but the political sense of retaining the emperor, Japan's defeat was unconditional, for in terms of lives, matériel and supplies, and territory lost, the United States and its Allies had wrought utter defeat on the

A Japanese man watches U.S. troops landing on the beach at Wakayama on Honshu in September 1945, when the American Occupation began. U.S. Army, *United States Army in World War II: Pictorial Record: The War Against Japan* (Washington, DC: Department of the Army, 1952), 459.

empire. Imperial forces were in retreat from India, Burma, China, and Manchuria and were either destroyed or isolated throughout the central and southwestern Pacific. Some 6.5 million Japanese were stranded overseas, nearly half in China and Manchuria. Among them were 3 million civilians who made their way back, were taken prisoner, or were killed. Americans were also spread out around the globe, as millions of troops awaited demobilization. Nearly 32,000 prisoners of war got their freedom and returned home to slow, sometimes chaotic, but still undeniable prosperity. America's superpower status, so evident in the war with Japan, remained undiminished for years.

Japan, on the other hand, was an impoverished nation. According to Occupation figures, Allied attacks on shipping and strategic bombing had destroyed one-third of Japan's wealth and up to one-half of its potential income. The country was left with one-fifth of its ships, one-third of machine tools, and just over one-quarter of rolling stock and motor vehicles. Farmers subsisted at 65 percent of prewar standards, but urbanites' living standards dropped to one-third of 1941 levels. Hardship was the rule. The Americans had flattened 40 percent of Japan's sixty-six major cities, leaving 9 million people homeless, who added to the ranks of the 3 million refugees created since early 1945. Just 35 percent of residences remained in the capital of Tokyo; the second largest city, Osaka, had just 43 percent left standing; and Nagoya, the third biggest, a pitiable 11 percent.

With its tremendous material superiority the United States had devastated Japan's material well-being and social cohesion to the extent that one wonders why the atomic bombs were even necessary. Production data (cited at the beginning of this study) showed America to be so far ahead in raw materials, food, and industrial output as to make comparison with Japan pointless. A U.S. strategic bombing survey noted that Japan could not have sustained itself past November 1945 because of the lack of raw materials. In fact, Japanese leaders acknowledged their helplessness, for their nation faced mass starvation during the winter.

Military capabilities also revealed a stunning gap, but the losses are just as staggering. In all theaters of World War II the U.S. lost (not including scuttling, capture, or internment) 167 warships (132 of these sunk by Japan) of all types between 1939 and 1945, whereas 402 Japanese ships went to the bottom, all in the Asian theater. Nearly one-half of the U.S. vessels were destroyed by air attack, and submarine torpedoes took care of another 22; the empire lost 173 ships to air attack and 145 to subs. Excluding kamikaze attacks, Japanese naval and air power sank just one American destroyer after January 1944. The comparison in aircraft provides an equally stark picture. Whereas U.S. operation losses in the Pacific numbered 1,699 planes, the lowest estimate for Japan was 38,105 aircraft destroyed, or over twenty-two times as many as the Americans lost. Discounting the kamikazes, for they were a product of desperation, it is clear that after November 1943, Imperial forces were simply ineffective.

Indeed, Japan could hardly respond in the face of the American avalanche of industrial, technological, and military output. So total was its defeat that the Americans had truly transformed the nature of warfare.

The coming of the nuclear age spoke to this fact, but so also did the advent of systematic amphibious warfare. Japan was the unfortunate victim of deadly U.S. invention, as well as power, although Americans themselves were a bit taken aback by their ability to destroy. As Douglas MacArthur proclaimed at the surrender ceremony, modern warfare proved that "Armageddon will be at our door" without global cooperation for peace.[13] No longer could Great Powers conduct a conflict without risking mutual annihilation.

It is hard to imagine that the final half of the war against Japan could have been any more brutal. Although precise estimates are impossible, given a variety of bureaucratic, political, and military factors, the casualties of the war were monumental, particularly for Japan. About 2.7 million Imperial military personnel and civilians died, or about 3.7 percent of the nation's 1941 population of 74 million people. Roughly 4.5 million of the servicemen returning from the war in 1945—another 6 percent of the populace—were wounded or sick. In addition, between 9 and 15 million Chinese died (second only to the Soviet Union's losses in World War II), plus millions of other soldiers and noncombatants in colonies and occupied territories. In sum, around 16 percent of Japanese navy seamen were casualties, and roughly 20 percent of the army personnel were killed or wounded.

Japanese figures imply that, relative to the other combatant forces, the U.S. services were the safest place to be. Total American war dead and missing in World War II amounted to 405,400 of over 16 million, and 670,800 million were wounded; almost one-quarter, or 100,997, of the deaths occurred in the Pacific theater, and more than 190,000 service personnel were wounded, sick, or unaccounted for in the area. Americans had a better chance of being hospitalized for heat prostration or disease than from firepower, yet the proportion of U.S. casualties was higher in Asia than in Europe. On average, divisions in the Pacific theater had 1 death for every 3.1 other casualties; in Europe, the ratio was nearly 1 to 4. Because of the intensity of amphibious assaults and of Japanese resistance, American divisions (12 of the top 20) in the Pacific theater had a higher proportion of casualties than in Europe. Marines took the heaviest toll, although the navy's ratio of killed to wounded (49.5 percent, or 36,950) was worse than that of the land forces.

The war's final two years were the most devastating in terms of lives lost. As historian John Dower has noted, the late summer of 1944 to the late summer of 1945 is best referred to as "the killing year."[14] Desperate

Japanese tactics led to a "frenzy of violence" in which tens of thousands perished. About ten times more Imperial than U.S. soldiers died on Saipan and Okinawa; twenty-five times more died on Tinian and in the Philippines. Civilian deaths rose into the several hundred thousands, especially on Saipan and Okinawa. For the Americans from July 1944 on, the death and casualty rates were less than Japan's, but they were still the highest of the war. Add in Japan's homefront deaths—as most of the deaths in bombed-out Tokyo, Hiroshima, Nagasaki, and sixty-three other cities occurred after early March 1945—and the "killing year" is an appropriate phrase.

World War II was a good war only because it ended. The war against Japan was a vicious affair with atrocities on both sides that ran the gamut of the most gruesome behavior on the largest scale ever seen. Men engaged in savagery and became savages themselves. The cruelty finally ended in August 1945, after eight years of Japanese aggression and four years of American counterassault.

The war's conclusion brought an end to Japanese militarism and imperialism, and it released the powerful forces of decolonization over the region, which eventually led to greater prosperity and lessened tyranny for millions of previously occupied peoples. The United States became a global leader, and Japan eventually recovered and prospered. These long-term consequences, however, do not submerge under the waters of history the bloody suffering and brutal terror wrought by Japan's futile effort to prevent its total defeat. The conquest of Japan brought out the best in many combatants, but it also exposed the tragedy of human nature.

 Notes

1. Spector, *Eagle against the Sun*, 544.

2. Edward J. Drea, *In the Service of the Emperor: Essays on the Imperial Japanese Army* (Lincoln: University of Nebraska Press, 1998), 152.

3. Murray and Millett, *A War to Be Won*, 520.

4. Grace Person Hayes, *The History of the Joint Chiefs of Staff in World War II: The War against Japan* (Annapolis, MD: Naval Institute Press, 1982), 714.

5. J. Robert Moskin, *Mr. Truman's War: The Final Victories of World War II and the Birth of the Postwar World* (Lawrence: University Press of Kansas, 2002), 102.

6. Douglas J. MacEachin, *The Final Months of the War with Japan: Signals Intelligence, U.S. Invasion Planning, and the A-Bomb Decision* (Washington, DC: Central Intelligence Agency, 1998), 31.

7. Gar Alperovitz, *The Decision to Use the Bomb* (New York: Vintage Books, 1995), 416.

8. Richard B. Frank, *Downfall: The End of the Imperial Japanese Empire* (New York: Random House, 1999), 267.

9. Cook and Cook, *Japan at War*, 393.

10. Herbert F. Bix, "Japan's Delayed Surrender: A Reinterpretation," *Diplomatic History* 19 (Spring 1995): 221.

11. Edwin P. Hoyt, *Japan's War: The Great Pacific Conflict* (New York: Cooper Square Press, 2001), 438.

12. Stanley A. Frankel, "The End of the War," *Frankel-y Speaking about World War II in the South Pacific*, chap. 17, Http://www.frankel-y.com/tape017.htm.

13. John W. Dower, *Embracing Defeat: Japan in the Wake of World War II* (New York: W. W. Norton & Company, 1999), 42.

14. John W. Dower, *War without Mercy: Race and Power in the Pacific War* (New York: Pantheon Books, 1986), 299.

Bibliography

Alexander, Joseph H. *Across the Reef: The Marine Assault on Tarawa*. Washington, DC: Marine Corps Historical Center, 1993.

_____. *Closing In: Marines in the Seizure of Iwo Jima*. Washington, DC: Marine Corps Historical Center, 1994.

_____. *The Final Campaign: Marines in the Victory on Okinawa*. Washington, DC: Marine Corps Historical Center, 1996.

_____. *Storm Landings: Epic Amphibious Battles in the Central Pacific*. Annapolis, MD: Naval Institute Press, 1997.

Alperovitz, Gar. *The Decision to Use the Bomb*. New York: Vintage Books, 1995.

Anderson, Charles R. *The U.S. Army Campaigns of World War II: Leyte*. Washington, DC: Army Center of Military History, 1994.

Andrade, Dale. *The U.S. Army Campaigns of World War II: Luzon*. Washington, DC: Army Center of Military History, 1996.

Bernstein, Barton J. "Understanding the Atomic Bomb and the Japanese Surrender: Missed Opportunities, Little-Known Near Disasters, and Modern Memory." *Diplomatic History* 19 (Spring 1995): 227–73.

Bix, Herbert F. "Japan's Delayed Surrender: A Reinterpretation." *Diplomatic History* 19 (Spring 1995): 197–225.

Bjorge, Gary J. *Merrill's Marauders: Combined Operations in Northern Burma in 1944*. Washington, DC: Army Center of Military History, 1996.

Brown, David. *Warship Losses of World War Two*. London: Arms and Armour Press, 1990.

Calvocoressi, Peter, and Guy Wint. *Total War: The Study of World War II*. New York: Pantheon Books, 1972.

Chapin, John. *And a Few Marines: Marines in the Liberation of the Philippines*. Washington, DC: Marine Corps Historical Center, 1997.

_____. *Breaching the Marianas: The Battle for Saipan*. Washington, DC: Marine Corps Historical Center, 1994.

_____. *Breaking the Outer Ring: Marine Landings in the Marshall Islands*. Washington, DC: Marine Corps Historical Center, 1994.

Cook, Haruko Taya, and Theodore F. Cook. *Japan at War: An Oral History*. New York: New Press, 1992.

Coppersmith, Morris. Diary. http://topshot.com/dh/Victory.html.

Crost, Lyn. *Honor by Fire: Japanese Americans at War in Europe and the Pacific.* Novato, CA: Presidio Press, 1994.

Cutler, Thomas J. *The Battle of Leyte Gulf: 23–26 October 1944.* New York: HarperCollins, 1994.

Denfeld, D. Colt. *Hold the Marianas: The Japanese Defense of the Mariana Islands.* Shippensburg, PA: White Mane Publishing Company, 1997.

Dower, John W. *Embracing Defeat: Japan in the Wake of World War II.* New York: W. W. Norton & Company, 1999.

_____. *War without Mercy: Race and Power in the Pacific War.* New York: Pantheon Books, 1986.

Drea, Edward J. *In the Service of the Emperor: Essays on the Imperial Japanese Army.* Lincoln: University of Nebraska Press, 1998.

_____. *MacArthur's ULTRA: Codebreaking and the War against Japan, 1942–1945.* Lawrence: University Press of Kansas, 1992.

_____. *The U.S. Army Campaigns of World War II: New Guinea.* Washington, DC: Army Center of Military History, 1994.

Dunnigan, James F., and Albert A. Nofi. *The Pacific War Encyclopedia, Vols. 1 and 2.* New York: Facts on File, 1998.

Ellis, John. *World War II: A Statistical Survey.* New York: Facts on File, 1993.

Fisch, Arnold G., Jr. *The U.S. Army Campaigns of World War II: Ryukyus.* Washington, DC: Government Printing Office, 1995.

Frank, Richard B. *Downfall: The End of the Imperial Japanese Empire.* New York: Random House, 1999.

Frankel, Stanley A. *Frankel-y Speaking about World War II in the South Pacific.* http://www.frankel-y.com/tape017.htm.

Gailey, Harry A. *Bougainville, 1943–1945.* Lexington: University Press of Kentucky, 1991.

Gayle, Gordon D. *Bloody Beaches: The Marines at Peleliu.* Washington, DC: Marine Corps Historical Center, 1996.

Gregg, Charles T. *Tarawa.* New York: Stein & Day, 1984.

Hard, Achira. "Japan: Guns before Rice." In *The Economics of World War II*, ed. Mark Harrison. Cambridge: Cambridge University Press, 1998.

Harrison, Mark. "The Economics of World War II: An Overview." In *The Economics of World War II*, ed. Harrison. Cambridge: Cambridge University Press, 1998.

Harwood, Richard. *A Close Encounter: The Marine Landing on Tinian.* Washington, DC: Marine Corps Historical Center, 1994.

Hayes, Grace Person. *The History of the Joint Chiefs of Staff in World War II: The War against Japan.* Annapolis, MD: Naval Institute Press, 1982.

Heinl, Robert D., Jr., and John A. Crown. *The Marshalls: Increasing the Tempo.* Washington, DC: Government Printing Office, 1954.

Hirrel, Leo. *U.S. Army Campaigns of World War II: Bismarck Archipelago.* Washington, DC: Army Center of Military History, 1993.

Hoffman, Carl W. *Saipan: The Beginning of the End*. Washington, DC: Marine Corps Historical Division Headquarters, 1950.

Hoyt, Edwin P. *Japan's War: The Great Pacific Conflict*. New York: Cooper Square Press, 2001.

Hynes, Samuel. *The Soldier's Tale: Bearing Witness to Modern War*. New York: Viking Penguin, 1997.

Ienaga, Saburo. *The Pacific War, 1931–1945*. New York: Pantheon Books, 1978.

Iriye, Akira. *Power and Culture: The Japanese-American War, 1941–1945*. Cambridge, MA: Harvard University Press, 1981.

Kraus, Theresa. *U.S. Army Campaigns of World War II: China Offensive*. Washington, DC: Army Center of Military History, 1993.

Linderman, Gerald F. *The World within War: America's Combat Experience in World War II*. New York: Free Press, 1997.

Lofgren, Stephen J. *U.S. Army Campaigns of World War II: Northern Solomons*. Washington, DC: Army Center of Military History, 1993.

_____. *The U.S. Army Campaigns of World War II: Southern Philippines*. Washington, DC: Army Center of Military History, 1996.

MacEachin, Douglas J. *The Final Months of the War with Japan: Signals Intelligence, U.S. Invasion Planning, and the A-Bomb Decision*. Washington, DC: Central Intelligence Agency, 1998.

MacGarrigle, George L. *The U.S. Army Campaigns of World War II: Central Burma*. Washington, DC: Army Center of Military History, 1996.

Moskin, J. Robert. *Mr. Truman's War: The Final Victories of World War II and the Birth of the Postwar World*. Lawrence: University Press of Kansas, 2002.

Murray, Williamson, and Allan R. Millett. *A War to Be Won: Fighting the Second World War*. Cambridge, MA: The Belknap Press, 2000.

Naito, Hatsuho. *Thunder Gods: The Kamikaze Pilots Tell Their Story*. Tokyo: Kodansha International, 1989.

Newell, Clayton R. *The U.S. Army Campaigns of World War II: Central Pacific*. Washington, DC: Army Center of Military History, 1992.

O'Brien, Cyril J. *Liberation: Marines in the Recapture of Guam*. Washington, DC: Marine Corps Historical Center, 1994.

Ross, Bill D. *Peleliu, Tragic Triumph: The Untold Story of the Pacific War's Forgotten Battle*. New York: Random House, 1991.

Schrijvers, Peter. *The GI War against Japan: American Soldiers in Asia and the Pacific during World War II*. Washington Square, NY: New York University Press, 2002.

Sherrod, Robert. *Tarawa: The Story of a Battle*. New York: Duell, Sloan & Pearce, 1944.

Sherry, Mark D. *U.S. Army Campaigns of World War II: China Defensive*. Washington, DC: Army Center of Military History, 1993.

Skates, John Ray. *The Invasion of Japan: Alternatives to the Bomb*. Columbia: University of South Carolina Press, 1994.

Sledge, E. B. *With the Old Breed: At Peleliu and Okinawa.* New York: Oxford University Press, 1981.

Smith, Charles R. *Securing the Surrender: Marines in the Occupation of Japan.* Washington, DC: Marine Corps Historical Center, 1997.

Smith, Gaddis. *American Diplomacy during the Second World War, 1941–1945.* 2d ed. New York: Alfred A. Knopf, 1985.

Smith, Michael. *The Emperor's Codes: The Breaking of Japan's Secret Ciphers.* Harmondsworth, U.K.: Penguin Books, 2000.

Spector, Ronald H. *Eagle against the Sun: The American War with Japan.* New York: Vintage Books, 1985.

Stewart, Adrian. *The Battle of Leyte Gulf.* New York: Charles Scribner's Sons, 1980.

Taaffe, Stephen R. *MacArthur's Jungle War: The 1944 New Guinea Campaign.* Lawrence: University Press of Kansas, 1998.

Tanaka, Yuki. *Hidden Horrors: Japanese War Crimes in World War II.* Boulder, CO: Westview Press, 1996.

Terkel, Studs. *"The Good War": An Oral History of World War Two.* New York: Ballantine Books, 1984.

Thompson, Robert Smith. *Empires on the Pacific: World War II and the Struggle for the Mastery of Asia.* New York: Basic Books, 2001.

Vatter, Harold G. *The U.S. Economy in World War II.* New York: Columbia University Press, 1985.

Werrell, Kenneth P. *Blankets of Fire: U.S. Bombers over Japan during World War II.* Washington, DC: Smithsonian Institution Press, 1996.

Willmott, H. P. *The Second World War in the East.* London: Cassell, 1999.

———. *The War with Japan: The Period of Balance, May 1942–October 1943.* Wilmington, DE: Scholarly Resources, 2002.

———. Memorandum to author on Japanese Performance. September 4, 2001.

Wright, Burton. *U.S. Army Campaigns of World War II: Eastern Mandates.* Washington, DC: Army Center of Military History, 1993.

Y'Blood, William T. *Red Sun Setting: The Battle of the Philippine Sea.* Annapolis, MD: Naval Institute Press, 1981.

Index